WHAT'S
LEFT
OF THE
JUNGLE

'Nitin Sekar has given us a tour de force of how the jungle's fate is interwoven with the myriad choices that individuals—and societies—make. India is for him a place of crisis and challenge, but also hope and renewal. In a land where conservation is so fraught a mission, he finds ideas and endeavours that offer hope and direction.'

Mahesh Rangarajan,
Environmental Historian and Vice Chancellor,
Krea University

'Nitin Sekar has written a fascinating tale of life in a Bengali village in the jungle, at the frontline of the human-wildlife conflict. *What's Left of the Jungle* needs to be very widely read, not only in India but by everyone with an interest in conserving biodiversity.'

Peter Singer,
Professor of Bioethics, Princeton University,
and bestselling author of *Animal Liberation*

'Full of intrigue, deception, family loyalty and hardships, *What's Left of the Jungle* offers a glimpse into the daily lives of the people who are the guardians of India's remaining wildlife and gives a much-needed dose of reality. It should be read by every well-meaning conservationist.'

Ruth DeFries,
Recipient of the MacArthur Genius Grant and
Professor of Ecology and Sustainable Development,
Columbia University

'All of us love the idea of saving the world's last elephants, tigers, lions, and other dangerous animals, but very few of us have to live with them in our own backyards. With uncommon grace, wisdom, and wit, Nitin Sekar explores how villagers in rural India manage to do so. It's a touching and important story, beautifully told.'

David Wilcove,
Professor of Ecology, Evolutionary Biology
and Public Affairs, Princeton University

'*What's Left of the Jungle* humanizes the people that sacrifice—invisibly, often involuntarily and generally without thanks—so that people around the world can enjoy the continued existence of majestic elephants and other species. Shining a light on these heroes and heroines gives their stories the power to inspire and transform conservation at a time when it is needed most. These are stories of deep empathy for both animals and the local people that make their continued co-existence possible.'

Paula Kahumbu,
CEO of WildlifeDirect and Host of *Wildlife Warriors,*
Winner of the 2021 Whitley Gold Award for Conservation

WHAT'S LEFT OF THE JUNGLE

A Conservation Story

NITIN SEKAR

BLOOMSBURY
NEW DELHI • LONDON • OXFORD • NEW YORK • SYDNEY

BLOOMSBURY INDIA
Bloomsbury Publishing India Pvt. Ltd
Second Floor, LSC Building No. 4, DDA Complex, Pocket C – 6 & 7,
Vasant Kunj, New Delhi, 110070

BLOOMSBURY, BLOOMSBURY INDIA and the Diana logo
are trademarks of Bloomsbury Publishing Plc

First published in India 2022
This edition published 2022

ISBN: PB: 978-93-54352-21-8; eBook: 978-93-54355-86-8
2 4 6 8 10 9 7 5 3 1

Typeset in Sabon LT Std by Manipal Technologies Limited
Printed and bound in India by Thomson Press India Ltd.

To find out more about our authors and books visit www.bloomsbury.com and sign
up for our newsletters

AUTHOR'S NOTE

This book was written using a variety of sources, but the most important were records from my time in the field and in-depth interviews and conversations with several of the characters in the book, especially Akshu Atri. Those interviewed for the book gave their free, prior, and informed consent for their stories to be used. Akshu went through the book with a teacher fluent in both Nepali and English to check for errors. Other documents, like scholarly papers, Forest Department documents, and newspaper articles were used to validate timelines and key facts. While this book is intended to be non-fiction, and while considerable effort was made by both me and my conversation partners to get the details right, there are a few ways in which the book deviates from what happened.

First, some characters in the book are composite characters that represent multiple individuals from the same place or institution. Furthermore, almost all the names in the book and many of the names of places and institutions have been changed. While this book is intended to give an accurate depiction of some of the power hierarchies and complications that come with conservation work and research, it is not intended to serve as an indictment of any individuals or a well-rounded portrayal of their character. This is especially important since, in preparing for the book, I did not capture the perspectives of all individuals involved in the narrative; the book is told primarily from my and Akshu's perspective, with targeted interviews with others for richness and triangulation.

Second, the order of events presented in this book deviates from the real historical order. In a handful of cases, this is deliberate, either as a consequence of the use of composite characters, to streamline storytelling, or just to consolidate related events that were spread out over time. In other cases, my interviewees said openly that even when they lucidly remembered many details of their narratives, they struggled with dates and chronology, especially from further back in their lives. While seasons were very relevant to them, the exact year and their age were not. We have made an extra effort to ensure that the sequencing is correct wherever it has implications for the interpretation or message of the book.

Finally, memories are fallible. Many of my conversation partners wrote almost nothing down of their past experiences and had few documents available, leaving only occasional opportunities to validate narratives. This was especially the case for personal life events. Where events described to me in conversation were also described by others I interviewed or in documents I independently found, they matched very well, generally validating the oral histories on which this book is built. Despite all our efforts, I am sure there are some (hopefully minor) errors in the book, and I accept responsibility for these errors. Finally, this book is a personal project that has not received oversight from any institution with which I have worked. The views expressed are my own and not the official positions of my organization.

PREFACE

Of all I have read on the topic of human-elephant conflict, I thought a 2010 Indian government task force report described it best:

'The stress, suffering, and loss are all too real. It is tragic for elephants as well as humans [...] Both [are] victims in the conflict. Both are victims of victims.'

The task force reported that over 400 people a year, mostly cultivators and labourers, lost their lives to Asian elephants in India, and that 100 elephants a year were killed by people. It described the at least 500,000 families who lost crops and property to wild elephants. All these numbers might have been underestimates, and they have grown by as much as 25 per cent since 2010. India's burgeoning human population has made elephant habitats smaller and less hospitable as people seek a better life. Elephants have taken more and more to crop-raiding as they've become accustomed to nutritious domestic crops. The boundaries between forests and fields are more contested than ever. Similar reports of increased conflict could likely be written about India's tigers, leopards, and bears. In many places and at many times, successful human development or animal conservation seems to make the numbers worse, the signs of either better reporting or an apparent zero-sum game.

The problem of human–wildlife conflict in part seems intractable because it is hard to know whom to root for.

On the one hand, conservationists never fail to remind us that the animals we have left are relics of what once was, and that we, humanity, are to be blamed for their widespread disappearance. The problem goes back thousands of years in some places, but the living human generations get a fair share of blame. Due to our hunger and exercise of power, populations of vertebrate species have declined an average of 68 per cent between 1970 and 2016. The situation is particularly stark for many of the charismatic terrestrial megafauna. Some species, such as African forest elephants and black rhinos, are mostly in the news because they are threatened by the illegal wildlife trade. But the situation in Asia shows that, even if the trade weren't a threat for such species, competition or conflict with economically aspirational humans eventually would be. Asian elephants that once roamed from the Middle East to China and the Southeast Asian tropics are now restricted to around 3 per cent of their historic range, numbering no more than 50,000 individuals in the wild globally. Wild tigers are down to a few thousand in patches mostly across south and southeast Asia. The Asiatic lion is down to a few hundred individuals in one state in India. While humanity's rise has proven devastating to species of all sizes, large animals—especially terrestrial animals larger than us humans—have been amongst the worst victims. Conservationists frequently ask us if this is who we want to be as a species: a people so avaricious, insecure, and violent that any creature larger than us is likely to be devoured or destroyed. If we're so brilliant, can't we find a way to coexist with them? Won't we miss the gleam in our children's eyes when they behold a charismatic, clever, magnificent creature? What will we tell them if they ask us why the animal in their children's book no longer exists or roams free?

When conservationists try to reverse the march of extirpation and extinction on the ground, however, they find they are no longer dealing with humanity as an abstract whole, but with specific individuals often underserved by society. Often, conservationists end up asking poor, marginalized people to share their living space with large, dangerous creatures. 'There is a five-ton creature with tusks eating all your crops, a 250-kilogram feline eating your cattle. Either could take your life with a single swipe. But please remember, there are very few of these creatures left in the world. Don't kill them! And don't remove much from their habitat. Invest in an electric fence, or a predator-proof kraal. We'll provide some support, but it's mostly your responsibility. Stay home, and keep your kids inside. Be careful when you're collecting firewood and in tall grass or sugarcane. Oh, and try not to be outside at night. If you need me, I'll be at the hotel down the road.'

No densely populated modern society has played by these rules. In the US, Western Europe, China, and Japan, people decimated their large-bodied wildlife long ago, often with their governments' support— only now, when their citizens can rest at ease inside sturdy homes in largely non-agrarian societies, are some countries gradually, out of a conveniently post-developmental conservation ethic, allowing the return of animals generally less dangerous than lions, tigers, rhinos, or elephants. It's not the Southern peasant's fault that humanity destroyed so much of the natural world before they were born. Why should they, those most left behind by modern development, now pay the price for conservation?

This dilemma between victims of victims is, to me, the most philosophically and practically compelling challenge in society's effort to reimagine its relationship with nature. I have long wondered what it is like to be one of the people living in the jungle, trying to make ends meet, expected to make sacrifices for biodiversity and for humanity's sins. And I have wondered what it takes to find a way out of the dilemma of victims.

Over a decade ago, I went to one of the frontlines of this struggle. I stumbled into a human story that captured the tensions and complications at the heart of modern conservation. It's a true story about poverty, ambition, democracy, elitism, murder, poaching, smuggling, love, and lust; it's a tale that has a cast of characters as diverse as an ecosystem. It intertwines the politics of counting cat feces, the clash of two of the planet's most intelligent terrestrial species, and the dumbfounding challenges of human transformation.

It's a story that taught me about how things work in the jungle, how difficult it is to balance the imperatives of conservation and development, and how things could be better. In a few pages, I will introduce you to the protagonist. But first, you should know something about where he came from. His story begins in a town in North Bengal, more than half a century ago...

INTRODUCTION

It was a crime that finally pushed the Atri family out of the town of Madharihat and into the jungle.

In 1960, when she was just ten years old, Satyavati Atri had moved to Madharihat from Sikkim to live with Motikar, a tall, narrow-nosed 24-year-old man whom she had married a year earlier. Now, they shared their home with six or seven others, including Motikar's brother, older sister, and aunt. Economically, it was never an ideal situation. Motikar earned ₹12 a month as a guard at the police station, not enough to support so many people. The land they rented and farmed ensured that they did not go hungry, and the cow they owned periodically provided some milk and a calf to sell—but they struggled to buy clothes and otherwise fulfill their material needs.

Then the robbery happened. Seventeen-year-old Satyavati clasped her infant son and stood by helplessly as a group of eight to ten people—armed with at least one gun—beat her husband across the back and stripped their hut of all their cooking vessels, plates, and metalware, leaving not even a tumbler from which they could drink. After the dacoits left, the neighbors came to visit the Atris. The Adivasi families told them that they were about to come help, but when they saw that there were so *many* thieves, they too had become afraid and had instead retreated to hide inside their houses. When Motikar reported the robbery to his superiors at the police station, the police came to the Atri household (a courtesy extended to Motikar, perhaps, because of his faithful work at the station). They dutifully looked around, and then they left.

Motikar was, of course, already intimately familiar with the corruption and inefficacy of the police, and his neighbors' reluctance to help him must have made the town of Madharihat feel very inhospitable indeed. He was also tired of giving 50 per cent of the yield from his rented land to the company that owned it. His little brother, Premdeep, on hearing of his troubles, was sympathetic. He invited Motikar to bring his family and live with other Nepalis in a forest village called Madhubangaon. 'Life is difficult here, too,' Motikar's brother admitted. 'You have to work without pay to keep your house. But come here—if we live, we live together. If we die, we die together.'

Motikar agreed, selling his cow and taking Satyavati, his son Chander, and his two buffaloes with him. Madhubangaon was a village of some 85 households nestled in the Buxa forest, around 10 kilometers from the nearest town. Premdeep occupied one of these houses, but, as he had just secured some new land some 3 kilometers away in the hamlet of Taazabasti, he had decided to shift to his new property. So Motikar and Satyavati moved into his house as Premdeep and his family settled down and farmed their new land.

The house that the young Atri family moved into was built with wooden planks and a thatched roof and mounted on stilts thick like tree trunks. There was room to tie up animals underneath. It was a relic of the colonial era, erected as an abode for labourers who served British India's Forest Department. While the British were no longer in the region, the extractive institution they had established was still functioning as intended, and the deal for the Atris was nearly identical to the arrangement maintained during colonial times. The officials ran Buxa Forest as a plantation, so they needed labourers to assist in logging and replanting the land. The Atris could reside in their house for free as long as one member of the household helped plant and maintain the Forest Department's plantations. This work would occupy one person per household for about six months of the year. Everyone else could dedicate themselves to earning a living. If no one from the house showed up to work at the plantation for a couple of days, the Department would show up and evict, or at least threaten to evict, the family. The government—a government to which the Atris and their neighbors felt little connection—held unparalleled power.

The Atris' three-roomed house was not so small by local standards, and they shared it with a nephew, a cowherd, and another Nepali man. The group had a substantial amount of work to do. Motikar, who had grown up in the region's forests, wandered the jungle gathering seeds for the trees he was to plant for the Forest Department. Satyavati and Motikar also had to oversee and assist the cowherd, who had 20–25 buffaloes in his charge. Buffaloes, unlike cattle, had large home ranges and had to be guided home regularly so they would be available for milking and not go feral. The Atris also cleaned the sheds and fed the calves that were too young to walk in the forest. Satyavati cooked for all the members of the household and looked after her growing family. Amidst all this, the couple looked for opportunities to generate more income, in part because the plantation work did not pay. Satyavati, for instance, washed dishes for more well-off families in the community. Finally, the group had to plant, maintain, and harvest crops on the two-odd acres of agricultural land over which they had stewardship.

To Satyavati, life in the jungle did not feel much better than life in Madharihat. Satyavati and Motikar continued to have children—after Chander, Satyavati gave birth to four daughters and two more sons—so the Atris found themselves constantly battling food shortages for almost two decades. They couldn't afford rice or wheat flour. They struggled many weeks to collect the ₹16 they needed to buy enough corn to stay alive. They didn't own a plough or oxen, so they always had to borrow these from others, which kept them in debt and limited how much of their land they could farm. The land was quite infertile, and, without cattle that stayed near the village during the day, the villagers did not have sufficient dung to make the land productive; initially, the soil could not support corn. Since they had sold their dairy cow, they were also short on milk. The fertility of the land improved very gradually. In the meantime, they made up the difference by serving as day labourers in and around the village. They also planted mustard, eggplant, and other vegetables in and around the plantations. Whatever the forest animals did not eat supplemented their diet at home.

The plantation work was no picnic. Eighty-five labourers were tasked with logging and then replanting about one compartment (15–30 hectares) a year. First, they had to cut down all the plantation trees with axes and kukris (traditional sickle-shaped Nepali machetes), load them onto bullock carts, and remove them from the forest to be sold by the Forest Department. Even cutting down one of the bigger trees with their metal tools could take two days. They would then light a contained fire to clear the remaining brush, break up the soil, create rows, and directly plant the trees' seeds. As the young trees grew and began to crowd each other, some were removed and used as firewood. During long hours of this work under the subtropical sun, the Forest Department provided no water to the workers, and, in the northern part of Buxa, there were few streams or rivers available in the dry season. Villagers could bring one bottle of water with them, but, after emptying it, they had to be creative. Satyavati would find a certain climber in the forest, slice it open, and squeeze water into her mouth. If that wasn't an option, Satyavati would look for a pool of water, perhaps even a wallow in which an elephant had rested. She would filter the water through her sari and drink it. Sometimes, Motikar would manage to fill a big vessel with water and take it with him to the plantation, where he and the other workers would share it. The Forest Department seemed indifferent to all of this—they simply required their labourers to work hard, or they would not be permitted to come the next day. The perceived attitude of the Forest Department toward its labourers was summed up by the apocryphal story of a pregnant woman from Buxa who, while toiling on a plantation, went into labour, gave birth, and—following the apparent expectations of her employers—secured her newborn in the shade and returned to work.

Malaria added to the hardship. Satyavati and Motikar never got the fever in Madharihat, but Buxa's region, the Dooars, was basically a swamp in the rainy season. During the monsoons, the river running through Madhubangaon and the Atris' land often flooded; paths became muddy and ensnaring in some places and treacherous and slippery in others. As the rains subsided, the water settled in pools perfect for *Anopheles* mosquitoes. The mosquitos were persistent and had to be regularly shooed away at night. Motikar cut open a burlap sack, tying one end to the ceiling and tying a wooden beam onto the other. At night, he would have his children sleep underneath the dangling beam. He would then swing the beam forcefully—the burlap pendulum would keep mosquitoes away for a while, like a fan—but, eventually, it would stop. Motikar would have to periodically wake up and swing the pendulum. Despite these efforts, people repeatedly fell ill, especially children. Just as one child recovered from malaria, another would fall sick, and then the parents themselves would fall victim to the disease. If they wanted treatment, Motikar would have to journey some 20 kilometers to Alipurduar.

To top it all off, Satyavati found her husband's behavior to be sometimes unhelpful. Motikar did not drink, or gamble, or pursue other women. His problem was different: reflexive generosity. Once, when Satyavati was sick, she sent Motikar to the market with ₹8 and a bag to purchase greens. Motikar returned with an empty bag. A poorer neighbor had told Motikar that his family had nothing, including food, so Motikar had handed him his purchase and returned empty-handed. When Motikar told Satyavati what he had done, she cried.

Somehow, though, Motikar still ultimately managed to hold up his part of the social contract. For instance, a wealthy acquaintance with full faith in Motikar allowed him to take over stewardship of a neglected herd of 20–25 buffaloes, a loan that Motikar paid back over time by selling buffalo milk and ghee. He then sold the buffaloes and purchased cattle, which had smaller home ranges and could make their way back home at night without a human guide. *Bhagwan* was looking after things for her family in part, Satyavati figured, because her husband was so generous.

The Atris' efforts to accumulate resources to survive were also hindered by their jungle-dwelling neighbors. As the villagers were gradually able to plant more corn and rice, macaques and elephants began raiding their crops. Initially, these animals didn't eat much. Only one or two elephants came each season. And in those days, if the villagers so much as approached an elephant with a small flaming torch, the animal would run away. Still, Satyavati estimated that wildlife took as much as one-seventh of the crop—presumably, this included losses to nocturnal crop raiders such as wild pigs, deer, and porcupines. Satyavati never saw these species, but Motikar spotted them in the jungle when he was herding livestock.

Motikar also saw other species that Satyavati never did: big cats. Though the predators rarely visited the cowsheds at night, they did pursue domestic animals in the forest; two to five times a year, Motikar would return home to report that one of the livestock—usually a calf—had been killed. Leopards perpetrated most of the attacks in the jungle, but sometimes a humongous striped feline would launch itself at a full-grown bull in broad daylight. There would be a little struggle, and the tiger would drag its quarry into the bush.

As the villagers were not compensated for such kills, they were pure losses of important assets. Villagers watching such kills mainly accepted them, feeling helpless or resigning themselves to the occasional cost of living in the jungle. But once Chander saw a tiger take down a neighbor's cow in the jungle. Chander told the neighbor, a man named Laale, what had occurred and guided him to the scene of the crime. Laale resolved to take revenge. With neighbors looking on from their own hiding places, he took a home-made pipe gun to where the cow carcass lay, climbed part way up a nearby tree, and waited.

The tiger returned to consume more of its prize. Laale shot, hitting his mark—but he failed to kill the cat. The injured tiger spotted Laale and charged. Laale tried to scramble further up the tree, but it was too late—the tiger dragged him down and killed him. The neighbors dug a grave right where the killing had happened and buried Laale. The tiger, too, later died of its injuries.

Just as the jungle took from Buxa's villagers, the villagers took from the jungle. Fruits, mushrooms, wild vegetables, climbers, firewood—when the season was right, the jungle provided a bounty.

In those days, it was not easy to illegally sell timber. There was no obvious and accessible market. Plus, villagers were afraid of being caught by forest guards. One neighbor, a *mondol* or village headman, was employed by the Forest Department to report illegal activities; the villagers feared and respected him. Residents of Madhubangaon were allowed to collect dry wood for energy but not to fell living trees, a rule the *mondol* enforced.

Illegal hunting was a somewhat different matter. Animal carcasses and skins were easier to process, hide, and transport—and there was always a market in the town of Jaigaon on the Bhutanese border. Satyavati once heard that officials had stopped a man with a basket on his bicycle as he went up the Dima riverbed. The officials asked him to open the basket. He said, 'Very well,' and he coolly opened the basket. Inside was a tiger pelt.

———

Throughout the 1970s, though life was still difficult, the Atris' condition gradually improved. In addition to rising agricultural yields, India's evolving democracy brought some benefits to Buxa's labourers. A leftist political party known as the Forward Bloc, under multiethnic leadership including both indigenous Rabhas and a Bengali man, orchestrated a march on Calcutta to demand that plantation workers be paid *hazira*. That is, they demanded that, in addition to being allowed housing, they be paid in cash for their labour. After persistent protest, around 1971–1972, the rules were changed—Buxa moved a step forward from its colonial history. Labourers were now to be given ₹2½ a day for their work. Collecting seeds for the plantations could also be a source of livelihood for those like Motikar who were comfortable wandering the forest. The Atris would even go through their cattle's dung to find seeds, clean them individually, and add them to Motikar's collection.

But the villagers were not initially privy to the rate they were owed by government officials, who apparently gave seed collectors half of what they were supposed to and pocketed the rest. When Satyavati finally found out what they were truly owed, she fumed at having gone through cow dung for seeds, cleaning each seed individually, to get half of what was owed to them. 'What's the point of that?' she asked in disgust.

The point was, of course, that Satyavati's family was poor, and she and her husband had to use whatever they had to stay alive. Motikar would diligently journey into the forest with little more than his kukri to collect seeds for sale to the Forest Department. This was the world he knew how to negotiate, taking long strides with his long legs, scaling trees when necessary, ever vigilant for elephants and tigers and snakes.

What he didn't know was that his and his children's world was being shaped by forces far away, in government buildings in New Delhi and Calcutta. In 1983, Buxa became India's 15th tiger reserve and, in 1986, some of Buxa's forests were declared a wildlife sanctuary. This meant that, at least legally, Buxa's primary purpose was no longer to provide timber but to help conserve India's rapidly depleting wildlife. The tiger was thought to be down to some 1,800 individuals all over India in 1972, a victim of a combination of colonial and postcolonial hunting, habitat destruction, and reduction in prey numbers. So Buxa was now declared part of a nationwide effort to prevent the Indian national animal from going extinct.

Motikar and Satyavati were not informed of this change or prepared for it in any way. As would happen so often in the coming decades, political decisions made far away would, slowly but surely, alter their family's relationship with the forest they depended on. With the pair largely unprepared to deal with the changes coming to Buxa, the responsibility for adapting to new realities would fall on their children—especially on one child, Akshu.

1

From the moment I met Bhuday and Dinesh at the New Jalpaiguri train station, we each had our own agenda. Dinesh, a sturdy Bengali man with thinning jet-black hair, hoped I would be his ticket to a post-doctoral fellowship in the US. Bhuday, the Nepali driver with a cartoon villain scar running through his eye, was hoping to charm me with his sycophancy. He wanted me to let down my guard so that he might continue to abuse his post. And I, a 24-year-old American PhD student, was determined to get Dinesh to fire Bhuday, his long-time ally. Now, as Bhuday drove us through dark green forests, sprawling tea plantations, and wide river flood plains fed by the early monsoon rains, my mind was focused on my friend Jilpa's warnings to me about my new companions. Jilpa, an elephant ecologist, had worked in North Bengal a few years earlier. She had advised me in detail about how to get settled in the region. She had said that Bhuday was an incorrigible drunk driver, thief, and alleged rapist, and that Dinesh knowingly tolerated Bhuday's behavior. Consequently, I didn't want Bhuday to learn about my expensive equipment, or where I would be installing it in the jungle. In retrospect, my preoccupation at that moment was a harbinger for my time as a researcher in Buxa Tiger Reserve, and then as a conservationist more generally. I might have come to North Bengal to study elephants, but, even setting aside logistics, the problems I would face would be 20 per cent ecological and 80 per cent sociological, economic, and political.

As our jeep hurtled east toward Buxa, I leaned over Dinesh's seat and engaged him in conversation, trying to get on his good side. He told me he had grown up in a village not far from Kolkata and that he had pursued wildlife studies out of sheer interest in the field.

'Your English is quite good,' I said. 'Did you go to an English-medium school?'

'No,' Dinesh said. 'I learned a little in school. Mostly, I started learning English-speaking in 2000 for my research.'

'Whoa,' I responded, genuinely impressed. 'That's incredible! In ten years, you've become this comfortable with English? I've been trying to learn Hindi for a few years,' I said. 'I took a few classes in the US, and I spoke a bit last year as I traveled around India, but I still am quite weak. I hope I get as good in Hindi as you are in English.'

'What is your native tongue?' Dinesh asked.

'Tamil,' I said, explaining that both my parents were South Indians, but that I was born and raised in the US. 'My Tamil isn't that great, either.'

'Well, you should learn Bengali here. After all, you are in Bengal.'

'I'd love to learn Bengali,' I said with tempered enthusiasm. 'But I think I should stick to learning one language at a time.'

'Actually, Bengali is not so different from Hindi,' Dinesh assured me. 'It will be easy for you to learn.'

We drove for five hours. I nodded off for the second half of the trip and, when I lifted my head, we were in a city: Alipurduar. As Jilpa had warned, the city was filthy—it was large enough to have the piles of garbage and putrid drain water of the larger cities I had visited in India, but not yet the restaurants, movie theaters, and metropolitan cultural attractions one could use to build an elite bubble in Delhi or Bangalore. It was the worst of both worlds.

'There he is,' Dinesh said.

'There who is?' I asked.

'That is Akshu.'

'Oh!' Akshu was the man Jilpa had recommended I take on as a field assistant. Jilpa had raved about him. 'He has little formal education, but he is a very sharp and responsible chap,' she had said. 'He can use a GPS, and he was the only person I trusted to videotape elephants for me in Kaziranga. He has loads of experience working in the jungle, and he will look after you and keep you safe from elephants. Without him I may not even be alive. And he is totally honest. If he owes you even ₹5, he will insist on paying you back, even if you have forgotten.'

I keenly peered out of the jeep. Gradually, I realized whom Dinesh was pointing at. He was underwhelming. Five-foot-eight, Akshu had a head of black hair and yellowish light-brown skin with brown splotches on his face. He was remarkably thin, with a short torso and muscle-free chest. He walked with a limp that could not be ignored—he was unable to bend his left knee, so he swung his left leg in an arc with every step. I had heard he was Nepali, but he looked North Indian to me. When he saw me, he immediately smiled, and I saw he was dramatically cross-eyed, with his left eye off trying to look around the corner. Inexplicably—because I have no idea what it was I was expecting of my village assistant—I was disappointed. Somehow, I found it hard to believe this guy would keep me safe from the jungle's denizens.

Akshu sat beside me and I greeted him warmly. It was obvious that he was just as amiable in person as he had sounded on the phone. We started a conversation in Hindi, but it fizzled out quickly. Small talk in Hindi wasn't something I was much good at.

What I really wanted to ask Akshu was if he had found a place for me to live. On behalf of the National Institute for Environmental Sciences, or NIES, Dinesh had established a field station in Alipurduar—for him, the city was where the action was.

'I think you would like it better in Madhubangaon, the village in the tiger reserve,' Jilpa had said. 'You would see how people live there. Elephants come into the village at night, so you could experience that. Alipur ... Alipur is just a city! It's dirty and noisy, and far from the jungle. I don't know why ecology researchers would want to stay there.' So Jilpa had asked Akshu to look for accommodations for me in his village. But I was reluctant to ask him about that when Dinesh was in earshot. Seeing how Dinesh made decisions, I got the feeling that he saw himself as being in charge of all of the Institute's research in Buxa, including mine. I was concerned that my interest in setting up my field station away from him would upset him.

We spent most of the day in Alipur running errands. Akshu helped me apply for an internet connection at the Vodafone store, which offered USB modems that worked even in Akshu's jungle village. Dinesh and I went to meet the deputy field directors (DFDs) of Buxa Tiger Reserve so that I could introduce myself. The DFDs were officials in the Forest Department and second in command of Buxa Tiger Reserve. After much waiting to meet the appropriate officials, I explained to them that my research was associated with the National Institute for Environmental Sciences, and that permissions should arrive from Kolkata shortly. They granted us a couple of nights at the Forest Department guest house in Madhubangaon, buying me some time to find more permanent housing.

Finally, as night fell, our group prepared to drive the nearly 20 kilometers to Madhubangaon, embedded 10 kilometers inside Buxa Reserve. As we were about to leave Alipur, Akshu asked if we could give his friend a ride back to the village, too. Dinesh assented, and a fellow named Puru joined us in the back of the jeep.

Puru spoke English, Akshu told me. He even taught it at a local school. Akshu, who was accustomed to working with researchers unfamiliar with any of North India's languages, spoke with me loudly and clearly in a Hindi seasoned with Nepali, Bengali, and English words. When he was unsure that he had used the correct English term for something, he would repeat himself using Hindi, hoping that one or the other would register with me. He was basically a walking Rosetta Stone.

'How did you learn English?' I asked Puru.

'Actually, Sir! I learned English in a refugee camp in Nepal,' Puru responded. He explained to me that he was a Nepali refugee from Bhutan. 'So, you speak Hindi?'

'Not very well,' I said. 'I'm learning.'

'Well,' Puru said, 'you will have to learn Nepali too. It is quite similar to Hindi.'

Since we were getting into Madhubangaon quite late, Dinesh said that the restaurant at the government's Jungle Lodge—the main tourist-oriented lodging in Madhubangaon—would be closed by the time we arrived, and he suggested we eat at a roadside hotel. I had my concerns, as such places often left me retching through the night.

I asked Akshu if it might be possible for me to eat at his home instead. I had previously found villagers' home-cooked meals to be far less treacherous.

Akshu was clearly surprised. 'Yes, of course!' he said.
He immediately invited Dinesh and Bhuday as well.

I suddenly realized I had imposed three guests on the
villager, but I didn't know how to undo the damage. 'It
won't be too difficult?' I asked regretfully.

'No, sir, no, sir. What kind of food do you eat?'

'Oh, anything vegetarian,' I said, hoping that would
take the pressure off—otherwise, I worried villagers
would struggle to find meat for a guest of my social
class. 'And please boil some water for me.' I was rapidly
depleting my multiple bottles of water in the Indian heat.

When we arrived at the Jungle Lodge in Madhubangaon,
I couldn't believe my luck: the opening match of the 2010
men's FIFA World Cup, the first hosted in Africa, was on
a TV in the restaurant! Then, well before half-time, the
monsoon winds caused a power outage that would last
through the night. By the time we left for Akshu's house,
it was raining furiously; when lightning struck, the
jungle around us appeared indescribably beautiful. To
get to Akshu's house from the paved-but-bumpy main
road, one had to go on a dirt path, which the monsoon
had muddied. Since the electricity was out, Akshu and
his younger brother prepared our plates by candlelight
inside. Dinesh and I waited outside, sitting on plastic
chairs on the kitchen's concrete patio, sheltered by the
tin roof. I took in the surroundings as the sky came
down. Akshu's house was just 5 meters away from the
kitchen. Like most of the houses in the neighborhood,
it was built on thick tree-trunk-like stilts a little taller
than me. I presumed the homes were raised to protect
them from flash floods. There were also a few cows
tied underneath the house, sheltered from the storm.

Whenever lightning struck, I could see palm trees in the field next to us. Akshu would later tell me they were areca nut trees.

Dinesh and I were called inside the kitchen to eat. I assured Akshu I could eat crouched on the 6-inch high stools they sat on, and Dinesh followed my example. The kitchen was built of wood, but the floor was this pleasant, brown, irregular, and bumpy surface that was somehow both like and unlike dried mud. The food was good—rice, lentils, and vegetables. It was also scalding hot—they didn't provide me a spoon, so I ate with my hand. I wasn't a stranger to this, but I hadn't quite mastered the art of eating piping hot rice without burning my soft skin. Thidey, Akshu's brother, noticed. 'Would you like a spoon, sir?'

'Why?' I asked with a raised eyebrow and then a smile. 'Am I not eating the right way?'

'No, no—nothing like that, sir,' Thidey said. He peered at me through the candle-lit kitchen, trying to understand if I was insulted or amused. He looked nothing like Akshu, with darker skin and eyes that looked straight. He had a scruffy beard and long nose reminiscent of my own. His front teeth stuck out just slightly, giving his face an endearing goofiness when he smiled. He was a little taller and a little thicker than his brother. He looked confident, like a leader.

Dinesh finished his food and went to sit outside with Bhuday. The rain was falling heavily on the tin and ceramic-tiled roof of the kitchen and patio. Comfortable that Dinesh was out of earshot, I asked Akshu if he had found a place for me to live. He said that he had tried but couldn't find any nice places. He wasn't sure, he said, what an American's requirements would be.

'Oh,' I stammered. 'I don't want to live in Alipur. I like this.' I motioned around me.

'You want to live here, in the village?' Akshu asked, surprised.

I nodded, saying I just needed a single room. Akshu said he had some ideas and that he would let me know the next day. I finished eating and headed back with Dinesh and Bhuday to the government lodge for the night.

The next morning at breakfast with Dinesh, I gathered the courage to shift away from pleasantries. Not knowing how to gently broach the sensitive topic, I plunged in. 'Dinesh, I heard from other researchers that Bhuday drunkenly raped a woman working at the field station in Chalsa.' Akshu had reported the allegation to Jilpa, who had conveyed it to me. Having dealt with Bhuday's incorrigible drinking habits firsthand, Jilpa had found the accusation entirely plausible. 'Do you know anything about this?'

Dinesh was caught off guard, but he quickly became dismissive. 'I heard such things also, but I don't think it is true.'

'Why not?'

'I asked Bhuday, and he said he didn't do it.'

I thought Dinesh was joking for a moment, but then I realized he was serious. 'Dinesh, why would he admit it? I understand there were even witnesses.'

Dinesh waved his hand at me. 'See, Bhuday is of a different caste than Akshu and the others,' he explained. 'So they do not like him. That is why they will say all sorts of things about him.'

'Did you talk to the young woman who was supposedly raped?'

'Actually, I went to talk to her some time ago. I met her mother. She said the girl died.'

My eyebrows flew up my forehead. 'Died? She was really young, wasn't she? What did she die from?'

'I think her mother said jaundice,' Dinesh said.

I pondered this as I finished my rotis and potatoes. It was possible that there was a caste vendetta involved in Bhuday's indictment, but Dinesh's dismissiveness was reinforcing what I had heard about him from Jilpa. I regarded Dinesh's assessment with suspicion. 'Well, OK—but I also hear that Bhuday drinks before he drives sometimes and is not very reliable. I don't want him as my driver. How about he still drives for you, but for my work I hire another driver? How do you think I can find one?' I hoped beyond reason that my asking his advice would soften the fact that I was questioning his judgment.

'No. We will have only one driver for the vehicle.'

I studied Dinesh. This wasn't the sort of reasoned discussion I thought I had been working toward the last couple of days. I thought about pointing out that, since I would be paying my driver for their services, I should be able to hire whomever I wanted. But I held my tongue. Dinesh had probably expected me, a foreigner ten years his junior, to be a pliant companion in this place he knew so well. He had not been prepared for me to challenge him. It felt a little too soon to let our relationship unravel.

I spent most of my childhood in Birmingham, Alabama, in the American South. My parents were in some ways stereotypical Indian immigrants—they had received a reasonably good education back home and made their way through advanced degree programs when they got to North America. When I was growing up, they weren't yet well-off, but one of their primary priorities was making sure their kids had the most enriching childhoods possible. When faced with the choice of sending me to summer camp nearby or to visit family in India, my parents would often put me on a plane, hoping I would grow up versatile and bicultural. When my mom discovered that her two-year-old son seemed particularly fond of animals, she purchased an annual membership to the zoo and took me every week. That wasn't enough to satiate me, so Amma checked out National Geographic documentaries from the library and sat with me at 8 PM every Sunday to watch *Nature* on PBS. I was captivated: my mother and grandmother talked about the animals' feelings and thoughts, and it seemed obvious to me that, while the creatures in front of me weren't smart in the same ways as humans, they knew things that we didn't know, could sense and experience things we simply couldn't. I would wonder what it was like to be the various animals I saw.

My mother loved seeing how happy animals made me. But she was also hoping that my interest in non-human animals might evolve into a passion for a certain field involving human biology. 'You were good at math, and you weren't squeamish around blood,' Amma told me later, wistfully. 'I thought it was a done deal.' But when I was 21, instead of applying to medical school, I showed up at the office of Dr L. Sivaganesan, National Institute for Environmental Sciences, hoping to work with one of the world's preeminent experts on Asian elephant ecology. I told the stately middle-aged scientist of my aspirations to work in animal ecology, wildlife conservation, and poverty reduction in India. 'I want to help create a society where India's poor can improve their situation without having to damage the natural and cultural heritage of the country,' I told him, my eyes surely glinting with ambition. I told him I needed research experience in India. Perhaps to test my mettle, Dr Sivaganesan introduced me to Jilpa Thurairaja and sent me with her to Mudumalai National Park for a month. I developed a research question and hired a couple of Adivasi assistants who—like Akshu—had worked with many previous researchers. A few weeks of following them around the jungle counting deer pellets and elephant dung, occasionally coming across a pile of tiger scat or dodging elephants, and I was hooked. With Dr Sivaganesan's support, I got into a PhD program in ecology and evolutionary biology in the US with the understanding that I would work under Dr Sivaganesan's mentorship in India. My first year as a PhD student, with a letter from Dr Sivaganesan in my pocket, I struck out on my own to establish a completely new research project on predator ecology in a set of tiger reserves spread across Central India. The whole year became an adventurous disappointment—I failed to secure much funding or permissions to do research or any useful data to address my research questions. With my tail between my legs, I proposed some less ambitious research questions and asked Dr Sivaganesan if I could work in one of the sites where he had already established himself. He took a liking to one of my questions, a question on the role of Asian elephants in seed dispersal. 'You can go to Buxa.' Using his considerable connections in North Bengal, he quickly made arrangements.

After my failed first year of efforts, I had landed in Buxa already on the back foot. I was determined to eliminate any barriers to collecting useful data. If my first field season in North Bengal didn't go well, my PhD might be in jeopardy. Dr Sivaganesan had eliminated the biggest barrier—the government bureaucracy—by ensuring that I would get permissions to do research inside the protected area, but the rest was up to me. Living far away from Buxa in Alipurduar would make me dependent on Dinesh and Bhuday to get to the jungle every day. If I made Madhubangaon my base, I could probably find another vehicle for rent, or even walk or bike into the field.

So I was relieved the next day when Akshu came to our lodge and quietly told me he had found a place for me to stay in Malabasti, a hamlet in Madhubangaon. It was just in the nick of time.

'Today,' Dinesh said, 'we will go back to Chalsa.' Chalsa was 100 kilometers west. Dinesh had his own work to do there, and he was unconcerned with my calendar. I had just over two months before I had to return to the US for a check-in with my faculty advisers. I told him I wanted to stay in Buxa and get started on my research. 'The field station in Alipurduar isn't set up yet,' Dinesh said. 'You can't stay there.'

'I don't want to stay in the field station, anyway,' I told him. 'I want to live here in the village. Akshu says he has a place for me.'

'Where?' Dinesh asked Akshu, who responded in Bengali. Dinesh turned back to me. 'It is very simple accommodations. Are you sure you can manage?'

'Do I get my own room?'

'Yes.'

'Then yes.'

Bhuday, Akshu, and I loaded up my stuff into the jeep and drove to a house just next to the Metal Road, right up the dirt path from Akshu's home. The house was a newer, sturdier version of Akshu's, with a similar kitchen and outhouse. It too stood on tree-trunk-sized round stilts and had a corrugated tin roof, but it was painted a pleasant light-blue color. The house had four rooms that formed a backward 'L' shape, with the rest of the rectangle left open as a south-facing patio. My room formed the protruding part of the 'L'; it connected directly to the patio and was unconnected to the other rooms. Perfect.

My room was about 7 by 11 feet. The wall between my room and the next was made of woven bamboo. The windows had shutters that could be chained shut, but no glass. The floor was made of uneven wooden planks that, once I was settled, would permit me to see my slippers at the foot of the stairs outside. As I would discover in winter, frigid air would draft up through the cracks. That day, under the June sun, the tin roof made the room an oven. There were gaps between the roof and the walls that a bat would use every night to fly through my room in search of a quick meal. As I looked around, it occurred to me that the camera traps and computer in my suitcase were worth more than the house. There was already a wooden bed in the room with a thin cloth mattress, a pleasant surprise. There was also an electrical connection. Remarkably, my mobile phone had reception, meaning I could speak to my family and girlfriend regularly—a huge bonus. The owner of the house spoke in loud, imperfect Hindi, assuring me that the space would soon have a desk. He said other things as well, but he spoke too quickly for me to understand everything.

'This is my *bhaia*, Hari Atri,' Akshu explained. *Bhaia* meant brother, although I quickly learned that the two were cousins. 'He too has done lots of research work with NIES.'

Hari was all smiles. I liked him immediately. He was several inches shorter than me and lean as well, but with knotted muscles on his arms and chest. His cheeks were sallow, his eyes expressive, and his teeth discolored. He was dressed in mourning white, his head shaven but for a single ponytail at his crown; his father had recently passed away. He shared the house with his wife Maili, two daughters Champa and Chameli, and mother—six people for one outhouse.

'How much is the rent?' I asked.

'Give as much as you see fit,' Hari said. When I pushed him for a number, he stood firm. It was a shrewd move. My willingness to pay was more than he would have asked for. I offered him ₹2,000 a month. I later would find out I was paying him four times as much as the previous tenant.

'OK, Sir?' Akshu asked.

'Yes, Sir!' I said. I was going to live in the jungle.

2

Not far from the Atri household, three of Satyavati's children decided to untie one of their goats—after all, they thought, no animal should always be tied up—and it wandered over to a *mickanay* climber near a jackfruit tree and began nibbling its leaves. The children—two adolescent girls and a younger boy—turned their attention to their chores. It was a while before they realized that the goat had gone missing. They immediately searched the area together. One of the girls, Rukmani, noticed movement amongst some plants in a long ditch that drained the field. 'It's probably the goat!' she exclaimed.

'Wait!' her brother said. Akshu, eight years old, was sickly and of the cautious variety. 'It could be a snake,' he warned. 'Don't go there! Use a stick to check.' Rukmani took a long stick and brushed aside the *negiro* plants. 'Snake! Snake!' she screamed. 'Oh my god, it is so thick!'

Hemkala and Akshu looked for themselves, and then the three children ran off yelling to tell the other villagers that a large snake had taken their goat. They came back with a bunch of men who quickly realized that the motionless snake was an *ajgar*. 'Oh goodness!' one said. 'It's a good thing that the snake didn't take you! It's not a small snake—it's a python!' The children had actually only found the tail of the snake. Realizing that the snake was motionless and must have eaten recently, the men cleared the brush over the snake and found that it stretched all the way to a sizeable *pithali* tree, which it still had enough body to then encircle. The monstrous creature's head rested atop its body. When the adults neared the head of the snake, it responded with a threatening open-mouthed hiss. But it was too weighed down by its recent meal to try and flee.

'If we don't kill it, this thing could take another of our goats next, or even one of our children.'

Akshu watched as the adults found thick pieces of wood and struck the snake with all their might. The snake seemed barely affected—its thick hide reacted like a fully stuffed couch cushion, denting slightly and then expanding back to its prior form. By now the python was clearly trying to move, but it was constrained—the villagers found the bulge in the middle of its body.

'It must have eaten your goat!' one of the men concurred. Assured that the python could not move quickly, the men lifted the snake onto a nearby path and stretched it straight. It was about 14 feet long. Some of the men escalated their weaponry, retrieving sharpened axes. Even then, when they struck the snake, there was no blood—there was a dull thud with each impact, but the hide stayed strong. The men started striking the tail-side end of the bulge where they thought the skin would be taught. The bulge in the snake started moving up toward the python's head, until finally the python vomited out the Atris' goat.

By now, it was clear to Akshu that the python was in poor shape. Even having regurgitated its prey, it seemed unable to move; perhaps the men had broken its bones or skull. But the villagers were not satisfied—the snake still seemed too alive to them. They took the injured creature to the military training ground that had been temporarily established in Madhubangaon. One of the soldiers shot the python in the head and measured its length. Then, as Akshu looked on, the men dug a big hole and buried the python and the Atris' goat together in a single grave.

―――――――

Throughout his early childhood, young Akshu often sat atop the steps to the Atris' house doubled over and covered in a shawl. His whole body was emaciated, his belly withdrawn and concave. He didn't have a fever—it wasn't malaria (though Akshu sometimes came down with that, too). But his illness was episodic and, for a few days, he would feel normal, going to school, stealing some corn and beans from the neighbors' farms, and trying (unsuccessfully) to catch wild jungle hens. Like the other village boys, he was particularly fond of his slingshot.

One day, he saw two red-whiskered bulbuls calling back and forth on a fig tree near the Atris' house.

'Look, Maa,' he called to Satyavati. 'I bet you I can hit that bird!' Akshu picked up a jackfruit seed and put it in his slingshot.

Satyavati gave Akshu a warning glance. 'Hit that bird? How about I hit you?'

'No no, just with the jackfruit seed!' Akshu said confidently. Before his mother could stop him, he took aim at the bulbul sitting on a fence post and let fly the seed. It hit the bird squarely, and the creature fell to the ground. Akshu ran over and, to his dismay, found that the bird was dead. Bulbuls are socially monogamous creatures, and the surviving bulbul chirped in distress and flew in circles near the scene of its partner's murder.

Satyavati pulled Akshu toward her and struck him firmly. 'Get out of here! You won't eat tonight, and you won't drink tonight! What was it doing to you?

Poor bird. Have you no sense? Have you no love?'
In some ways, though, Satyavati was also glad when
Akshu misbehaved like the other children, seeing such
normalcy as hope that he would eventually overcome
his recurring ailment.

For Akshu himself, there was no starker reminder of
his limitations than the fact that he was seldom allowed
to go into the jungle. His father and elder brother would
go to herd cattle and collect seeds and vegetables; his
mother and sisters collected firewood and fodder. All of
them would sometimes go to work in the plantations.
Other young boys frequently acted as cowherds. And
then there were the forest guards who would enter the
forest from Madhubangaon on their way to patrol the
jungle for poachers and smugglers.

So Akshu assumed that the jungle was where all the
action was and begged his father to take him along.
'You're too young,' Motikar would say; but he was
primarily concerned about Akshu's health. On days
when Akshu was doing alright, he would encourage him
to go into the forest just outside the village to herd cattle
with his brother Chander, who was 13 years his senior.

Chander was one of those fruits that had fallen
far from the tree—growing up, he had played hooky,
choosing to lounge at the river. He avoided farm chores
when he could and instead looked for shortcuts to make
money. For instance, Chander would go to a nearby
colonial-era water tank to cut off iron bars on the lower
part of the structure to sell. When Motikar warned him
that he was taking too much risk—what if the tower
ultimately collapsed on Chander?—Chander responded
in anger. Unlike their compassionate father, Chander
did not speak affectionately to his siblings. Nonetheless,
perhaps hoping Akshu would ultimately take over for
him as cowherd, he took his younger brother along into

the forest and taught him what grasses and climbers were palatable to their cattle. Chander showed Akshu where to find wild mangos and wild *kusum* fruit. Chander had a particular fondness for jungle tubers—what they called 'jungly potatoes'—and was very talented at finding them.

'Oooooh,' Chander would say excitedly, 'see that yellow-yellow plant beneath that tree? Go check that out.' Akshu would obey and, sure enough, he would find a large tuber. 'See, this tuber's plant has four leaves,' Chander would explain. '*Panithura* potato is like this; *panglang* is like this...'

Akshu loved the attention from his elder brother, but Chander was not interested in sharing his favorite activities with Akshu. The one thing that got Chander more excited than the wild tubers was the round dens he found at the bases of trees. 'Stop, stop! Let's see what we have here...' Chander would say lustily. He would note the exact location of the den, leave his little brother at home, and come back alone with his spear. Chander would return to the village with at least one but sometimes several (once, he came back with six) dead porcupines, ready for consumption.

Chander would also catch fish in the rivers. On one occasion, someone had poured poison into the river, and Chander and a friend opportunistically gathered as much of the dead fish as they could. There was much excitement when he returned home with the haul. But before they could cook the fish, they discovered that the friend that had gathered fish with Chander was ill. Within a couple of hours, the boy died. Chander had seen him drink water from the poisoned river. The Atris elected not to eat the fish.

Since Akshu was generally restricted from visiting the jungle, his main exposure to the denizens of the forest occurred when they visited the village. Some creatures were visible during the day, such as peacocks and jungle fowl that traversed the village looking for grain, hornbills and parakeets that came to eat figs, king cobras that nested not far from Akshu's home, and flying foxes that visited the papaya trees at dusk. Akshu and his friends would compete over whose house hosted more weaver bird nests, and they stared curiously when the rare gharial crawled onto the bank of the creek east of the Atris' home. But most of the creatures visited only at night, so, to Akshu, these creatures were largely a collection of disembodied sounds—like the forlorn howl of the jackals.

One night, the Atris awoke when a cow tied up under their house began mooing frantically. In the bright moonlight, Motikar saw something white and small moving quickly away from the house. 'The cow's child has gotten loose,' Motikar told his family as he dashed outside. Agile and long-legged, Motikar caught up with the calf, now on the ground. She was prostrate, and she wasn't OK. Motikar had just found her wound when he heard the growl. Motikar turned to confront the leopard—he yelled, half-threatening, half-terrified, and the predator fled. Motikar brought the injured white calf back home and administered some traditional medicine to its wounds; after two or three days, she resumed drinking her mother's milk and recovered.

Then there was the chicken thief. The Atris kept eight hens that slept on a pile of firewood next to their house under a tin sheet. One hen would often peck at another, and the latter would screech. One night, they heard this usual sound—'Kaaah! Kaah!'—and Motikar growled gutturally back at them—chicken-speak for, 'Cut it out.' There was peace, then—silence.

The next morning, they realized one of the chickens was missing. 'Maybe someone stole it from us,' Chander suggested. Later that week, just after the Atris had gone to bed, a hen called out frantically again—but this hen continued to call as it was taken away. 'KAAH KA—ah kaah...' The Atris followed the sound away from their home until it stopped, and the trail went cold. Not long after, a third hen was taken, and the Atris followed the sound even farther before death stilled the victim. The Atris, now clear that the culprit was an animal, saw the matter as quite serious; they had lost almost half of their hens. In the morning, the Atris started looking for hen feathers and found a trail of them leading from their home into the bushy area between the settled village and the creek. There, again, the trail ran cold.

Not long after, an Adivasi woman from the village was in the village outskirts to answer nature's call when she saw a dark, furry animal climbing into a hole in a tree. Remembering the Atris' account of the chicken thief, she led Akshu along with two of his neighbors, twin boys named Narad and Om Ojha, to investigate. They climbed the tree and examined the den; it was filled with chicken feathers. 'Oh ho!' they exclaimed. 'We found the chicken thief!' And the culprit was there! Deep in the den, the shape of a stocky cat with a long tail, the size of a small dog—it was a common palm civet. It was the first time Akshu had seen such a creature.

The boys couldn't reach the civet, and it was near nightfall. But Akshu received word later that a group of boys had managed to permanently end the chicken thief's reign.

Predators might have launched occasional, high-cost incursions into the village of Madhubangaon, but as the

Atris planted more crops, herbivores were mounting a growing offensive. Muntjacs would sneak into the crops as the sun set. Wild pigs would dig up the villagers' yams and eat their corn until village dogs chased them off. Macaques would make a meal of their corn until the village children chased them across the creek; once, Akshu's friends abducted one of the monkeys' babies as punishment, holding it captive for several days until the baby's and mother's calls of distress became unbearable.

The biggest offenders, too dangerous to be dealt with by dogs or children, were elephants. Every year, when Madhubangaon's corn or rice lured the pachyderms, the men of the village would climb into *tongs,* tree houses or towers, and spend the nights sleeping in the fields. If an elephant (inevitably male) interrupted the night, the men would awake and begin hollering, 'Hoy, the *haathi* has come! *Haathi ayya ray!* The elephant has come from this side! Hey, Adhikaari Naani—wake up!' until all the other men and often the rest of the village was up and shouting at the intruder. Akshu would join the women and children on the village's paths and look out at the elephant in the crop fields, illuminated by moonlight or torch or battery-powered flashlight, alternatingly making noises at the elephant to scare it away and speaking admiringly of the marauder. '*Aaaaiiii! Oooooh!* Look at how big the *haathi* is!' the children would say. 'Such a big *haathi*!'

For the children of Madhubangaon, the fact that elephants were taking a share of their food was not something that immediately tarnished the crop-raiders in their minds. Elephants were still a source of real wonder in the village. On rare occasion, *doll haathis*— herds of female elephants and their young—would even emerge near the village during the day, and the villagers would all look on in awe as the calves played with their siblings, aunts, and mothers. Akshu loved to watch the elephants' ears flap as they grazed, to see their giant tongues as they chewed. The village adults tolerated the elephants, often resigned to the fact that God, in the form of an elephant, would take *some* fraction of their crops as patronage. The villagers with farms on the outskirts of the village would do a puja over a section of their fields, offering it to Lord Ganesh in a ceremony that, as Akshu understood, basically attempted to negotiate with the deity. 'Ganesh Bhagwan, don't damage our crops, OK? This is your share, so eat this.'

As Akshu began to connect the dots between his family's poverty and their inability to accumulate resources, including food, his feelings toward male elephants began to shift. Akshu's family could only afford to buy him one set of clothes a year; to preserve it, Satyavati would often have Akshu run around wrapped in just a *gamcha*. The Atris couldn't afford soap, so they used dried *rita* and *pangra* fruit when they bathed, boiled ashes to clean their clothes, and mud after having relieved themselves. As there were no power lines in the village, the Atris didn't have electricity, and they couldn't imagine owning a phone.

Satyavati and Motikar suffered many familiar challenges of the poverty trap—for instance, they did not own a plow, and they did not have savings to pay for a trip to the doctor when they or their children got seriously ill—so they were repeatedly forced to take out loans to make ends meet. The moneylenders charged interest in the form of rice—about 200 kilograms per year for a ₹1,000 loan—meaning that most of the rice the Atris successfully defended from the elephants would go to their bankers, leaving the Atris mostly corn to eat. Some families, like that of Om and Narad Ojha, didn't lose nearly as many crops from their lands, which were closer to the center of the village, buffered from attacks from the jungle by farms like those of the Atris. Akshu protested when the moneylenders took his family's rice, but he also began to associate his family's problems with the elephants that raided their fields.

Once, Akshu saw Narad's mother giving leftover rice to the dogs that lived on their property. 'Even the dogs in Narad's house get real rice,' Akshu complained. 'But we only get cornmeal.' Satyavati—who was probably both amused and a little saddened by this reality—mentioned her son's comment jokingly–seriously to Narad's mother. In response, the latter called Akshu into her home later that week. 'Come,' she said, offering Akshu a plate full of rice, dal, and vegetables. 'Eat as much rice as you want! All the rice you want!' Akshu gorged himself with rice, but it was a one-day offer. From the next day, he was back to corn—and, now, having just had a full meal of rice, he hated the corn more than ever. Sometimes, he idly wished that all male elephants would die.

If Akshu was beginning to resent the animals that raided their crops, his brother was downright indignant that they had to deal with the elephants at all. 'Why am I having to eat corn? Why did you leave Madharihat?' Chander demanded of his father. 'You had such a nice, salaried position there. Why did you bring us to this damned jungle to live amongst the elephants? If we had stayed in Madharihat, by now we would have become rich! Instead, we are stuck here.'

His anger overflowed onto his sisters. Once, dissatisfied by the quality of the vegetables they had cooked, he scolded them relentlessly. 'What can we do? the girls asked. 'We just cook the vegetables we are given. If you bring us good vegetables, we will cook them.' Unhappy to get such lip from his little sisters, Chander continued to yell at them. Akshu spoke back to him that day for the first time. 'They're right!' Akshu observed. 'They didn't buy the vegetables, they just had to cook what they were given!'

'Oh, so you're on their side too now, are you?' fumed Chander. He grabbed a piece of wood and made toward his siblings as though to beat them, and they all fled from the kitchen.

It was ever so small a rift that formed then between Chander and Akshu. The little boy could not possibly know how his defiance toward his brother would shape the rest of his life.

———————

Akshu's illness still recurred regularly. Now about ten years old, he was doubled over again on the steps to the Atri house. He ate less than both his older and younger siblings, and he looked on as they laughed. 'He isn't doing well. He never sits well,' Motikar complained. 'All the other children go to play and wander and find food, but he doesn't go with them. He just sits there.' Akshu's handsome younger brother Thidey was only about four years old, but still he and his cousin were able to harass Akshu with impunity, pelting him with small stones and calling him names until their sweet sister Bhagavati intervened. By now, Satyavati knew that it was not Akshu's personality to tolerate perceived injustice. He was just too weak to assert himself.

The traditional medicines Motikar gathered in the forest had no discernible effect on Akshu's health. In Satyavati's mind, he was actually getting worse—and then, one day, Akshu got up off the steps and moved a few meters from the house. He hunched over, and his abdomen convulsed—Satyavati realized he was struggling to vomit. It was a prolonged affair, but eventually Akshu was able to get it out. And from the vomit, to Satyavati's dismay, emerged a flat, white, leech-like wormy creature.

For the Atris, a 20 kilometer trip to see a doctor in Alipurduar was not to be taken lightly—it was expensive, so they relied on traditional medicines for milder ailments. Many of their traditional medicines had proven to be fairly effective, and they couldn't afford to seek modern medical attention (which was often of dubious quality anyway) for every affliction, many of which resolved naturally. But in this particular case, the Atris had miscalculated by not seeking formal treatment. After Akshu vomited the worm, Motikar took him to Alipur. Akshu received treatment, a few pills.

Akshu improved markedly. While he was still prone to common illnesses—the fevers and diarrheal diseases that plagued Buxa's seasonally swamp-like forests—he was no longer debilitated. Motikar and Satyavati held their breath for a few months before they allowed themselves to believe that their son had been transformed.

Motikar began taking Akshu into the forest. His thin, cross-eyed son was an eager student.

First, Motikar showed Akshu what one could eat in the forest. Jungle foods were not plentiful enough to provide all the calories a family needed, but they served as a vital source of diverse nutrients. Motikar collected *amla* fruit to pickle with spices into an *achar*. *Chalta* fruit, which were hard, sour, half-kilogram specimens particularly liked by elephants, could be sliced with a kukri and eaten with salt or pickled. Akshu learned that he should slice up *chalta* fruit and feed it to his cattle to increase the volume of milk, give it a pleasant taste, and rid the cows of intestinal worms. The buds of the *semul* tree, if removed just before blooming, could be cooked up into a delicious dish, and the tree's cotton-like fibers were used to stuff mattresses and pillows.

There were also all the medicines. Take the seed husks of the *harra* tree, grind it up, mix it with milk into a paste, and put it on a person's tongue—it could treat a severe cough, his father told him. A patient with a really bad head-cold may be treated using a climber-like plant called *abhijalo*—by breathing in the fumes after wrapping it in banana leaves and heating it in smoldering ashes. Climbers, fruits, sap, roots, and even bark from the right tree were used to treat everything from gastric problems to jaundice and typhoid.

Finally, Motikar showed Akshu the best wood for constructing houses and taught him about plants like the *komalkoti* that, if processed and ground up and mixed with mud, helped improve the quality of mud houses. He told Akshu which plants had fibers good for making rope. And he gathered fruit husks of the *chukrassi* fruit, mature seeds of *birdarrow*, and certain mushrooms that could be sold as decorations.

Of course, now that Motikar was taking his son with him into the wilderness, he also had to help him stay out of harm's way. Motikar taught Akshu to identify the winding track of a python and to be vigilant for venomous snakes and big cats, although these were rarer than the various dangerous herbivores of the jungle. Once, Motikar and Akshu were collecting decorative mushrooms, walking on either side of a thick fallen tree. Suddenly, they heard the frantic sound of an animal moving rapidly through the vegetation a short way off.

Akshu looked up—there was no sign of an elephant. From his height, all he could see was plants disappearing as they were trampled by an approaching animal—it did not look so large, and Akshu did not feel threatened until he heard his father. 'Son!' Motikar hollered, 'climb onto the tree! Climb onto the tree!' Akshu scrambled onto the fallen tree just in time to see a huge wild boar with curved tusks charge right past the log, exactly where he had been moments before. The boar must have been over 100 kilograms; Akshu realized it would certainly have overturned him had he not obeyed his father. The boar, clearly in a rush, disappeared into the brush.

Like most villagers, Motikar's and Akshu's interest in the jungle was primarily in that which was practically useful. Akshu was eager to learn about the plants of the forest, for instance, but he saw no use in learning about the diversity of birds. When it came to elephants, Motikar's interest was primarily in safety. To help ensure his son would not surprise or be surprised by a herd of Ganesh's comrades, he taught Akshu to track elephants—to observe the pattern of flattened grass and to find the toenail marks of elephant footprints on hard and dusty ground. When they did have to run from elephants, Motikar taught Akshu to pull himself up into the thickest tree around—to use a vine or climber if the tree was too thick or smooth to scamper up—so that the elephant would be unable to knock down his refuge.

By this stage, much of Akshu's youthful enthusiasm for the giants had subsided; he watched them with vague interest. When Akshu stood on a hill or rise and saw elephants below, he would note where they were going and how fast. He wasn't really interested in, say, what they were eating. Akshu figured that if they left the elephants alone to do their work, he and his father could do their own. Occasionally, though, the elephants broke this unspoken jungle-dweller's pact. Once, Motikar returned home without his usual jungle harvest. He explained that he had climbed a tree and was felling *guruja* climber to cook and eat with rice. He had then watched helplessly from above as a herd of elephants appeared, devoured what he had painstakingly harvested, and disappeared back into the jungle.

Akshu had experiences with his father that very few people in future generations would ever have. A couple years after his recovery from chronic illness, they were collecting decorative mushrooms on one side of a small and drying pond, perhaps 15 meters wide. Without any warning, five large bovine creatures emerged from some bushes across the pond. They were spectacular— the largest individual's horns spanned nearly 2 meters, spreading almost perpendicular to the animal's skull, the end turning skyward. Akshu, immediately recognizing that they were wild water buffalo and that they were now rare, was transfixed, while Motikar, who had seen such creatures on occasion, was keenly aware that he and his son were in danger. 'Look for trees to climb,' he whispered to Akshu. 'Thicker than 6 inches.' Apparently, wild buffalo could fell a thin tree much like an elephant. Akshu stared at the buffalo closest him. Its eyes were at about the same height as his. The bovid lifted its head, sniffed the air, nodded, and dipped its head down deeply, and then repeated the procedure. Motikar was weighing his options when, suddenly, the buffaloes grunted, turned, and bolted. Motikar sighed in relief. 'If they run away, they won't come back,' he said. Akshu smiled, pleased that something so large could be afraid of him.

3

During my first week in the village, I painstakingly tried to communicate with the people around me, often relying on Akshu or Puru to interpret for me. My landlord's daughter, Champa, a vivacious 16-year-old, looked at my laptop with great interest, so I sat her down and started teaching her to open and close programs and type, also making a failed bid to teach her to play Minesweeper. Villagers made a point of dropping by wherever I was to steal a peek at me, and for Hari and Maili, having an American as a guest seemed to be a point of pride. I could not help but enjoy being the object of so much attention.

For meals, I would walk down the dirt path to Akshu's home, where his wife and mother would prepare me food. While most meals involved rice or rotis, they would occasionally break out a different Nepali dish like momos, *sel rotis* resembling funnel cakes without sugar, or lo mein noodles. They served vegetables ranging from potatoes and cauliflower bought at the bazaar and bitter gourds and mustard leaves grown on their land to a variety of climbers and greens and tubers they collected from the jungle. They got milk from their own cows, which meant it ebbed and flowed with the season and presence of calves. Eggs came from their chickens and neighborhood ducks, but were even rarer. Once a week, Akshu would bring home fish or, occasionally, goat meat from the market. Satyavati was a vegetarian like me, so she and I would instead get locally made paneer. The dal they served was extremely watery, but the rest of the food was delicious. I paid the family a little extra to get an occasional egg or yogurt for me to try and keep from losing weight, but it didn't work.

In those early days, dinners were also a time of fascinating conversations and cross-cultural exchanges. Akshu's house was chock full of people: his wife Kusum, his seven-year-old daughter Kanchi, his newborn baby Nirman, his parents, his brother Thidey, a distant relative with an apparent mental illness, and the two Bhutanese refugees Tula and Puru. These ten people lived in a creaking house that was smaller than Hari's. I was glad Akshu had not asked me to cram in with them, but the supper company was fantastic. The Bhutanese refugees knew just enough English to close the gap between Akshu and me. Early on, I tried to integrate myself into their community. 'Stop calling me "sir". I'm younger than all of you except Tula, and he's only a couple of years junior to me.'

'Sir—sorry—what should we call you, then?' Puru asked.

'Little brother,' I said in Nepali.

They laughed and shook their heads. 'No way.'

'Why not?'

'Because you are so educated,' one of them said. 'You deserve respect for that.'

'No, that does not make sense,' I responded. Relying on Puru, I switched to English. 'I am more educated because I had the opportunity to go to good schools. I was lucky. You all haven't had that opportunity. And you know so much more about the jungle, and about how to farm. I have no practical skills.' Once the men fully understood my point, they seemed a little stumped by this logic for a while. But only for a while. Over the next few days, the debate reignited whenever I tried to wriggle out of the honorific.

'No, it does not matter how you became educated—only that you are. Thus, you still deserve to be called "sir",' they said.

I said, 'Well, actually, Akshu, you are teaching me about the jungle. That is why I have hired you, to be my teacher. And when students pay Puru and Tula to be their teachers, the kids call them "sir". Not the other way around!' As the message was clarified and filtered through the group, there was another wave of laughter. Akshu just shook his head obstinately. 'I am working for you. As long as I am taking money from you, I need to show you the proper respect.'

'Fine,' I said. 'But I will call you Guruji.'

Akshu's brother Thidey was not to be outdone, and one day he presented his logic to me. 'When I call you "Sir", it is not with regard to you,' he said. He tapped me on the chest. 'I am speaking to the god seated inside of you, the god of education. That god has never come to me, so you cannot call me "Sir"!' He smiled triumphantly.

I looked at him blankly. 'Thidey ... isn't the god of education, Saraswati, a goddess?'

Thidey nodded yes.

'So ... shouldn't you be calling me "Madam"?'

After dinner, two of the men would walk with me in the night back up to Hari's house among flashing fireflies. They made me shine my flashlight in every direction from whence an elephant could come, and they made me look carefully for snakes on the dirt path. It was training; Akshu would not allow me to walk by myself at night until my second field season.

A few days after Dinesh and Bhuday had left Buxa, I felt I was settled enough to try and start my work. I asked Akshu what Jilpa had told him about my research. 'She told me to show you the fruits that elephants eat,' Akshu said. 'Right, Sir?'

Labouring in Hindi, I tried my best to help Akshu understand my research question. I endeavored to explain that in ecology, one major question was how each animal or plant species affected other species. For instance, some bee species were important because they helped pollinate flowers of wild plants and crops. Trees affected other species because they helped prevent erosion, stored carbon, and provided food and habitat for many animals. But scientists didn't yet know if most species did something unique, or if most species were replaceable. For instance, if one bee species were to go extinct, then maybe other bee species or pollinators would start eating more nectar and pollinating more flowers—maybe they would replace the extinct bee species, and the ecosystem wouldn't actually miss the insects that had disappeared. Ecologists were working to predict how losing species or groups of species would affect ecosystems.

One theory was that species that had really unique bodies or behaviors—like elephants—may be less replaceable if they disappeared from an ecosystem.

'I want to understand if elephants do anything that affects other species,' I stammered in Hindi. I told Akshu that scientists had shown that African forest elephants in particular dispersed a lot of seeds. I tried to explain to him that ecologists thought this sort of seed dispersal by elephants might be crucial for some tree species. If all fruits fell and remained near their parent tree, then the seeds from those fruit would have to compete with the parent tree for light and nutrients. And if all the seeds were together in one place under the parent tree, they could easily be found and consumed by, say, a rat or by a fungus. Since elephants could swallow lots of big seeds and defecate them far from the parent tree, I tried to explain, the seeds would have a better chance of surviving.

The conversation was a chore. I had never practiced discussing seed dispersal, functional ecology, or elephant dung in my Hindi classes. When I picked enough of the right words, Akshu had no problem grasping the concepts—as a farmer, he knew far more about plants than I. But my vocabulary was wanting. After 15 to 20 minutes of struggle, Akshu still didn't understand my research question. But he understood the most immediate point—that, to start my project, I needed to find fruiting trees.

My plan was to focus on two or three tree species and quantify how much fruit elephants and other animals ate from those species, and then estimate how important each animal species was for dispersing those trees' seeds. Dr Sivaganesan had suggested a few tree species—*Careya arborea*, or the slow match tree; *Dillenia indica*, the elephant apple; and *Mangifera indica*, the wild mango. I told this to Akshu, who immediately recognized all the scientific names. He had helped Dinesh put together a list of the area's tree species matching their local and Latin names.

'I see, Sir. So you want to go find some *kumbhi* and mango trees? *Chalta* doesn't fruit until the dry season.' *Chalta* was the Hindi name for *Dillenia indica*.

'Yes!' I said. Then I picked up a boxy-looking thing in a boxy-looking metal case to show Akshu. 'And I want to put this camera trap on the tree. If an animal eats the fruit, it will take a picture.'

Akshu looked at me, puzzled. 'How close do you need to be to take the picture?' Having spent considerable time trying to chase elephants from his crops without getting trampled, he seemed concerned about spying on elephants as they ate.

'No, no,' I told him. 'This is a camera trap. If the animal comes, it will take a photo by itself.'

Since we didn't have a vehicle, Akshu suggested we walk into the jungle outside of Madhubangaon to look for *kumbhi* and mango trees. Excited about getting into the jungle, I agreed. Walking would not be a long-term solution since I wanted to collect data throughout the 760-square-kilometer reserve, but all I needed for now were a few trees on which to test my camera traps.

It was not yet noon, but it was already a scorching June day. I wore hiking boots which I had slathered with waterproofing. The creek between the village and forest was swollen, so I took off the boots and crossed. I again donned my hiking boots and trod 15 meters when we came to another depression, this one laden with stagnant water. I repeated my operation. The next obstacle was a mud pit—I tried to just stomp through it, but the mud grabbed onto my foot. The more I struggled to pull out one foot, the deeper the other went. It wasn't quite quicksand, but I suddenly had a visceral appreciation for how that would work. Akshu wore slippers, sliding them off and carrying them as he limped through these wet patches. I took off my boots and walked barefoot for the next half hour.

We reached the first *kumbhi* tree but found it had no fruit. Akshu then took me to a mango tree. This time, there clearly had been fruit, but they had been removed—Akshu showed me the signs that villagers had climbed the tree and harvested the fruit, often lopping off branches that were too thin for them to scale so they could remove the mangoes from the fallen branches.

'A few monkeys have been here too,' Akshu said, referring to Buxa's wild Rhesus macaques. 'Many of the mango trees began fruiting last month, so we have come a bit late.' We moved on to a third tree—again, this *kumbhi* tree simply had not fruited this year. These trees were not close together, and I was impressed that Akshu knew where they all were. He responded that while his was a small world, he knew it pretty well.

'You should … must … might have seen so many animals living here!' I stammered out in Hindi. 'Have you ever seen a tiger in the jungle?'

'Just once,' Akshu said. 'When I was quite young, maybe 10 or 12.'

We returned to the village after three hours in the jungle. It wasn't all that long, but I was still exhausted; I was just recovering from an illness, and my bare feet had been smothered with hundreds of ant, mosquito, and leech bites. Akshu, amused, said my skin was like that of his newborn son. Where the bugs had subsided, the subtropical sun had been merciless. The canopy of the forest areas we had treaded was not closed, as the vast majority of the area was some sort of plantation. While the plantation planners had deliberately left some fruit trees to stand, they were rare, so other villagers had already beaten us to them. Akshu clearly was not the only one who knew where he could find a jungle snack. We had not found a single tree with fruits.

Over the next couple of days, Akshu and I searched different areas of the forests near Madhubangaon. On the third day, after four hours in the grueling sun, we approached a humongous mango tree, whose dark green leaves were obvious from a distance even to me. We worked our way through the brush to the tree and immediately found a fruit on the ground. I was thrilled. I started taking off my backpack to take out my camera trap. The idea was that we would put this automatic camera on the tree, pointed at a few fruits. Later, when an animal removed the fruit, my camera would be triggered and 'trap' a picture of it, and we could see whether it was an elephant, macaque, or some other creature. Over a couple of years, if we randomly selected trees across Buxa, we could get an idea of what proportion of fruit was removed by elephants and what proportion by other species. This would be the first step in calculating whether other species could replace elephants as seed dispersers for the mango. As I prepared for our first trial with the camera, Akshu burst my bubble by pointing out that there weren't any mangoes on the tree.

Stare as I might, I could not discern a single fruit. There were lopped off branches on the ground around us, stripped of their fruit. Other villagers had been here, too. Monkeys would reject or sometimes toss unripe fruits, leaving at least some fruits for someone else, but people just took unripe fruits home so they could ripen there. The elephants didn't have a chance.

Akshu handed me a second fruit. 'What do we do with two fruits? Should we put up a camera?' he asked.

I looked at him a bit defeated. Putting a camera where there was such heavy human traffic, and for just two fruits, seemed like a good way to get a camera stolen for little chance of gain. I handed him one of the two fruits. We sat down and ate the mangos. They were sweet and delicious in the midday sun.

Clearly, people had found and eaten most of the wild mangos within walking distance of the village. This was my first clue that Buxa, despite being a protected area, was not going to provide insight into how important elephants were in a 'natural' system, mostly unmodified by humans. And I decided that wild mangos, being so delectable to humans, were probably not the ideal study species. With Akshu's help, I identified another large-fruited tree species we could study, this one called the '*lator*', or jungle jackfruit. It was a soft-fruited species with seeds about 1.5 centimeter long, so we could see if elephants were more important for its dispersal than, say, hornbills or parakeets.

Next, I focused on trying to secure a vehicle. After a day with an expensive rental vehicle whose owner and driver both struck me as unreliable, I began negotiating with Dinesh again. He and Bhuday had returned about a week after they had left, this time to stay for the rest of the field season. Dinesh and I sat down and discussed how we could share the jeep, since the two of us had very different geographic requirements. We decided that Dinesh, an early bird, would have the vehicle from 7 AM to 2 PM Monday through Thursday. I would then have the vehicle from 2 PM to sunset those days and for the full day on the remaining three days of the week.

With the schedule amicably settled, I spent several days unsuccessfully trying to coax Dinesh into letting me work without Bhuday. I was running out of time to begin my research. I either had to spend a bunch of money on another vehicle and driver or risk working with Bhuday. Dinesh had a stranglehold on the NIES jeep, and he was wearing me down.

I had up to this point been relying primarily on Jilpa's long list of complaints about Bhuday to inform my actions. I had hesitated to try and ask Akshu—in Hindi, at that—about something so sensitive as rape. But I began to wonder—maybe I had weighted Jilpa's testimony too heavily? Now that Dinesh and Bhuday knew I was a stickler for decency, perhaps they would behave? Maybe Bhuday would stay sober? And maybe Jilpa, who also was not a native Hindi speaker, had misunderstood Akshu's account of the rape, or maybe Akshu did have some sort of vendetta against Bhuday. Having lost my sense of control over the situation, I began to hope that I had been overzealous in my opposition to this whole hiring-an-alleged-rapist-drunk-driver thing.

Late that afternoon, I found myself alone with Akshu in his kitchen. Taking a deep breath, I asked Akshu as sensitively as possible, 'Guruji, Jilpa told me that Bhuday raped a woman at the Chalsa field station. She said you told her that. Is that true?'

Akshu spoke more quietly than usual. 'I wasn't in Chalsa when it happened,' he said. He told me that a drunk Bhuday had forced himself upon a young village woman who cleaned the field station. Her pleas of distress from Bhuday's closed room were heard by the repairman-construction worker, or *mistree*, who was working in the field station. The *mistree* did not intervene, but he did report what he had heard to the neighbor's brother. Later, when Akshu went to the Chalsa field station to work, he gradually befriended the young woman. One day, she tearfully told Akshu, in socially acceptable vague terms, that Bhuday had laid his hands on her, ignoring her pleas not to do so. The neighbor's brother independently brought up the *mistree's* account to Akshu, validating the young woman's story.

'I told Dinesh what Bhuday had done,' Akshu said, 'but he did nothing. So when I went to work with Jilpa, I told her what had happened.' Jilpa took the matter up with Dinesh. That must have spurred him into action. 'But by the time Dinesh visited her home, the young woman was dead.'

'What happened to her?' I asked.

Akshu lowered his voice further. 'I don't know for sure. The girl worked for the neighbor too, and his wife said she had seen the girl bleeding a great deal. In this wife's opinion—and in mine—the girl became pregnant from the rape. Her mother was from a very poor Muslim family, and she found someone to do an abortion—but he did a poor job, and the girl died.'

Akshu left the kitchen to milk his cows, and I sat there stunned. It suddenly occurred to me just how ludicrous it was that I—or Dinesh, or Jilpa, or anyone—ever thought that this was something that a bunch of ecologists could take care of on our own. These were serious accusations that required professional investigation, not whatever the bumbling authoritarian Dinesh could manage between field outings, probably with Bhuday lurking behind him. It was clear that no one believed involving the cops would be productive, and I—who arrived a couple years after the crime, lived over 100 kilometers from the witnesses, and didn't speak a lick of Bengali—clearly wasn't the guy to try and summon them. And I was skeptical that the cops would be interested in pursuing justice for a deceased Muslim girl with only a poor mother, anyway.

One thing was clear to me now, though. Jilpa had watched Bhuday drive drunk, and Akshu had strong reasons to believe Bhuday had raped a young woman. I definitely did not want to work with this man. Through dinner, I sat pensively, wondering whether I should go ahead and hire the other vehicle and driver despite the considerable expense. Thidey asked what was wrong, so I told him.

'Listen, Sir,' Thidey said. 'You're never going to be able to get the evidence to fire Bhuday for rape. You have to try something else.'

I was open to new ideas. 'What?'

Thidey thought for a minute. He was the creative political type. 'Well, why don't you just tell the girl's community what Bhuday did? They're Muslims—they'll take care of Bhuday for you.'

I immediately told Thidey that wasn't an option. Even if Thidey's stereotypical assumptions about Muslims happened to apply to the young woman's community, sparking religious vigilante violence was pretty firmly on my 'things not to do' list.

'Well, then,' Thidey said, 'just wait. Bhuday has no control of himself. Do not act strict with him—just watch him well. Then, he will one day drink on the job. Then you can fire him.'

I shook my head. 'I don't want him working with me for weeks, learning how expensive my equipment is, seeing where we put my camera traps—then he could harm my work later.'

Thidey grinned his goofy grin. 'Weeks? If you're nice to him, you're not going to have to wait that long.'

On our third day working together, Akshu, Bhuday and I went to check the camera traps and replace any fruits that had been removed. The jungle road was completely flooded in places, and Bhuday skillfully sloshed our four-wheel drive vehicle through almost knee-high water. We came to a tree that had fallen on the road, and Akshu and Bhuday took their kukris and went to hack the end branches off the tree so we could drive around it. Fallen trees and floods would, as it turned out, block off many sample trees from us over the course of the season; the roads and bridges of Buxa were in poor shape and easily made impassable or dangerous by the monsoon. I pulled off my boots and joined the Nepalis, insisting on trying my hand with the kukri. Both Bhuday and Akshu were soon laughing at my ineptitude. They gave me a quick lesson, but my improvement was scarcely noticeable.

By the time we got back to the village after work, it was past 7 and dark. I heartily commended Bhuday on a good day's work and asked if he was returning to Alipurduar. He said he would have dinner with his wife first, and then leave at 8 PM for town. His home was in Madhubangaon, not 10 minutes away from Hari's.

I went to dinner, came back to enter my data from the day, and got into bed. There was light rain on the tin roof, so I could not hear much of what happened outside the house. Around 10 PM, I was on the phone with my girlfriend in the US when there was a knock at the door. At first, I ignored it. My relationship was new, and I was keen to keep it alive despite the distance.

'Sir!' It was Hari.

'Yes?' I asked, annoyed.

'Sir, please come out! Someone is here for you!'

It was Bhuday, and he was hammered. He gave me the keys to the jeep, slurring that he had started driving through the forest to get home but had decided to spend the night in Madhubangaon. 'Sure,' I said, taking the keys. 'Just tell Dinesh you're doing that, OK?' Over Bhuday's objections, I called Dinesh and handed Bhuday the phone. They spoke briefly, and Bhuday handed the phone back.

'Do not let him drive!' Dinesh said to me. I held myself back from rubbing the situation in his face. 'Put the jeep under Hari's house so it is safe from elephants, and I will come tomorrow morning by auto rickshaw,' he said. I called Akshu, and the two of us with great difficulty maneuvered the jeep between the stilts holding up Hari's house. I marveled at Thidey's forecasting.

I had leverage now. Dinesh knew I could reveal to Dr Sivaganesan that he had knowingly harbored a chronic and unrepentant drunk driver for the university vehicle. The next morning, Dinesh was left with no choice but to fire Bhuday. With Dinesh on the back foot, I usurped primary responsibility of the vehicle. Akshu helped us find a new driver, a former truck and auto rikshaw driver from the village named Narad Ojha, and I told Dinesh that the vehicle and its driver would stay in the village with me during the night.

In a matter of weeks, I had freed myself of Dinesh in just about every way. Akshu and others who had worked for Dinesh in the past seemed impressed that I had been able to get rid of Bhuday so quickly. I started feeling pretty good about myself, thinking I might have gained the fine balance of principle and political wherewithal to navigate the intrigues of working in the field.

In fact, it was just beginner's luck.

4

As Chander had hoped, the now-healthier Akshu inherited primary responsibility for herding the family's cattle when he wasn't in school. The families in Akshu's hamlet shared herding responsibilities so, when it was his turn, Akshu was charged with taking both the Atris' dozen or so cattle and his neighbors' animals across the creek into the jungle to feed, making sure none were lost or stolen. Akshu was seldom if ever completely on his own. His herd would combine with those of other cowherds. Nonetheless, by about noon the conversation would have died down, and Akshu and his companions would be bored of walking alongside their livestock. Generally, the activities the boys engaged in to stave off boredom seemed innocent enough—for instance, they would scramble up slopes near rivers and streams looking for kingfishers' nests, dig out their eggs, and suck out their contents. On one occasion, though, Akshu found himself up in an *assare* tree, cutting small branches with his kukri to feed the calves under his watch. Suddenly, he realized that he wasn't alone—six or seven forest guards had spotted him. 'Why have you come alone into the jungle?' one shouted. 'Why are you cutting fresh wood?'

In those days, young, fit forest guards patrolled the forest regularly on foot, looking for violators of conservation laws. They commanded a great deal of fear, and Akshu, of course, was still a child. He almost wet himself as he scrambled down the tree. His father had warned him not to cut green wood—the villagers living in Buxa were only permitted to collect dead, dry wood from the forest floor for fuel. But Motikar's tendency of framing things in terms of ethics instead of practical implications such as risk of punishment had not resonated with his son.

'If I ever catch you cutting fresh wood again,' the forest guard continued, 'I will take you straight into custody. You are NEVER to cut fresh wood.' Akshu mumbled that he was just there to graze his cattle and ran back to his herd, never to cut fresh wood again.

Akshu might have often felt bored as he herded cattle, but he was unwittingly developing a deeper relationship with the forest ecosystem and its denizens. His typically unexciting days were punctuated with the sublime and the terrifying. On one occasion, Akshu and a middle-aged companion named Magar Dai were driving some 50 or 60 cattle east on a dirt road coming from Madhubangaon. The trail stretched straight into the forest as it crossed several of Buxa's creeks. At one of the streams, there was suddenly a disturbance. The cattle that had passed the creek continued forward, but half of the herd just behind the creek abruptly stopped. They looked agitated, but before Akshu could ask Magar what was happening, the problem made itself clear. A huge *makhna*—a male elephant without tusks—stepped out of the forest. Immediately, it turned its massive head in the direction of the humans separated from him by just a small group of cattle.

Akshu instinctively turned to flee, but Magar whispered, 'There's no need to run. There are so many cattle, he won't come after us.' Akshu stuck by his elder. The *makhna* flapped his ears toward them, but he didn't trumpet or snort. Finally, he turned and began walking in the same direction as the cattle.

Though they appear to be lumbering, elephants can walk quite fast, and the cattle in front of the *makhna* found themselves trotting to stay ahead of their new companion. The cattle behind the *makhna* soon got with the program as well and began to follow the elephant, first cautiously and then more comfortably. Akshu and Magar looked at each other, shrugged, and followed their cattle; their tension was quickly replaced with great pride that their herd included a wild elephant. The *makhna* occasionally stopped, stood askew, and pointed his trunk, still wet-tipped from his drink in the creek, toward the jungle, sensing things that Akshu could not. Finally, after about a kilometre or two of this, the *makhna* turned toward the thick jungle of Buxa's core area and disappeared from view, leaving Akshu both relieved and happy.

In general, herding was a fairly safe activity for Akshu and the other boys. Wild animals didn't see the cattle as a threat, and since the herd moved slowly and deliberately and often included cows wearing bells, they never really surprised the jungle's denizens. Elephants in particular, while dangerous in one sense, were also discerning; they could react poorly if surprised in the forest, but when away from the crop fields where they confronted people directly, they seemed less prone to violence. Given prior notice that cattle and humans were en route, they could be quite tolerant.

Of course, children in a jungle still managed to occasionally stumble into trouble. A 12-year-old Akshu was once herding cattle with two of his cousins at the Bala River in late fall. The river was a seasonal one that spread as wide as 70 meters in the monsoon, but then contracted to just a stream by autumn. That day, the riverbed had been recaptured by a sea of tall *Cassia* grass with white flowers blooming in the post-monsoon, pre-winter climate. It was a hot day, so Akshu and his cousins lounged under a tree on the west bank of the Bala as their cattle fanned out across the alluvial plain to graze. As the afternoon began to grow old, Akshu's older cousin Manoj told Akshu and Natkhat to retrieve the cattle.

'You,' he told Natkhat, 'go south, go east across the river and then drive the cattle back toward me. Akshu, you do the same for the cattle to the north.'

Akshu and Natkhat set out to rein in the dispersed herd, largely invisible in the tall grasses. Akshu soon looped back west over the riverbed, tapping any cow he met with his stick to encourage them back toward Manoj. The herd seemed to be responding. Akshu wound through the grass, looking for stragglers. He sensed an opening in the grass ahead, expecting that a resting cow had flattened the vegetation or that maybe a large stone or log had obstructed its growth. He was just a few meters away when he saw the stripes of a tiger.

It was lying on its side. What surprised Akshu about his first tiger sighting was just how long the cat was— the tiger's paws pointed west, so, coming from the east, Akshu could see the whole eight- to ten-foot length of its body, from its head pointing south to its tail pointing north. Flies buzzed around the creature as Akshu recognized what it was, but he thought the feline was sleeping—after all, flies even crawled over Akshu and his family as they slept. Perhaps it was the buzzing of flies that prevented the tiger from hearing his approach as it slumbered? Or maybe it was dead.

Nonetheless, Akshu found himself shivering, his heart racing—millions of years of evolution told him he was in danger. He couldn't have stared at the prostrate predator for more than a couple of moments; he backtracked slightly, quickly tiptoed south, and then raced west toward his cousin, imagining that the black and orange stripes might appear from the wall of grass around him at any moment, and that it would be the last thing he would ever see, if he saw it at all.

Akshu arrived back on the western bank of the Bala and breathlessly told Manoj what he had seen. 'It's a good thing it didn't get you,' Manoj responded somberly. As the cousins began to drive their cattle home, Akshu's racing mind slowed, and the euphoria from having survived an encounter with a big cat settled in.

'It might have been dead,' Akshu said.

'It's a good thing you didn't check,' Manoj joked. 'Sometimes a tiger kills a cow and drinks much of its blood, and then it falls into a deep slumber.'

But the three of them began to imagine the benefits that could be had from a dead tiger. Akshu had seen others who had somehow acquired the claw of a leopard and made it into a pendant—how cool would it be if he could have a *tiger* claw as a pendant?

In the next day or two, the boys came back to the river to find the tiger, reasoning that only a dead tiger wouldn't have moved in the interim. Afraid to split up, they covered the part of the river that Akshu had been charged with together. Soon, they found the spot where Akshu had seen the tiger—and the great cat wasn't there. His cousins asked if he was sure this was the spot. 'I'm completely sure,' Akshu responded. Maybe some other villagers had heard of the boys' discovery and came to find the prize themselves; maybe the tiger had been killed and left there by poachers who had since recovered their quarry. Or maybe the tiger had been a living one, drunk on the blood of a cow or sambar deer, and Akshu had all but stumbled into an encounter with Buxa's largest predator that was unlikely to have ended well.

Akshu's years as a herder coincided with a time in which the Atris' land was reasonably productive, before the elephants began fully exercising their power. Thanks mostly to the villagers' diligent use of cow dung, Malabasti's residents had managed to make their land far more fertile than when Motikar and Satyavati had come in the 1960s, and the adult Atris spent a fair amount of their time working the fields. In February or early March, before the pre-monsoon rains, they would plant corn. Interspersed throughout the maize, and thus difficult to find for crop-raiding jungle animals, were vines of beans, cucumbers, and pumpkins that wound up the corn stalks. Corn grown in higher-level land would also be inter-planted with chili, and some land was set aside for ginger and potatoes. The corn would be harvested in late May and early June. Farmers would feed some of the green leaves of the corn crop to their cattle. Whatever had dried and remained there, they would cut up and leave on the soil to fertilize it. After the monsoon rains hit in mid-June, the decomposing remnants of the corn stalks and cow dung would make the soils dark and rich, and the farmers would plant their rice in nurseries to grow thick and bright green as they plowed their fields. They would then plant the rice seedlings in July–August. The short-grained rice would begin to be ready for harvest in late October, but most would not be ready until December. The Atris would then grow a crop of mustard, which would flower into a golden plain in an otherwise drab winter landscape; they would harvest the mustard in early February, drying its leaves to make *gundruk* that would last for much of the year and could also sell for a few hundred rupees a kilo. The Atris would then plow the land three more times, and it would be ready again for the corn. Land not under cultivation for corn or rice was used to grow hundreds of banana plants. Thus, the Atris essentially used all their farmland year-round to support themselves.

Yet, despite the progress they had made in agriculture, the Atris—who had to feed seven voracious children— faced palpable shortages of income and food in those days, and economically they were amongst the hardest years of Akshu's life. Almost all the rice the family grew still went to pay back money lenders, who charged interest rates as high as 10 per cent a month, even for loans for medical and family emergencies. Particularly after the elephants took their share, the Atris didn't have enough corn to feed themselves throughout the year. Government rations in those days were a reliable source of kerosene but not of food. Since Buxa had been declared a tiger reserve and was supposed to serve wildlife conservation over timber production, the big Forest Department plantations of 1,000-plus hectares that Akshu's parents had worked on had been gradually reduced to small spaces of just 20–25 hectares. These smaller plantations didn't provide as much work for Buxa's forest villagers, whose families had also expanded. A maximum of only one of the Atris could now do paid work on the plantations, and that was Akshu's oldest sister Devi. His other older sisters were unable to find work, and Akshu, his younger sister Bhagavati, and Thidey, the youngest, were in school and too young for regular employment, anyway. So the Atris focused primarily on subsistence activities. By herding cattle, Akshu helped provide a much-needed source of milk and cattle for sale. Chander worked the land with his parents, occasionally disappearing for his own purposes. Motikar continued to milk the cows and collect mushrooms and a couple other non-timber forest products to sell. And Satyavati looked after the housework and cooked most of the daily meals.

Since income was tight, the Atris would experience acute food insecurity in June and July, when the last year's corn had run out and the current year's corn was still drying. Akshu and his younger sister and brother would eagerly anticipate Wednesday evenings, when Devi would receive her weekly pay for her plantation work. Devi would keep going to the road to see if her compensation had arrived. As soon as she received it, she would go to the bazaar and buy some flour and cornmeal, then come home to start making rotis. Her siblings would gather around the fire pit in the kitchen, calling dibs on warm rotis made very small and thin so that the flour might last further into the week. 'This one is mine!' one of the youngest children would shout, playfully snatching each roti and eating it plain, their diminutive nutrition-forsaken bodies absorbing everything possible from the bread.

Over the next four to five days, the Atris would stretch out the bazaar-bought food, mostly cornmeal, supplemented by jungle and garden veggies. Almost without fail, the family would skip a meal or two on Wednesday until Devi brought home the dough. Sometimes, though, the food would run out on Tuesday or even Monday. Motikar covered the gap by collecting food, especially jungle tubers, from the forest. If the Atris had family or other guests visiting, they would borrow a bowl of cornmeal from their neighbors; somehow, they would find a way to return two bowls the following week.

The scarcity of food—especially protein—in the community may have contributed to the persistent and innovative hunting culture in Buxa. Families like the Atris could occasionally afford to slaughter one of their goats, but the rest of the year was leaner. Thus, villagers fanned out over Buxa, capturing a huge variety of foods. While he was herding, Akshu watched villagers fish and capture freshwater turtles throughout the day. He ran into hunters that, like Chander, had speared porcupines and monitor lizards in their burrows. Some hunters took dogs with them to capture Malayan giant squirrels. They would use slingshots to try and knock a squirrel down from the tree, but if they couldn't, they would pursue the squirrel as it fled through the canopy into a short-treed area until it had to cross a patch of ground, at which point their hunting dogs would pounce on the colorful rodent and make the kill.

Perhaps most ingeniously, some villagers found a straightforward way to kill snakes. On his way back from herding, Akshu and his friend once ran into some hunters skinning a 12-foot python. The hunter explained that all a hunter had to do was take a stick, carve out a small cavity on the end, and put some tobacco inside. Once a python was found, it would inevitably open its mouth in a threat display and maybe even lunge toward the hunter. 'Push your stick into the snake's mouth and drop even a little of the tobacco inside,' the hunter explained, 'and the python will be dead soon. It's very toxic to them.'

Akshu also watched as his neighbors set out at night to capture animals more easily found after dark. Hunters realized that black-naped hares would stare unmovingly once caught in the sights of a flashlight—so, while one person stayed steady with the light, the other would circle around and take the hare out with a long club or a slingshot. Villagers would brave snake bites and elephants to capture long-bodied fish from the rivers with flashlights and kukris when they emerged after dark. Hunters would sometimes find a jackal's footprints on a jungle trail; they would then dig a hole in the path and cover it with brush. In the evening, they would hide off the path and howl. A jackal would soon trot down the path, lured by the apparent sound of a friend or intruder, only to be shot or fall into the pit trap, where it would be dispatched from above with a bow and arrow. Wily though they were in some ways, Motikar told Akshu, it was very easy to kill a jackal.

Of course, hunters also pursued less exotic quarry. In addition to the bows and arrows owned by many villagers, a select few even had village-made pipe guns. Akshu saw people bringing back wild pig, chital deer, and muntjac meat from the forest. Thidey briefly joined a group of hunters and observed their customs. The successful shooter, he found, got one perfect leg to take home, while the rest was split amongst everyone. The head was never to be brought home, so the hunters would cook the brain with some oil, half a chili, and some salt and turmeric in the jungle, using large leaves as plates.

Needless to say, all of this hunting activity within Buxa Tiger Reserve was illegal. In the common parlance of conservationists, everyone—from the boys wielding slingshots to the organized hunters—would qualify as poachers. But villagers only vaguely knew what was and wasn't legal at that time; forest guards did not provide much instruction, and forest patrols, who were few and far between, seldom got far beyond the fringes of the village. In contrast, villagers knew the jungle intimately. To Akshu, his one run-in with forest guards notwithstanding. The law was not a major concern. And the idea of conservation—that species, if not protected from overhunting, could disappear completely from the landscape or even be wiped from the face of the Earth—was simply beyond the comprehension of a boy who knew little of the world beyond walking distance. Instead, Akshu's mixed feelings toward hunting were probably a direct consequence of the mixed messages he received about animals from his family and community. On the one hand, both Satyavati and Motikar seemed to have a fairly moralistic attitude toward animals. Motikar instructed his children to be compassionate to animals—he embraced the common Hindu belief that they had the same souls as people, and that they could suffer. He got upset when Akshu tied bamboo thorns to a fence to protect their maize from a feral bull, worrying that the animal might be injured. Motikar did not easily anger at the elephants when they raided the Atris' crops, reasoning they needed to eat as well. However, aside from Motikar and a couple of elder Adivasi men, Akshu knew no one in Madhubangaon who voiced disapproval of the pervasive hunting throughout the jungle. And even these naysayers were not opposed to benefiting from the slaying of animals: those Adivasis, Akshu observed, partook in meat when someone else brought it to their home, and his father still ate goat meat. The potential ethical costs of eating meat also seemed largely offset by social benefits. If a guest was provided a nonvegetarian meal, they would spread the word: 'Ohhh, they fed me meat, they fed me fish—they really respected me.' If a guest was fed a meal without fish or meat, their review could signal a lower status for their hosts.

Young Akshu apparently saw nonviolence toward animals as a nice idea but omnivory as a practical necessity (and the local norm) in the jungle. In Madhubangaon, food, especially protein, was often too scarce for anyone to be picky about what they ate. Most of the neighborhood just didn't seem to often consider whether hunting had ethical ramifications. Still, several Hindu and Buddhist customs implied the ethical value of nonviolence toward animals— they seemed to imply that ahimsa was a positive but non-mandatory practice that brought people closer to divinity, similar to charity for many faiths. For instance, in most of Malabasti's Hindu households, no one would consume fish or meat for at least 13 days after a close relative had died, fretting that such violence would perturb the peace of the deceased's soul; Akshu's more devout family would abstain for an entire year. Throughout India, more broadly, vegetarian traditions had often been framed around an abstract concept of purity and used to drive a wedge between the castes, becoming more about a profoundly problematic social hierarchy than ethical considerations of animal welfare. But any sincere consideration of the meaning of short-term vegetarian practices or ritual offerings to forest animals would precipitate reflection on the belief that animals experienced joy and suffering and had souls like humans. Thus, just as many holidays in various faiths provided an opportunity for adherents to contemplate the value of charity to the needy and compassion to other people, customs and practices that honored the well-being of various animal species planted a seed that could sprout real behavioral change. For instance, after Satyavati's mother passed away, she undertook traditional restrictions on her diet for a year—but then she never began eating meat again, saying it no longer felt right to her. She thus became the first and only vegetarian in the Atri household.

'You keep eating,' she told her family upon her decision, 'but I no longer will.'

Obligingly, Akshu kept on eating. But he must not have been completely uninfluenced by the animal-considerate messages he was receiving from the more spiritual members of his community. One day, he and some other cowherds were in the forest, and they were looking for something to do.

'Let's catch a jungle hen!' one of the boys said.

'How?' Akshu asked. While he no longer carried a slingshot, he was keen to catch some game. None of the other boys had their weapons either.

The boys were discussing various traps they had heard about and experimented with when the oldest cowherd, a man in his forties named Muktan, joined the conversation. He was from the mountains, and he had far more practice as a hunter than the boys or even most of their parents.

'I'll show you the best way,' he said. As the boys followed him, Muktan plucked about 30 hairs from the tail of a cow, making sure that the hairs still had their sticky follicle ends intact. He tied the hairs together so that they formed a nearly meter-long rope made more robust by the sticky follicles. He then flowed effortlessly through the forest, quickly identifying a thin trail that had the hallmarks of being used by small animals. 'You set the trap in this sort of animals' road,' he explained. He went to a point on the trail already sandwiched by two trees and further narrowed the gap with brush. 'Get me some cow dung.' The boys brought a fresh cow pie, which Muktan placed in the narrowest part of the path. He made the cow-tail rope into a noose and tied it to a sturdy branch, which he bent back until it was held lightly in place over the cow dung by a thick nearby branch. The noose was held wide open by brush, the bottom embedded in the dung. Finally, he sprinkled some mustard seeds that he carried with him in the middle of the cowpie, pressing them lightly into the dung. 'This should work well,' Muktan said to the bemused but skeptical boys.

They left the trap overnight and came back the next evening to check on it. Amazingly, the boys saw a jungle hen had indeed hung itself—the branch had sprung up when disturbed, and the cow-tail-hair noose had successfully snared its victim. The boys extracted the dead hen, started a fire, and roasted and ate Muktan's quarry. It tasted like chicken.

Akshu was thrilled. A few days later, he suggested to a fellow cowherd that they repeat the set-up in a few places. It was a wonderful diversion from the boredom of herding cattle. They finished three traps, and Akshu went home daydreaming about the meat he would get to eat in the coming days.

None of the traps was immediately successful like Muktan's but, a couple of days later, as Akshu approached from a distance in the evening forest, he could see the silhouette of something hanging from the cow-tail rope they had used.

'That's not a hen!' Akshu's companion exclaimed.

'It's not!' Akshu said excitedly. He could see the creature had a thick body and could make out several limbs. 'It's ... it's a muntjac!'

The boys rushed toward the animal, their mouths watering at the thought of barking deer venison for dinner—when, suddenly, Akshu saw the silhouette split into two and an animal scamper away. The escaping animal was a baby monkey, and the hung creature...

'Oh, Bhagwan...' Akshu muttered. The hung creature was a female Rhesus macaque, its eyes closed, its face pink, its head tilted as though its neck had broken unevenly. Akshu realized that the animal had looked like a deer because its baby had been clinging to her chest, still drinking her milk. Akshu felt horrible; he looked into the jungle after the baby macaque. He imagined how much he would have suffered if his mother had been killed when he was still breastfeeding.

Akshu pinched his ear lobes and bowed his head, vowing never to set another such trap. He never hunted again.

It was a late autumn day when Akshu's younger sister fell terribly ill. Bhagavati had a sudden and violent bout of diarrhea and a fever. 'It's very bad,' Satyavati told Motikar. 'I'm worried.'

Bhagavati, nearly 12 years old, was the doll of the family; she was a positive and peaceful girl, and her sudden and drastic decline was enough to convince the Atris that modern medicine might be immediately necessary. Motikar got the money somehow, and he and Satyavati hired a private vehicle to take Bhagavati the 20 kilometers to Alipurduar. The trip over the potholed road took about an hour, and they weren't intercepted by the dacoits that sometimes patrolled the road. They arrived by early evening. The government hospital had a women-only facility, so Motikar waited outside the gate as Satyavati and Bhagavati were shown to the emergency waiting room. After some time, a hospital employee came to speak with them. She didn't look them in the eye or hold Bhagavati's little hand.

Bhagavati was finally admitted, and they again waited. Hours passed, and Bhagavati continued to suffer from diarrhea. By the time the doctor saw her, it was around 11 PM, perhaps five or six hours after their arrival.

The doctor didn't introduce himself when he called them into his office. Instead, he engaged in the same rapid-fire, barky evaluation that most Indian villagers expect from small-city doctors.

'What's wrong?'

'Fever, diarrhea…'

'Since when?'

'From the morning, it has been very bad…'

'OK.' He wrote a prescription for several medicines and handed it to Satyavati. 'Go on!' he said, ushering Satyavati and Bhagavati out. Satyavati could tell that Bhagavati had worsened, so she immediately acquired the medicines and began feeding them to her daughter. They hunkered down in the hospital for the night, Motikar still waiting outside. Bhagavati wasn't improving—she was still having diarrhea, and her fever was still bad. It was one of those nights that seemed to last forever, but then it was over shockingly fast. Between 5:30 and 6 AM, Bhagavati died.

Here, in the early 1990s in North Bengal, Satyavati didn't think to ask the hospital staff why her daughter had passed away, and the hospital staff didn't bother to explain it. The hospital wasn't really accountable to the villagers they served—the Atris suspected that the doctors weren't very good and may not have been properly trained, but they hadn't a clue how to assert themselves or complain that something that seemed so curable would be allowed to take their beautiful girl. Instead, Satyavati and Motikar departed with what was left of Bhagavati, their grief, and a deep anger that their child's life hadn't been valued.

As far back as Akshu knew, it was the Atris' first major family loss since their arrival in Madhubangaon—for all their troubles thus far, the Atris had managed to stay alive in the face of everything, from malaria to unsympathetic moneylenders to animal invaders. Yet, despite having been at a government hospital, they didn't see what had happened as a failing of the State—they didn't see the State as responsible or having responsibilities. Instead, they were angry about the indifference of the particular doctor they saw. But they didn't know what they could do to punish him.

Akshu coped with the loss by daydreaming about Bhagavati—Bhagavati studying diligently for school, Bhagavati mediating disputes among their peers, Bhagavati eating *phatooki* fruit in the cornfields or the ripened black fruit of lantana under the water tower, staining her mouth purplish black. Their father had called her 'Pindi', so Akshu (very cleverly, he thought) had given her the nickname 'Bindi'—so now he thought about Bhagavati whenever he saw okra. Soon, though, Akshu began to think about what happened to his baby sister after her death.

'Their souls take root in another body,' Motikar had told Akshu of the dead. 'That's why you should never be cruel or kill another creature. Any animal could be of *"aafno manchhe"*.' Our people.

So Akshu started wondering where Bhagavati was now. Was she one of the insects he saw buzzing around? Maybe one of the hens pecking at other insects in the dust? Or even one of the elephant calves that came into the outskirts of the village to play with its mothers and aunts? On significant days, like the anniversary of Bhagavati's death, the Atris kept their eyes open for stray dogs or other animals that might try and join their family; on a typical day, a new stray would be chased off for begging for food scraps, but on a death anniversary or the like, it was assumed such creatures might be a returning relative. A dog that happened to show up on a significant day would luck out, earning an offering of leftovers from the family at the end of every meal, never to be chased away.

One day, Akshu really felt—felt deep inside—that he might have found his sister. He was milking cows in the cowshed, and he had untied the calves to let them frolic nearby. The calves would often run up and down the path to the shed and in the fields, exercising their new legs, shaking their heads, and kicking backward as they played. Most calves tended to be disinterested in humans; after all, people only began to feed them after they were weaned. One calf, however, walked up to Akshu and nuzzled him.

'Bindi?' he said. The calf studied him closely as he rubbed her neck. For at least a moment, Akshu believed—wanted to believe—that his sister had come back to him.

***

The two-year period of food insecurity the Atris experienced came to an end for a few reasons. Akshu and his older sisters began getting occasional work as labourers in the cornfields and rice paddies of others, giving the Atris an added source of income and food. The Indian government's ration system also began offering more rice and wheat flour to families below the poverty line (BPL); this food was of limited quality, the rice and wheat flour often being old and sometimes inedible, but at the least it served as animal fodder. In addition, the expansion of commercial interests in Buxa provided thousands of extra rupees to Motikar and other experienced forest dwellers. Whereas, previously, a single company would pay Motikar and other villagers to gather decorative mushrooms, now two other companies arrived, and they began ordering large amounts of a diverse line of non-timber forest products (or NTFPs) that could be gathered from Buxa: *theenpalli, checkrassi, birdarrow* fruits, *pangra, narkheli*. Villagers didn't know why outsiders wanted these plants, but orders were far larger than before, for 10,000, 20,000, or even 100,000 specimens. So many village families were able to help fulfill the orders. The villagers vaguely knew that what they gathered was to be used as either decoration or medicine—otherwise, all they knew was that the forest products would make their way to Cooch Behar, then Calcutta, and then perhaps other parts of the country. Villagers also recognized this as an opportunity to produce new demand—Motikar, for instance, introduced one of the companies to *buensikatoos*, a plant he used for buffalo fodder but that one of the companies recognized as a potential decorative plant. They sent samples to company headquarters, and soon a new order arrived for this product as well. For Buxa's villagers, the forest was now providing yet another resource to fuel their daily survival and slow climb out of poverty.

Despite this noticeable improvement, Chander didn't seem any happier. The taciturn young man, now in his late twenties, was tame as a mouse in public, but at home he behaved like a disgruntled boar, angry and resentful that the family was still poor. As the other Atris began making enough money to ensure the family could make ends meet, Chander became increasingly unproductive and spent much of the cash he acquired on lottery tickets. He would then go to the temple or come home and pray to the gods for a win.

When he didn't win his way to wealth, he would lash out at his parents, singing the same refrain Akshu had heard from him for over a decade. 'Why did you leave

Madharihat and bring me to this damned jungle? We could have been rich by now...'

'How can we explain this to you?' Satyavati would cry. 'We were so miserable in Madharihat. We were robbed of everything we had—gold, money, metal vessels—they took everything from us, they beat your father. It was a miracle we left with our lives.'

'Well, then why didn't you at least claim some land in Jaigaon when you had a chance? Why did you have so many children—if you hadn't had so many, I could have had a decent life.'

Akshu, now 14 or 15 himself, was no longer cowed by his brother; he hated to watch Chander make his parents so sad. 'This is lunacy,' he would yell. 'You were a six-month-old baby when you left Madharihat, when Papa was herding buffalo near Jaigaon—who knows if we would've been rich or poor over there? Our parents have spent decades collecting seeds, herding other people's buffaloes, washing other people's pots and pans—why don't we do something to support ourselves now? We're young, we're fit. We shouldn't depend on them anyway!'

Chander sometimes fought back when Akshu took him on; at other times, he just looked at him and listened, his thoughts unshared. Chander appeared to be experimenting with various forms of emotional blackmail. Once, he spent several days acting very angry, ignoring anyone who asked him what was wrong. For nearly four days, he marched about grumpily, often skipping meals. Motikar finally yelled, 'What's going on, just tell me already!'

'You have a wife, you sleep with her,' Chander hissed. 'I want a wife too.'

'Oh,' Motikar realized. 'He wants to get married.'

Akshu was beside himself. 'You fool!' he said to Chander. 'How dare you treat our parents like that? We asked you what was wrong for so many days. You could have explained calmly that you wanted to get married!'

Despite Chander's tantrums, Satyavati and Motikar saw the core of Chander's request as legitimate—it was their responsibility, after all, to find him a wife. So they began spreading word through the Nepali Brahmin community that their son was available for marriage. An acquaintance in Jaigaon told Motikar that he knew a family in town with a daughter of marriageable age. Motikar took his son to visit the family. Chander and the young woman saw each other, and Chander expressed interest. 'My son likes your daughter and would like to marry her,' Motikar told Prem, the young woman's father. Both families agreed to go through with the union.

The usual wedding preparations commenced. The main event would be held in Jaigaon, where the bride-to-be was from, and then another celebration would take place in Madhubangaon, where the couple would settle into Motikar and Satyavati's home. Each side would pay for the festivities in their respective villages, and though this meant the woman's side would pay somewhat more, there was no dowry. Both sides began making investments and arrangements for the ceremonies—hiring priests and buying coconuts and incense and flowers. Before the actual wedding, there would be engagement rituals at the bride's home. The bride's family prepared lots of food in anticipation of the Atris' arrival and, in Madhubangaon, Chander's parents, siblings, uncles, and closest cousins readied themselves for a trip to Jaigaon to make the engagement official. Everyone was ready to go when Akshu's cousin's wife, Maili, came down to tell Motikar, 'Chander doesn't want to go.'

Motikar was bewildered. 'What! Why?' He and several others ran into the house to find Chander. 'You said you wanted to marry this girl—why aren't you ready to go?'

'She didn't even speak with me when we visited,' Chander complained.

'Are you joking?' Motikar fumed. 'You know that's not how this works—her duty was to just serve tea when we visited. You know that. If you wanted to speak with her, you could have gotten one to two hours with her—you should have asked then!'

But Chander was recalcitrant. He no longer wanted to marry this woman. Motikar was distraught; even Satyavati, usually level-headed, became very tense. 'My word is my greatest asset,' Motikar said shakily. 'Without my trustworthiness, what am I? What do we do?'

Satyavati had only one idea—and it was, in this cultural context, the obvious one. 'We could offer them Akshu's hand in marriage instead…but…'

'…but he's too young!' Motikar finished. 'If you were a little older,' he cried to Akshu, 'and you agreed, I would marry you to this girl. But she's much older than you, and I don't want to ruin your future. But now what to do? My honor is now worth not even two rupees…'

Akshu observed all this with great sadness. He wanted to say, '*Joom*, I'll marry her!' and save the family's honor. But he felt far too young—he wasn't ready.

The family wrung their hands, trying to think of a way to resolve the dilemma, but there really was no way out. Finally, the Atris sent an intermediary to inform Prem that Chander had changed his mind. Prem's family was furious—this was a tremendous insult.

'Send him here!' Prem roared to the messenger. 'Bring him, and I will cut off his head with a kukri.' Prem's sons also threatened the Atri family. They would come after Chander, they said.

After a period of expecting some form of retaliation, the Atris sighed in relief. They heard that Prem's family's temper had cooled to less violent resentment—the immediate danger had passed. However, while getting cold feet before a wedding (especially to someone one had never spoken to) might be seen as defensible in many times and places, Chander's remorseless change of heart and disregard of cultural norms made even clearer to the Atris that Chander was not just immature and temperamental but somewhat unstable. For a poor jungle-dwelling family in 1990s India, however, little could be done about this. There was no language, there were no services available to address this danger from within.

5

With Bhuday out of the picture and Dinesh out of the way, I was free to begin my research in earnest. Since the monsoon fruiting season for both the *lator* and *kumbhi* fruits would last less than two months, I was hungry to collect as much data as possible on which animals were eating the fruit. As we were sharing the jeep with Dinesh four days a week, Akshu, the new driver Narad, and I worked every day.

Since my childhood of marathon sessions watching National Geographic and hearing my grandmother's stories of various forest animals, I had always dreamed of a job that would take me into India's jungles on a daily basis to commune with wildlife. But in the monsoon season, Buxa was not terribly revealing. While the South Indian protected forests I had visited at least guaranteed seeing some wild pigs and chital deer almost daily, in Buxa, the only mammal I was fairly confident I would see most days was the Rhesus macaque, a monkey visible even in the streets of Delhi. It was unclear to me whether this paucity of sightings was primarily due to low animal densities in the jungle or the monsoon. The core area of Buxa was mostly classified as semi-evergreen vegetation but, after the rains began, there just didn't seem anything 'semi' about it. The jungle was thick with vines and climbers and epiphytes and tall herbs and tall grasses—so many leafy bushes, so many leafy trees. There was water everywhere, so staking out a waterhole wouldn't increase my chances of seeing wildlife. Watching a three-ton elephant disappear in the grass right next to a forest road underscored to me how difficult wildlife was to see in thickly vegetated parts of Buxa. With the almost constant din of cicadas and other insects, hearing nearby animals wasn't easy either, even when we were on foot or sitting silently in the vehicle. In fact, in the monsoon, what Buxa really offered abundantly were invertebrates. Butterflies and moths of all sizes and shapes, in hues of blue and yellow and purple and red, were the most conspicuous, sometimes landing on me to dab at my salty skin or clothes with their long proboscises. There were also stick insects of spectacular shapes; metallic-black spiders with long bodies and wiry legs, shaped like nothing I had seen before; colorful beetles, iridescent flies, true bugs, and so on. By simply paying attention, one could see several novel creatures a day.

Now that I had access to the jeep, my first job was to rapidly find as many trees of our study species as possible and try to identify what animals were eating their fruit once they fell to the forest floor. I had six camera traps, and we began putting them on the *lator* and *kumbhi* trees right away. Akshu and Narad and I would go into the jungle, count the fruit in and under our target tree, and mount a camera trap on a tree overlooking some fruit. If an animal moved into the camera trap's frame, the camera was supposed to sense both the movement and the temperature difference between the animal and the background environment, triggering the taking of a series of photos.

Many of the trees we found that first field season were within 100 meters of jungle roads passable by jeep. Yet the monsoon jungle was still no picnic. The rains caused the rivers and creeks to swell, making them tricky or impossible to cross. My clothes never seemed to dry, and I would sweat so much that I felt like changing three times a day. After a couple of weeks, I discovered that the humidity from the forest was wrecking my camera traps, fogging the images from two of the cameras and jeopardizing my ability to identify the animals eating fruit. Ants and mosquitoes bit me constantly; even my water-resistant bug repellant would wash off in the rain and sweat. Wasp nests were hidden in clumps of leaves, and I accumulated close calls with the worst wasps, *powla*, and stings from the second-worst wasps, called *barula*. Initially, I couldn't identify the 'itching plants' Akshu pointed out to me in time, and I would get rashes from rubbing against them. By far, the most bothersome inhabitants of the jungle to me were the leeches. The rubbery creatures came in a variety of colors, from a monotonous tree-bark brown to black with bright yellow body-length stripes, a reddish underside, and subtle blue ends. The smallest leeches were less than a centimeter in length and about the width of a needle, and the biggest could be 2.5 centimeter long and thicker than shoelaces. The persistent and acrobatic creatures would climb up my body until they found a place they liked, bore into my skin, and pump me with an analgesic so I couldn't feel them and an anticoagulant so that my blood would flow freely. Generally, the leech bites just left me with annoying blood stains in my clothes, but when I wore chappals instead of boots to negotiate the flooded forest, the open wounds they left became infected by fungi abundant in the moist jungle, troubling me for weeks.

None of the invertebrates seemed to bother my assistants very much. In the thick and noisy monsoon jungle, they had different concerns. One gray tropical afternoon, Narad, Akshu, and I went to install a camera trap on a *lator* tree not far from the 22-mile watchtower. The rain pitter-pattered on the jungle's leaves and the cicadas called loudly, and I was chatting gaily with my team. Suddenly, there was a clap like thunder, but instead of coming from the sky, it came from the forest, perhaps just 15 or 20 meters from where we stood. The source of the sound was shrouded in vegetation. Without a word, Narad and Akshu immediately took off, running toward the vehicle. Confused and excited, I followed immediately. Narad was far ahead, but Akshu, hindered by his unbendable leg, moved slower, swinging his leg in a frantic semi-circle with each step. I caught up with Akshu easily but jogged behind him, glancing back now and then to see if there was something chasing us. We reached the jeep without event.

'Not bad, right?' Akshu said, smiling his cross-eyed smile. 'I can still run, right? Not bad?'

I didn't answer. The truth was that I couldn't imagine Akshu outrunning anything at his speed. But then again, I was not sure any of us would have much of a chance if truly pursued by a wild animal. 'What was it?' I asked, still mystified. 'That sound? It sounded like thunder.'

'*Thund-ar*?' Akshu asked, for I had said the word in English.

'Meaning … lightning? Electricity from above when it is raining? It makes this sound?'

'Sir! It was an elephant!'

'An elephant! How…?'

'Sir, it takes a log in its trunk and then—*badung*!—it slams it against a tree or another log or the ground.' I would later read that elephants could actually make the sound by snorting and bounding the tip of their trunk on the ground simultaneously.

'Why?' I asked.

'It's a warning, Sir! It heard us and knew we didn't know it was there. So it made a big sound to say, "I am here! Don't come any closer."'

It was marvelous to think that wild elephants and villagers could communicate in this way. 'So we can't go back and put the camera up...?' I asked.

Akshu and Narad laughed. Akshu's eyes twinkled. 'I don't think we should, Sir. Maybe we can come back in the evening. But if you want to go back now, sure, I'll go with you!' Now I was laughing, too.

I looked longingly toward the tree. Most likely, an elephant was eating some *lator* fruit, and now we wouldn't have any evidence of it. I disliked that I was losing data.

Outside of work hours, when I was in the village, I found myself beginning to feel more isolated. My presence in the community was no longer novel, and since the language barrier between me and most of the others was significant, my new neighbors understandably stopped trying to work around my limited vocabulary. To offset the loneliness, I started trying to befriend the village's free-roaming dogs. They were unconcerned by my incompetence in local languages, and their happiness to see me helped, but the fact that they were generally covered in dirt and ticks made me reluctant to really embrace them. I missed my regularly bathed and flea-free mutt back home.

I began to try harder to ingratiate myself to the community. I offered Hari's daughter Champa more time on my computer. When someone had a headache or stomachache, I shared my over-the-counter medicines and explained the dosage. I learned a few words of Nepali and used them when I could, generating substantial laughter.

I gradually realized that it was my proficiency in English that made me most useful to my new neighbors. One evening, there was a commotion beneath my room in Hari's elevated house, and Champa yelled out to me. 'Brother, brother, there's a snake!' I rushed out of my room and down the stairs, where Hari searched in the evening light.

'Grandmother saw it,' Champa explained. 'It went right past her as she sat here.' She pointed to the bottom steps. She and Hari told me it was venomous.

'Sir! It went in there,' Hari said, gesturing to a pile of bricks about 10 feet wide. 'Snakes really like it in here.' He rushed upstairs and returned with a packet of strong-smelling stuff. 'This will get it to come out,' he said, and he began sprinkling the powder on the hard ground between the house and the bricks, a sort of grassless yard in which adults lounged and children played.

'What is it?' I asked.

'It's a medicine,' he said, sprinkling more powder with his bare, nimble fingers. 'Don't worry, it won't kill the snake. Just confuse it and make it still.'

Curious about what this magic potion might be, I followed Hari upstairs and asked to see the powder.

The back of the packet was written entirely in English, without a trace of the Devanagari or other indigenous scripts my hosts could decipher. It warned of the toxicity of the powder, which was identified as 'phorate' and described as an organophosphate insecticide and a potent neurotoxin. Those handling the contents were recommended to wear a mask and gloves; inhalation could result in anything from nausea to neurological damage and would require the immediate attention of a doctor.

Alarmed, I called out, 'Hari Bhaia, go wash your hands—do not touch your mouth or nose. This stuff is poison.' I did my best to explain the power of a neurotoxin with my limited vocabulary. 'It can cause your brain to stop working properly. You may not be able to move your hands or legs. You may go crazy. See this?' I pointed to the skull and bones symbol and explained that it meant the contents could be deadly. I pointed to the picture of gloved hands. 'What do you use this for? Why do you have this?'

'To kill insects on our crops. We only use it once in a while,' Hari assured me.

'You shouldn't,' I said. I wasn't actually familiar with the chemical, but I was fearful that an attempt at a more nuanced warning in my rudimentary Hindi would lead to disaster. 'If you put it around your house, your kids may not die from snake poison, but they will die from your poison.'

Hari and his wife Maili quickly found a plastic bag. They put the phorate inside, put that plastic bag in another plastic bag, and put it in a gallon container that they tucked away in the kitchen. Hari washed his hands.

The toxin on the ground could not be removed, and it stayed there overnight. While Hari might not have understood the danger it posed him, he did understand its power over reptiles. The next morning, Hari woke me up. 'Sir! The snake came out! Come see.' I jumped out of bed wearing shorts and a t-shirt, grabbing my camera but forgetting my glasses as I rushed downstairs. The snake was striped black and yellow, somehow looking venomous to me. It was, I would find out later, a banded krait, a swamp- and lowland-loving snake with highly neurotoxic venom. As predicted by Hari, the snake just lay in the grassless yard, senseless. Hari fearlessly picked up the serpent by its tail and moved it to an unplanted plot of land next to his home. This land was in a depression next to (but many meters below) the bridge of the main path running from the Metal Road. I and many villagers, especially children, gathered on the path, ogling at the venomous snake. The kids chattered excitedly about it. Its head sometimes seemed raised above the ground, suggesting it was still alive. As word spread, more people came to see the snake. I had to leave for work but later heard that the Forest Department came and removed the banded krait.

My efforts to be useful to my neighbors in Malabasti weren't just motivated by the desire to feel less alone. I was also motivated by a sense of responsibility, and a sense of guilt, as an aspiring conservationist.

Being raised on zoos and nature documentaries had its downsides. Along with the joy of watching animals would come devastating news about the state of our planet. The bad news might be the last few lines on the sign next to the rhino exhibit, or the last five minutes of the wildlife documentary. It would be about how humans were destroying the animal's natural habitat at some unfathomable rate, huge sections of rainforest knocked down every day for farms or mines or timber. It would be about the poaching, the hunting, the fur coats, the ivory, the bush meat, and the paper and furniture. It would be about the drastic decrease in population or the impending threat of global extinction for just about every interesting species I learned about. The effect of all this on the psychology of a small child was profound. I felt that humankind was just so *greedy*. Why did we take away the homes of all the animals? Why were we making so much out of wood, coal, and metal? If we just could be happy with what we had, if we just took less, then maybe we could coexist with all these other delightful creatures?

Years passed, and my mild misanthropy was aggravated in the schools I attended in Alabama. I grew wary of the big white kids' taunts about how Indians were weak or weird and all Hindus would go to hell. I wanted to get away from the cruelty of humanity.

When I visited India growing up, I tried to find my escape. I would beg my Kumar Mama to take me to a wildlife sanctuary. My uncle was disinterested in wildlife, but he lovingly humored me—we saw crocodiles in Ranganathitu, gaur in Nagarhole, wild dogs in Mudumalai. But everywhere we went, we also saw people. At some point, I expressed frustration that we couldn't get away from them.

'There are a billion people in this country! There are too many, you can't get away from them,' Kumar said.

'But they shouldn't be in the protected areas,' I protested.

'Why not? They live here. This is where they are from. It's their home,' my uncle responded. He always complained about India's high population and chaotic democracy, wishing his country had gone the way of China. But he enjoyed arguing with me, challenging the nephew who thought he had all the answers.

'Sure, but this is the animals' home. Why should they be here? They have cut down trees in the middle of the forest to build a village.'

'Where you live was also once a forest,' Kumar responded. 'Bangalore was also once a forest. Why do you live where you live? Look at how poor these people are. They have built their home here. Where are they supposed to go?'

'That's different!' I said defensively. 'This is a national park. They should be moved. This place should be only for wildlife. People have enough space.'

Kumar guffawed. 'People have enough space, meaning? These people are taking far less space than you. You have a brick house with a nice big yard in America. Look at how small that fellow's hut is. How does it matter to these poor beggars that other people somewhere have a big house? If you in America have two cars at your house, how does it matter to this fellow who only has an old bicycle? Who is going to move them? Are you going to build these people a new house, give them a new job?'

'The government could move them…'

Kumar laughed a laugh whose merriness for the spirited exchange seemed completely at odds with his cynicism. 'With the corruption in this country, these poor beggars will just get *poorer*.'

I wouldn't admit to Kumar that he was right—especially as a teenager—but I realized he had a point. There was a contradiction between the way I lived and the way I regarded the people living in and around the national parks we visited. I didn't know why some people were so much poorer than others, but I certainly didn't think it was the poor people's fault. So it seemed unfair to blame them for having to eke out a living in the forest. As a child, I had stared out of a car at the children my age begging on the streets of Delhi and Bangalore, realizing it was a matter of pure luck that they were on the outside and I was on the inside.

It wasn't until I was in college and graduate school that I learned just how treacherous my attitude toward local peoples had been. I read about how Yellowstone National Park, the US's first national park, was created by kicking out the Eastern Shoshone, a Native

American tribe that had coexisted with wolves and bears for longer than they could remember. When I studied abroad in South Africa, I learned about how the colonial and Apartheid governments had evicted various black African communities like the Tsonga to form Kruger National Park. In these and many other examples, those dispossessed in the name of conservation faced a future of uncertainty, poverty, and worse. This model of displacement for conservation was replicated throughout North America and colonial Africa and Asia, often by governments of the same white people that had exterminated charismatic megafauna in Western Europe and much of the US. The hypocrisy of these colonial-era conservationists stank of the same white supremacy I had caught sniffs of in some of my classmates in Birmingham—a sense of entitlement that superseded any concern for moral consistency or human decency.

But there was another lesson I learned well in college: that people of all backgrounds and cultures have the same capacity for error and abuse. Once in power, African and Asian leaders replicated the conservation models of colonial administrations. In independent India, from 1973 to 2006, the Indian government relocated at least 80 villages and 2,900 families from forests that the government—without the consent of the local people—had declared as tiger reserves. The vast majority of these were involuntary displacements, forced upon some of India's poorest and most marginalized peoples, including Indian Scheduled Tribes (Adivasis), by a government keen to save the few remaining wild tigers. Many of those relocated ended up destitute. Without access to the forest for firewood or food and without the skills or land for agriculture, they lacked the means to support themselves. In their new locales, Adivasis often ended up at the bottom of caste hierarchies with no way to resist oppression. In addition to becoming homeless or food insecure, many of those relocated were depressed at being ripped from the land they loved. Research found evidence that morbidity and mortality in these groups increased significantly due to their displacement. Modern India, I realized, might be a democracy—but the Adivasis and other forest-dwellers relocated for conservation were, for much of India's history, too disempowered and spread out to organize politically or form a significant voting constituency.

Yet, despite learning of all the human harm and suffering caused by wildlife conservation, I couldn't let go of my original sympathy for the animals that humanity was edging out. There was evidence that even indigenous peoples were capable of driving species to extinction, and this seemed only more likely as wildlife and poor people were forced to share smaller and smaller blocks in the landscape. Somehow, I thought, our society had to figure out how to coexist with other species without screwing over already-marginalized people. Obviously, we could not stop hunting and fishing and deforestation altogether, but surely we could minimize it so more creatures would get a shot at a fuller life? Clearly, it wasn't fair to force poor forest-dwellers to sacrifice everything for conservation, but perhaps we could help ensure their aspirations were honored while safeguarding wildlife?

When I came to Buxa, this was my mentality. I knew there was something fundamentally unfair about expecting very poor people living in or near the world's protected areas to make *more* sacrifices to protect wildlife while I, a middle-class American who had never had malaria or been truly hungry, went on safaris around the world and returned home to a lifestyle they could only dream of. Yet I feared that if we left human action and consumption ungoverned in protected areas, people would understandably exploit their forests and savannas for whatever resources they needed in the short term and maybe even kill off the dangerous animals—like elephants and tigers—that plagued them. There had to be a way to help communities near wildlife find a path out of poverty without exhausting forest resources or decimating local wildlife. I wanted a socially equitable model of conservation—one where people like me bore the costs necessary to simultaneously serve both marginalized people and wildlife—and living in Buxa gave me my first opportunities to start to piece together, in a real-world setting, just what such a model might look like.

A central tenet of my emerging philosophy on conservation was that a good conservationist should learn to listen to local people about their problems and their ideas for solutions. One morning in July, I got my first chance to try and exercise that philosophy.

Akshu intercepted me on my way down to breakfast. 'Sir! A leopard came into the village last night!'

'Huh?' I asked. I struggled to find the words to ask how he knew.

But Akshu anticipated the question. 'It killed a goat at my neighbor's house,' he said.

'Oh! Is the goat still there?'

'Yes, yes,' Akshu said. I ran to get my camera and followed him to the home of a widow just next to Narad's house. As we walked, Akshu explained that the widow, Sangita, had struggled since her husband's death several years ago. She had no regular source of income, and she had twins around eight years of age. It was a real pity, he said, that the widow had lost a goat.

Sangita's house was the first an animal would encounter along the main northeastern path into the village from the creek and forest. It had never occurred to me, but apparently slight variations in geography helped determine who bore the brunt of local human–wildlife conflict. Houses like Akshu's and Hari's were situated such that elephants coming from the forest would immediately end up in their rice paddy, making it easy for them to sneak in and raid crops at night. In contrast, other families' crop fields were situated perhaps 350 meters inside the village, surrounded by houses and others' rice paddies on all sides. Elephants almost never got that far in before being detected and shooed away, so such families could count on reasonably healthy yields every year. Sangita's house was the first line of defense for interior houses—an ever-present altar of sacrifice to the wayward predator. Risk was not evenly distributed, even among the poor of the same village.

Sangita seemed to be complaining when I walked into her compound. She immediately stopped talking when I came in with Akshu. 'He wants to see the goat the leopard killed,' Akshu said in Nepali.

I asked Sangita if I could take pictures of the goat. I tried to tell her I could provide the photos to the Forest Department if she needed help making her case for compensation. Akshu explained, and the widow bashfully assented. The goat had been tied up by its neck to a pole, she said, pointing to one of the sturdy log-sized stilts that held up the house. The leopard had come in the night, quickly pounced on the goat and subdued it. Unable to drag the goat away since it was still tied up, the leopard began to consume its quarry there next to house. The widow and her children woke up and hollered at the leopard, driving it back into the forest.

The once-white goat now lay unbound near the house. There were matted pools of deep red blood on its neck behind its head and on its foreleg. Its stomach was bloated, and its back leg was detached from its body. The leopard had taken at least a couple of bites from between its back legs before fleeing. A line of feline footprints ran from the gate to the house—too small to be a tiger's and too big to be anything else other than a leopard's.

I asked Akshu what the process was for compensation and he explained that forms from the Gram Panchayat village government office needed to be filled out. I offered my assistance, but Akshu told me that the forms were in Bengali and that he would take care of them for the illiterate widow.

Later that day, Akshu asked for a different favor. 'Sir, this isn't the first time this leopard has come into our village,' he said. 'She has taken a few other goats in the past.' Akshu was confident it was the same leopard based on the size of its paw prints and some other factors, and he suspected it was a female. He told me that the Forest Department had a trap to catch problem leopards like this, and that the range officer would let them use it if I asked him. The range officer would then transport the leopard north into the core area away from their village.

I was immediately torn. On the one hand, nothing seemed more exciting than trying to catch a leopard that was harassing local villagers. On the other, I had read a little of the growing body of knowledge showing that relocations of dangerous animals led to a slew of unintended consequences. The work of biologist Vidya Athreya and her colleagues had demonstrated the dangers of relocating leopards from agricultural areas to forests in Maharashtra. Dr Athreya pointed out that we forget that wild animals are individuals and often think of them as interchangeable pebbles that can be dropped anywhere. Instead, her research suggested that every leopard knows every square meter of its territory, allowing it to hunt and evade humans effortlessly. We think of leopards as solitary, but they still have social networks and hierarchies of dominance and subordination, with females potentially having relationships with their grown cubs. If we move an animal with such a complex relationship with its environment to a new location where it will have to fight new battles for dominance and struggle to understand a new territory, why would we expect it to stay there? Dr Athreya demonstrated that relocated leopards generally tried to return to their old habitat, in the process often passing through human habitation with which it was unfamiliar. These lost and desperate carnivores were thus more likely to have run-ins with the local people. Once relocated, a leopard was likely to wreak more havoc, not less.

At the time of Akshu's request, though, my grasp of these issues was far more tenuous. Akshu's suggestion that the leopard be moved deeper into the forest assuaged my concerns about a potential returnee. The leopard would not have to cross human habitation to come back to its territory. Still, it seemed like an awful lot of effort for no obvious pay-off. 'Guruji, won't the leopard just come back? What if she has cubs?'

Akshu shook his head. 'Maybe she will come back, but maybe she will just find more food in the core area and be content.' Seeing I was still unconvinced, he added, 'Sir, if we don't do anything, the leopard will keep coming to our village, and one night one of our children might go out to the outhouse and be taken. Then we will be sad about not having taken action.'

'Does that actually happen?' I asked, surprised.

'Yes, every year or two a leopard will take a child. Usually from the tea gardens,' Akshu said.

Well, I certainly did not want to feel responsible for *that*. Feeling that I did not know as well as Akshu and the others what would be best for them, and allured by the prospect of catching a leopard, I agreed to help.

One night that week, Akshu, Narad, and I went to the nearby range office to fetch the trap. The range officer heard just a few words from me and agreed to loan it to us. He also offered us a truck with a bed that could carry the trap to Malabasti, the hamlet where Akshu and the widow lived. Akshu said that if I hadn't been there, the officer would certainly not have acted so swiftly.

It was a gorgeous, dark, and starry night, and some nearby villagers helped us lift the huge trap and put it on the truck. The truck's headlights were not working, but I insisted that we get the trap moved then and there— I didn't want this side adventure to interfere with my research in the daytime—so the truck chugged behind our jeep to Akshu's hamlet. There, Akshu summoned his neighbors, and 12 of us moved the trap to the beginning of the path that the leopard had taken earlier that week. We covered the trap with a dark tarp and brush so it blended in. While Narad used the jeep to escort the truck back to its place, Akshu and I began baiting the trap.

The trap had two compartments. Village-side was a small compartment, which we could open, place live bait in, and close from outside. This small compartment was separated by a thick metal grate from the large compartment, meant for the leopard. The entrance to this compartment would be set open facing the creek and forest, and when the leopard entered and tried to get at the bait, a trigger on the floor of the cage would slam the door behind it. The widow had already buried her slain goat, so what we needed now was a live animal for bait. Akshu suggested we use a female goat with small kids at home so that she would call throughout the night, drawing the leopard into the trap. Suddenly, the volunteerism I witnessed when we were moving the trap evaporated—no one wanted to put their animals in the cage. 'Is it because they are afraid the animal would die of fright?' I asked.

Akshu nodded. 'But it won't.' His female goats were pregnant, and he was afraid if a leopard attacked, they could miscarry, so he would not risk one of them. Since Narad and the others refused to provide a goat of the ideal demographic, Akshu and I brought a young black male, just over a year of age, from Akshu's goat pen. As I held him, he baaed plaintively, but he did not fight me. I fell in love with him instantly. 'You're sure he won't die of fright?' I asked.

'Goats are tough,' Akshu assured me. We put him in the trap with some straw and left him baaing, hoping to catch the marauding cat by sunrise.

Of course, we did not catch the leopard that night. Nor the night after, or the night after that. A week or so passed in which Akshu and I set the trap every evening, carefully looking out for elephants under the night sky, retrieving the goat every morning. 'Why isn't it working?' I asked Akshu one morning. I had never had high hopes for this endeavor—I had set up traps for smaller animals in my prior field work, and I knew it could be tricky—but if we were going to try to do this, I felt we should make a calculated effort.

Thidey overheard me. 'Did you talk to Narad?' he retorted. Narad's house was not far from the trap. 'The goat you put in the trap is too brave.'

'Huh?' I asked.

The goat, Thidey said, just cried for 15 to 20 minutes and then went to sleep. 'He probably knows he is in the safest place in the village! How is the leopard even supposed to know he is there?'

I had grown bored of this exercise by now, but Akshu kept at it. He replaced the goat with a chicken, and almost every night set the trap. The chicken clucked uncomfortably the first night or two, but then it too grew complacent. Habituation was working against us.

Finally, Akshu set a deadline. 'When I have tried for a month unsuccessfully, I will stop,' he said. The last night of the month, I ceremoniously helped Akshu set the trap. The following morning, I ran to his house with mock excitement. 'Did you catch her?'

Akshu sighed. 'No. I heard that the leopard came into the village this week, but we didn't catch her.'

'What? Did she kill something else?' I asked.

'She entered from the south,' he said, pointing down the village path from his house. 'She killed two goats over there. She must have known that this was a trick!'

I smiled. I had learned during my field training that it was hard to catch wild animals, so I wasn't surprised at how things had turned out. But I had hoped that our efforts would help the community. Maybe locals like Akshu just didn't know enough about catching wildlife.

6

Thanks to Satyavati's dedication to education, Akshu had been able to complete the eighth grade. From sixth grade onward, no school was available for Akshu within walking distance, so Satyavati saved money generated from selling chicken eggs to pay the two-rupee round trip fare to send Akshu to school in Alipurduar. But when Chander stopped plowing the family's fields, Satyavati really began to struggle to protect Akshu from having to help sustain the family. Akshu realized his parents could no longer support his education, and he told his mother he would be quitting school. He felt he was supposed to help his parents make ends meet. He took up primary responsibility for plowing the fields.

Even so, Akshu had to find other work. After fulfilling his responsibilities as a farmhand and a cowherd, he still had time to spare, especially after the fields were planted. He spent some of this time at the *chowpathi*, the intersection of the main road and the road to his hamlet, asking around for leads on employment. He would watch admiringly when his cousin set up shop at the intersection to sell marked-up goods he had purchased from Alipurduar. Akshu appreciated entrepreneurship.

'How much do you profit?' Akshu asked his cousin.

'Four *anna*, eight *anna*,' he responded. That was one-fourth to one-half of a rupee. It was a measly amount, but Akshu noted that he was there very irregularly and for short periods of time. When Akshu's cousin opted to return to herding cattle, Akshu seized the opportunity. He took on his cousin's remaining wares and convinced his family to scrounge together ₹75 for him. He went to Alipurduar and purchased paan, bidi, cigarettes, and biscuits. He couldn't afford to build a structure for his store, so he took a bamboo mat from home and set up shop near the *chowpathi*. Akshu would start as early as 6 AM and stay until about sunset. His sister Rukmani would eat her meals and then cover for him as he had his. Akshu's reliability and persistence began to pay off. He was soon making a profit of around ₹20 a day. He was quick to reinvest, adding mustard oil, flour, salt, turmeric, and masala to the store's offerings. Eventually, he even started buying soap. Instead of taking money from the store, the Atris began to use some of this inventory; by buying in bulk and using supplies that might otherwise be wasted, the Atris tied themselves optimally to the store. Akshu felt pretty good about his business acumen during these days, especially since it was in broad display to his community. He was particularly happy when his friend Kusum stopped by.

'Ram Ram! Have you eaten yet, Akshu?' she said once on her way home from school. Kusum was a little younger than Akshu and had been a playmate of his sister Bhagavati. With cinnamon-colored skin and a kind smile, she was a fairly no-nonsense type, avoiding the empty chatter that so many of their peers liked, but she made a point of dropping by to see Akshu when he was at the store or while he was plowing.

'I had some rice at noon,' Akshu assured her with warm familiarity. Her house was not 200 meters away from his, and they had known each other longer than either could remember.

'How are sales today?' she asked.

'It's going,' he responded, grinning his disarming cross-eyed grin. Kusum's parents were among the wealthiest villagers in Madhubangaon outside of the bazaar, and Satyavati and Motikar had worked part-time for Kusum's parents for years. Akshu felt particularly satisfied to show Kusum that he and his family were enterprising.

'I saw that you dropped a jar of biscuits yesterday,' Kusum said sympathetically. 'I wish you could have a proper shop here so you wouldn't have to carry all your supplies home every day.'

Akshu wasn't thrilled that she had seen that, but at least she didn't have the haughtiness of her parents. As always, she seemed genuinely caring. 'Yes, it was a loss of ₹25. But if we leave the biscuits here, we will lose a lot more than that.'

'Yes, the monkeys would probably take them!' Kusum said, a smile spreading across her generally serious face. 'I'm hungry, I'm going home. See you later.'

Akshu resisted the temptation to offer her some biscuits as she turned away.

———

As the store became more integrated into the Atris' survival portfolio, other members of the family helped share the burden of shopkeeping. So, Akshu would rotate among the family's other economic activities. Such rotation was crucial partly because malaria continued to be a serious problem in the region, afflicting just about every individual in the Atri family almost every year. The local health center would give a person with a fever some chloroquine, take a blood sample, and send the sample off somewhere, and often the test would only come back when the patient had already recovered or, on at least one occasion, already died.

One morning in winter, Akshu's older sisters were all down with malaria, and it fell upon him to work on the plantation. He showed up at the *chowpathi* to board the truck going to the plantation for the first time.

'Who are you?' the beat officer in charge asked from atop his motorbike.

'I'm Motikar Atri's son, Akshu Atri.'

'You're too young,' the beat officer declared. 'You're just a kid. Go get someone else from your house.'

'No no, he's old enough,' the *mondol*, or leader, of Akshu's hamlet said. Akshu was around 16, but he didn't look it. 'His sisters are all ill. There's no one else in his house to work.'

The beat officer relented. Akshu and the others were driven to a plantation nearby with young saplings. The rains had been good in the last several weeks, and the little trees were surrounded by competing grasses, forbs, and climbers. The beat officer, a Bengali man named Manik Barman, ordered the villagers to clear all this brush, but not to harm the young trees. Some of the villagers went to work on the grass with sickles. Akshu used his kukri, slicing woody vegetation and climbers low on their stems. He effortlessly distinguished saplings from forbs and climbers. When he saw a climber that had started to grow onto a *sirish* sapling, he efficiently cut it down with one swing.

'HEY!' shouted Manik. He ran up angrily. 'I can't believe this! You cut down a *sirish* tree! I told the *mondol* not to give such a young kid work, now look what you've done.'

Akshu shook his head, puzzled. 'No—no, that's the *sirish* tree there. I just cut a climber.'

'Oh, so now you're going to teach me something?' Manik fumed. 'I'm a beat officer! You fool...' and he unleashed a rain of insults.

The *mondol* and other villagers gathered. The *mondol* picked up what Akshu had felled. 'This is just a climber, sir,' he said.

'I have so much experience,' Manik yelled. 'And you're telling me I'm wrong? I'm a beat officer!'

But a third, fourth, and fifth villager all sided with Akshu. They pointed out another *sirish* sapling to the beat officer for comparison. 'This is a tree,' they said. 'That was a climber.'

The beat officer was a city dweller from Alipurduar. He was outmatched when it came to identifying trees. But he wasn't going to concede to a bunch of villagers. He stormed to his motorbike and drove off, feeling embarrassed and disrespected.

The incident reflected an ongoing change from when Akshu's parents had arrived in Buxa. In the old days, the Forest Department had a dominant, paternalistic, and sometimes oppressive relationship with the forest villagers. The Department's officials were not to be questioned. More empathetic officials would ensure the villagers' homes and bridges were well maintained. The Forest Department had effectively ensured that the plantations were productive, ruling over their labourers with an eye toward efficiency. Furthermore, even if Forest Department patrols had been far from comprehensive, they seemed to have provided some check on how Buxa's villagers used forest resources, for instance, by keeping livestock out of the core area. The Forest Department, with the help of the forest villagers, was also quite effective at preventing people from outside of Buxa from taking too much from the forests. At that time, due to their regular work in the plantations, forest villagers felt some sense of responsibility for the forests they had helped plant, and they would report outsiders who came to Buxa to cut wood or hunt to the Forest Department.

The hierarchical arrangement of that time period did not allow the villagers equitable decision-making or much upward mobility, but it appeared to have maintained a degree of order and sustainability.

By the mid-to-late 1990s, such top-down control gradually eroded. Soon after they won the West Bengal state elections in 1977, the Left Front political alliance began decentralizing power from the state government to local (democratically elected) village councils called gram panchayats. In the early 1990s, the Indian Parliament followed West Bengal's example, passing constitutional amendments mandating the formation of panchayats across most of India. The purpose of these reforms was to make government more responsive to local needs and spur development for impoverished rural people deep in India's hinterlands. As a result, local governments gradually gained the power to spend revenue on public works like school buildings, irrigation projects, and local roads, and communities could participate in helping decide how local funds were spent and hold authorities to account.

In North Bengal, empowered panchayats appear to have filtered in gradually; tea gardens and forest villages like Madhubangaon only had panchayat elections beginning in the mid- to late-90s. Before the panchayat reforms, political parties had only occasionally reached the villages surrounding and inside Buxa Reserve. More local control of money and power incentivized political parties to expand across rural India. Winning panchayat elections meant they could use local coffers to deliver goods and services to their local constituents. These voters would then be more likely to not only support their party in local elections but also in state and national elections. Local elites and ambitious peasants seized the opportunity to join such parties, seeking anything from a chance to skim off some of the funds to the realization of a more empowered, responsive local government.

The expansion of panchayats, in some ways, resulted in exactly what democracy is supposed to accomplish: politicians vying for the support and affection of all their constituents, including poor, rural people. But decentralizing power also led to problems. For instance, the political parties were geared toward providing short-term benefits to their supporters, irrespective of long-term considerations like environmental sustainability or rule of law. If a Forest Department official captured a person milling about the jungle and arrested him for poaching or smuggling, especially near election time, local party leaders would leap on their motorcycles and show up at the official's office. The various party leaders would then vie to secure the captive's release.

'He wasn't doing anything wrong in the jungle! He's a cowherd,' one of the party leaders would say.

'You grabbed him from the jungle; he was just bringing dry firewood,' would say a second.

Eventually, the Forest Department officials—faced with fighting influential parties instead of a single villager—would release the individual, whether he was an innocent cowherd or a career smuggler. 'Don't be afraid!' party leaders took to telling villagers. 'We are here for you!'

For villagers in and around Buxa, exploiting the forest for resources—whether for grazing, non-timber forest products, firewood, or for illicit activities like timber smuggling or poaching—was the most obvious available means to supplement their limited agricultural income. So villagers often embraced this new political support to gain access to the forest around them, both for legitimate and illegal purposes. The increased pressure on the forest from villages on Buxa's periphery was especially significant since, prior to this new political order, such villagers and tea-estate workers were in principle not allowed in the forest.

The problem with the blooming local democracy might not have been that local people didn't value sustainable use of the forest—in fact, the elders in Akshu's community seemed aware that overharvesting natural resources would impoverish the forests. But the new political order didn't incentivize anyone to *vote* on sustainability. Forest villagers lacked any legal control over forest, so they didn't believe that they would benefit in the long run from sustainable use of the forest. As a result, they didn't punish political parties that defended poachers and smugglers. In contrast, when political parties rose to the defense of villagers found in the forest (whether engaged in legal or illegal activity), they gained those villagers' votes. Thus, despite India's strong national conservation laws, the short-term interests of resource exploitation began to win out over the long-term interest of conservation. India's young democracy was being constructed on systems of patronage—and there was no more easily accessible fuel for patronage than public forests, minerals, and wildlife.

These problems were exacerbated by uncontrolled immigration. When the Atris had come to Buxa in the 1960s, the government tightly controlled habitation in the forest. Motikar and Satyavati moved into one of 85 government-constructed houses, but new villagers couldn't come in without explicit permission from the Forest Department. In 1993, Akshu noticed a sharp change in his community. After a monsoon flood in Madhubangaon, several displaced families built temporary homes in a nearby plantation. When the Forest Department did not react, it opened the floodgates: growing village families began to build new homesteads in the plantation as well.

One day, Akshu found out that an outsider from the neighboring state of Assam was buying some of this commandeered land from a village family, and immigrants from throughout North Bengal, the northeastern states, Bihar, and Bangladesh began moving to Madhubangaon without the Forest Department's consent. The villages expanded like a blooming suburb—just as the landscapes surrounding Buxa became more crowded, so did the forest itself. If the original villagers had felt as though the land being settled illegally belonged to their community, perhaps there would have at least been efforts to make the expansion of the community more systematic. But, again, the original villagers felt that they had no legal claim over the forest and, when the panchayat arrived, the political parties were happy to have more potential voters to vie for. So Buxa's villages brimmed with people who needed or wanted a new home and free access to natural resources.

In this new political order, the Forest Department was also less capable of confronting those violating the conservation laws meant to protect Buxa's forests. Over the years, employees of West Bengal's Forest Department had become unionized. As unions had the support of Bengal's leftist ruling coalition, the union made it extremely difficult for the Forest Department to fire ineffective or even corrupt forest staff who enriched themselves off the forest. With few people immediately hurt by the reduced effectiveness of forest conservation, there was no interest group to offset union power. Furthermore, locals perceived that the forest guards and officials, most of whom were from outside of North Bengal, were not invested in the region's people or sustainable use of Buxa's forest or wildlife. Many of the guards supposedly weren't even comfortable in the forest. 'They mistake sal trees for teak trees,' villagers joked.

'They are even afraid of leeches!' The relationship between the uninspired forest guards and the forest-dependent villagers became very thin, making it that much easier for the villagers (and forest guards) to take what they wanted from the jungle without remorse.

Given the increased pressure on the forest and diminished forest protection, perhaps it is unsurprising that the jungles of Akshu's late teenage years were so different from the jungle of his childhood. The black-naped hares, peacocks, jungle fowl, and giant squirrels that had been trusting enough to wander the village were now only visible deep in the forest. Cattle egrets and weaver birds, though left untouched by Akshu and his friends, also vanished from the village, maybe due to the use of pesticides. Fishers no longer could find the long-bodied fish they used to hunt at night.

Most of the large hooved animals—gaur, deer, and wild pigs—had become far rarer in the forest. When he was younger, Akshu used to frequently come across the quills of porcupines in the jungle, but now he seldom did. Oriental pied and great hornbills, kingfishers, pythons, and monitor lizards were also harder to find in Buxa.

As far as he could tell, many species had disappeared from Buxa. He never again saw a wild gharial, giant turtles, or even fish over 5 kilograms in Buxa's rivers. Akshu heard that the wild water buffalo he and his father had seen were no longer to be found in Buxa. Flying foxes no longer came to hang upside down from the papaya trees in the village or forests, and the howling of jackals had ceased. He realized he seldom heard anything about live tiger sightings anymore. With the prey in Buxa so reduced, perhaps those predators that had survived the poaching themselves were looking elsewhere for food.

Of course, especially with the coming of markets for NTFPs, villagers like the Atris had also extracted plenty of vegetation from the forest. In addition to grazing tens of thousands of cattle and buffaloes in the reserve and collecting plants for their own subsistence, the villagers had taken to collecting and selling NTFPs like an otter takes to water. The reeds found near the Dima and Bala Rivers that could once hide an elephant had been cut and sold to companies making sitting mats. *Birdarrow*, *batlawry*, and bamboo—all plant species that elephants loved to eat—had been stripped from Buxa in huge quantities.

In short, Akshu knew he was coming of age into a jungle that was diminished. He sensed that some of the killing was gratuitous. He felt some sympathy for the pain that hunted animals must have felt in the moments before their death, and for the sadness that their relatives would feel in the absence of their companion. But he did not mourn the disappearance of species from Buxa—extirpation and extinction were still concepts beyond his grasp—and whatever momentary sympathy he did feel for the jungle's animals would disappear as he pondered his own problems. Akshu and his family had little time to consider the complicated political economy that was chipping away at their forest home and, in any case, without a conservation organization or environmentally oriented political party to unite behind, it was far too big a problem for one family to take on.

––––––––––

It was a surprise when, in the late 1990s, the Atris all awoke to a thud and crack in the middle of the night.

The clang of falling metal cookware followed. Motikar and Satyavati sprang up, with Akshu and their daughters on their heels, all hollering. This had never happened to them before, but they knew intuitively what was occurring. An elephant was invading their kitchen.

The raised wooden structure of the Atris' home was several paces away from the mud and bamboo structure with a thatch roof and mud-dung floors that they used as a kitchen. Separating the kitchen reduced the risk of a fire in their wooden home and prevented the smell of smoke and spices from overtaking their sleeping and living areas. In addition, it had protected them by placing the most attractive items for an elephant safely away from the sleeping family.

But the Atris were quick to try and chase away the thief. '*Hoy! Haathi ayya!* Stop! Run away!' the Atris and their neighbors yelled at the elephant. From the window and porch of their home, the elephant looked humongous, a shadowy giant towering over the silhouette of the little mud kitchen. Before the Atris could light a torch or pull out firecrackers, the elephant fled toward the river. The Atris examined the damage as best as they could with candles and kerosene lamps in the moonlight. It looked like the elephant had broken only one of the walls of the kitchen, apparently knocking it down with its upper trunk and perhaps its foot.

'What did it want?' Satyavati asked; there had been hardly any rice or flour left in the kitchen to begin with. Without a refrigerator to preserve food, an unimaginable possession as they didn't have electricity, they had fed all the leftovers to the livestock and stray dogs. 'Did you leave a bag of salt in there?' she asked.

'No,' Motikar responded. 'Remember, I bought that bag of *gokul dhana* for the nursing cows? That is missing.' Sure enough, the next morning, their neighbors would discover drag marks with an uneven trail of spilled *gokul dhana* in the direction of the river.

The Atris looked sadly at the kitchen. They were relieved that it wasn't worse. Since only one wall had been knocked in, it would take just four to five days to repair the structure. But they also felt at a more fundamental level, like much of the village, quite trapped. Slowly but surely, the elephants were becoming more disruptive and aggressive. From February until May or early June, tuskers and *makhnas* had started invading the village fields more frequently. In particular, the elephants had realized that on rainy pre-monsoon nights, villagers could neither see nor hear them in the corn fields, and the invaders could raid the fields with relative impunity, eating not only corn but pumpkins, beans, and squashes. Each year, the Atris lost 20–30 per cent and occasionally as much as 50 per cent of the corn crop to elephants. Some of the villagers fought back, spending more nights in the tongs in the fields where they could alternatingly sleep and keep vigil. The young men of the village often felt triumphant: they would yell and shout, maneuvering to outflank and outwit and chase away the divine elephants when they took more than the share due to them. But this was far more work than in the old days, when elephants feared their torches. Over the course of the growing season, the sleepless nights would wear on village sentries.

Still, these efforts kept corn profitable enough to keep growing it. There seemed to be no way to salvage some of the other crops. Elephants had taken such a liking to basmati rice in the fall that the Atris and others stopped planting it, even though it was worth nearly three times more than the short-grained rice they otherwise planted. Elephants also seemed to have gradually realized just how wonderful bananas and banana plants were. No matter how quickly the villagers responded to the sound of elephants in the night, they weren't fast enough; the elephants executed precision strikes, ripping whole bunches of bananas off their plant and fleeing to the dark jungle so they might eat in peace. Trying to keep elephants away from bananas was like trying to keep flies away from a goat carcass, and the attacks were so comprehensive that the villagers, one by one, discontinued growing bananas altogether. Invading elephants had similarly made growing coconuts nigh impossible as they went for the fruits while they were still small, and once the *haathis* realized what was embedded in the spiny, crunchy skin of the pineapple, well—*kaa-runch*, *ka-runch*, *crunch*—that was over too. After the farmers abandoned bananas and pineapples, expectant and disappointed elephants went after the farmers' tall, elegant bamboo, which was used to build fences and houses. The elephants would break the bamboo with their trunks and maneuver them in and out of their mouths like toothbrushes as their tongues stripped off the bamboo leaves.

The cause of the increased assault on all these crops was a mystery to the villagers. The villagers had been there for decades, so why were attacks increasing now? Previously, elephants had been afraid of humans bearing torches even at a distance. Now, the flames had to be brought closer, the noise people raised had to be louder to chase the marauders away. Sometimes, burning clothes and jute bags had to be hurled at the animals to scare them off. Why the change?

Unbeknownst to the people of Madhubangaon, what was happening in Buxa reflected a larger pattern across South Asia—male elephants were becoming increasingly specialized as crop raiders in South India and Sri Lanka as well. Ecologists had a hypothesis to explain this. Crops like corn and bananas offered a rich, concentrated source of nutrients generally unavailable in the jungle, where food was more spread out. Stopping at a village farm and gorging themselves on crops was way less work for an elephant than searching the jungle for a fruit tree here, some edible grasses there. The catch was, of course, that this highly concentrated resource came with the risk of being harassed, injured, or even killed by the humans that lived near these crops. Particularly for a herd of female elephants with calves, this risk was generally unappealing. As long as there were safe ways to meet their nutritional requirements in the jungle, the females would prefer them. The potential gains of getting nice and fat from crops didn't offset the risks of losing a calf or a leg.

For male elephants, however, the value proposition was very different. As a polygynous species in which females do the child-rearing, any given male elephant was free to mate with as many females as he could. Getting females to mate with them required not only that they woo their female partners, but also that they fend off other suitors. Since bigger male elephants generally won fights over smaller elephants, buffing up on easy-to-access food could mean the difference between being big enough to maintain access to a great many of an area's receptive females and having access to none at all. While a female elephant's reproductive success wasn't likely to change much if she got that extra nutritious meal, a male's whole love life might hinge on it. For him, the extra nutrition might be worth the risks of squaring off against those pesky primates with fire, rocks, firecrackers, and even arrows and bullets. This was all the more true in an age where conservation laws and the threat of punishment made people even more reluctant to retaliate against an animal widely considered a manifestation of god.

Madhubangaon's villagers might not have been familiar with this particular hypothesis at the time, but they did identify other reasonable ecological explanations for what might be happening. As NTFP markets were established in Buxa, villagers watched as truckload after truckload of wild plants like *birdarrow* and cane were driven out of the jungle. Villagers knew that they had stripped the forest of many of the elephants' favorite foods. 'Poor elephants,' Akshu heard some of his relatives and neighbors say. 'Elephants have such big stomachs, and humans have taken all their food from the jungle. They too just want to survive—is it any wonder that they come out of the forest for food?' In a sense, the villagers thought, maybe the elephants were even a form of karma—the elephants were invading the fields more often because humans were invading the animals' jungle more often. Even if this theory was incomplete, it reflected the likely truth that less food in the forest would make food in the fields, despite the risks, more appealing to elephants, especially for males looking to bulk up. And the fact that some villagers in Madhubangaon had this perspective underscored two beliefs that are not so uncommon across India. First, that animals were entitled to try to meet their fundamental needs to survive. And, second, that in the cosmic struggle for survival, for humans to undermine the survival prospects of other creatures was, even if necessary from the human perspective, somehow suboptimal, or maybe even a little unfair.

So, in the face of this increasing onslaught, the villagers of Madhubangaon offset the lost crops the best they could. They made do with newly expanded government rations, NTFPs, and the income that came from the villagers' other legal and illegal activities. On Chander's recommendation, the Atris began growing *suppadi* (areca nut) trees in place of all the fruit trees and bamboos, since elephants were apparently disinterested in eating them. Other families joined in, and the slender palms were soon grown everywhere in Malabasti that grains and vegetables weren't. Many villagers were undoubtedly angry and frustrated on occasion, and some were outright livid at the elephants, but they still continued to tolerate elephant crop-raiding as a fact of life and, at least in some cases, a consequence for their own transgressions against the forest.

At this point, to say things were going Akshu's way would have been an exaggeration. He was over 18 and, thus, an adult, but he didn't have many of the things an adult might want to have. He didn't have a high school degree or a job, nor any real prospect of economic independence from his family. However, Akshu did think he had the other thing most young adults want.

It was unspoken, but it was clearly there. Whenever Akshu and Kusum saw each other, they looked at each other knowingly, they smiled more readily, they laughed more easily. Village life in northeast India enjoyed less restrictive norms for male–female interaction than those known in some other parts of the country. Boys and girls would chat freely as they sat at the *chowpathi*, the bazaar, or, so long as others were present, even in the homes of the village. Kusum and Akshu had had plenty of opportunity to get to know each other as they had grown up in the same hamlet, and they were able to read each other's signals. This was good, for Akshu and Kusum's language of affection had to be painstakingly subtle. Somewhere between batting eyelids and a seductive wink was a line that would set off alarms. Casual romance was simply not accepted.

Sincere intention for matrimony was all that one could openly express, but even that had to follow a specific protocol and was only considered appropriate between certain people.

So when Kusum's relatively well-off family had several photos of her taken and printed, Kusum had to find a fairly innocuous way to get Akshu one of them. The prints were laid out on a table in her home. She invited several of her friends inside to see them before inviting Akshu—with one of his friends—to take a look as well. Akshu and his friend came in and politely complimented the photos. 'Can I have one of them?' Akshu said in his amiable way.

'Of course,' Kusum replied casually, playing along with the Platonic ruse. 'Pick whichever one you want.'

Akshu carefully picked one that captured the essence of the girl he liked, and he and his friend left.

Akshu felt good about his odds. He and Kusum *clearly* liked each other. She was kind and thoughtful, and while he knew that his cross-eyed gaze was not considered a hallmark of handsomeness, he also knew that Kusum had seen so much more of him than that— she had seen his kindness to others, his dutiful service to his family, his penchant for responsibility. People in the village knew who was regularly involved in drinking or timber smuggling, and she knew Akshu wasn't engaged in either. She surely knew that Akshu had liked her for a long time, that he would likely be loyal. Both Kusum and Akshu were a little different than their neighbors, or even most of their families. There was something more principled and less materialistic about how they conducted themselves. And, crucially, they were both Nepali Brahmins, and he got along fine with Kusum's parents and brothers. He had no reason to suspect that the union wouldn't ultimately work. He just had to find a way to make a living before he could ask his parents to approach Kusum's.

It turned out that this perspective was naïve. One of Kusum's neighbors observed Akshu and Kusum's interactions when they had been perhaps just a little indiscrete, and she went to Kusum's mother and informed her. 'These two are doing something wrong,' she stated. Perhaps Kusum's neighbor embellished what she told Kusum's mother, or perhaps the latter simply assumed the worst. Either way, Kusum's mother was furious. With little delay, she charged to the Atris' kitchen and found Akshu there, chopping vegetables for dinner.

'Hoy!' she roared at Akshu. 'How dare you try to seduce my daughter!'

Akshu was completely caught off-guard.

'You know what you did, don't lie! You are not qualified to marry my daughter, do you understand? Look at where you live! You live in a hut that's falling apart. My daughter lives in a palace! You don't have a job, you don't have an education ... How would you care for my daughter? What will you feed her? If you have children, how will you raise them? You are a beggar! You are too poor! *Sala*!'

Kusum's family members and neighbors had now joined in the melee, while Akshu's family also gathered, confused and worried that the village's elites were making accusations. 'You should be beaten for your insolence,' declared the brother of the woman who had ratted out Akshu.

It was precisely in anticipation of this sort of reaction that Akshu and Kusum had decided, without a word between them, to keep their mutual affection a complete secret. When a social hierarchy is challenged, it is difficult to know where those privileged by it will stop in the effort to maintain their supremacy. To have to deny any sort of palpable action, like a kiss or even an open expression of love, in such a situation would have been risky for them both. But there had been no such dishonorable action. And Akshu made that clear.

'*Aare*!' he said, with a mixture of defiance and consternation. 'Call the girl here and ask her! Ask your daughter if I have said or done anything to her!' When Kusum's family and neighbors continued to threaten him, Akshu stood up and repeated himself. 'You have no proof! Go ahead, call Kusum here, see what she says!'

Kusum, by this time, had either been called or caught wind of what was happening and appeared.

'Kusum,' Akshu said, his indignation masking his affection for her. 'Did I say or do anything untoward to you? Or did you to me?'

'No...' Kusum said in a 'what-are-you-talking-about' tone. 'No one said or did anything wrong, you to me or me to you...'

The denial wasn't enough for Kusum's mom. 'You son of a dog,' she told Akshu. 'Do you know that until yesterday, your father was guiding our cattle, and your mother was washing our dishes? And now you have the nerve to make advances on my daughter?'

For a brief moment, Akshu considered standing up for himself and his family. Of saying that a person's worth isn't dictated by their wealth, that he was not ashamed that his parents had washed others' dishes or herded others' cattle, for it was honest work. But he sensed that to say anything that asserted himself would just cause Kusum's family to take action to separate them beyond repair. He was just about to say, 'OK, well, I haven't done anything...'

But Kusum was more exasperated. 'No! I'm not at all affected here. Why are you yelling at him?' And that was all her mother and father needed to hear. For Akshu wasn't the only one who had known Kusum her whole life—so had they. In her defense of Akshu, they could hear an affection that confirmed their worst concerns. And they knew that these two had deep similarities in attitude and personality. It wasn't just Akshu—it was both of them, and it was real.

Kusum's parents acted swiftly. They reached out through their networks to find what they considered a suitable spouse for Kusum. They found a well-educated boy in the city of Siliguri that matched their specifications, and who (or whose family) quickly took a liking to Kusum; just like that, Kusum and this boy were officially engaged. The wedding was set, and Kusum's family invited Akshu and his family, hoping to dissuade them from disrupting the ceremony.

Akshu had no idea what Kusum thought of all this— they were not permitted to communicate more than a passing word. Akshu had already reasoned that if Kusum wanted to escape this arrangement, it was on her to do something. He couldn't intervene without knowing that she actively preferred him to her fiancé. Of course, after having heard her parents insult Akshu so publicly and after hearing Akshu fail to publicly declare his affections, it seems likely that Kusum would have also wanted some sign from Akshu that he was still interested. By preventing communication, Kusum's parents were winning.

On the day of the wedding, Akshu joined the rest of the wedding-goers at the *chowpathi* to see the groom. He looked at him, welcomed him with everyone else, but didn't speak with him. Having satisfied his self-injurious curiosity and stifled village speculation of a vendetta, he returned home and cried. He vowed that he would take Kusum back even if she came back to him after consummating the marriage, even if she came back to him with a child, with two children from this man. He wanted Kusum—Kusum without ears, Kusum without her mouth, Kusum without her eyes—any, *any* version of Kusum.

He looked at the photo Kusum had given him some months before. He felt like he was going to die. He felt more poignantly than ever that his poverty was a problem for every aspect of his existence.

7

After a couple of months back in the US, I returned to Buxa for my first fall/winter season there. Akshu's father Motikar had passed away two weeks before my return, so I spent a few days readying myself for field work as the Atris completed their mourning rituals. When Akshu was ready, I explained with visual aids to him and Narad that we had to systematically search for trees of our study species by vehicle and by foot. Now that the monsoon floodwaters had disappeared and the thick foliage had receded, we could travel much more safely through all parts of the reserve, from the Himalayan foothills to the deepest parts of the core area.

We completed the tree survey, and I randomly selected a sample of *chalta* trees to rotate through for the first three months. The camera traps were used to understand what species ate the *chalta* fruit, a green fruit about the size of a softball with a gooey, 6 millimeter-seed-filled ball of pulp at the center. The thick outer layers of the fruit were so hard that a human couldn't really hope to bite into a fresh *chalta* fruit without first slicing it into small thin pieces and perhaps even cooking it. *Chalta* trees were distributed through most parts of Buxa. Unlike the *lator* and *kumbhi* trees that dropped their fruits rapidly during the monsoon, *chalta* trees fruited and dropped their fruits gradually over about five months during the dry season, providing plenty of time for data collection.

One day, early in the season, our jeep happened upon Mr M. Petkar, one of the deputy field directors of Buxa. I chatted amiably with him about my research. 'Ahh, that's right,' Mr Petkar said. 'You have camera traps.' I told him that we hadn't captured many exciting pictures yet in the monsoon—mostly just Rhesus macaques and some elephants.

'Do you have any extra traps to spare?' Mr Petkar asked.

'I have two I could spare at this point,' I said. 'Why?'

Mr Petkar said, 'We have not gotten a photo of our tigers here for many years. It's such dense forest, you know, and there isn't a lot of tourism or many people that go into the core.' He mentioned there were places in the reserve that tigers were rumored to frequent. 'Perhaps you can take a camera trap to such places to capture a photograph of the animals?'

I was a little surprised. The idea seemed futile—one camera trap in an area, unless trained on a tiger kill, a known tiger thoroughfare, or a path to water in a dry area, was unlikely to capture a tiger. But the request seemed modest enough and a good way to build my relationship with the Forest Department. I agreed to the task, adding locations Petkar suggested to my routine.

Over the next several months, my camera traps under fruiting *chalta* trees turned up all sorts of interesting creatures. Only a handful of these species seemed to actually eat the fruits. The Asian elephant was one of them, eating more of the fruit from in front of the cameras than any other species. Gaur, the world's largest wild relative of the cow, also seemed to enjoy the hard, sour globes. Macaques, rats, and small squirrels went after the fruit mostly once they had begun to soften and rot, with the pulp and seeds apparently still worth salvaging. But a host of other species not interested in the fruit happened to cross into the frame. Wild pigs, Himalayan crestless porcupines, jungle fowl, peafowl, muntjacs, and sambar deer all made cameo appearances. A variety of stunning small birds—including the Indian pitta, Siberian rubythroat, rufous-bellied niltava, and orange-headed thrush—would all eventually make appearances in my traps. There were also a host of small carnivores. Leopard cats, fishing cats, large and small Indian civets, common palm civets, small-toothed ferret badgers, crab-eating mongooses, and even full-sized leopards all appeared on camera. Akshu was dazzled by the variety; he'd never heard of or seen some of the small carnivores despite a lifetime wandering the jungle. 'Our jungle still has a lot!' he said with a smile.

'Still?'

'It used to have more.'

Other camera-trap pictures helped explain how things might have changed. In addition to the wild species that ate *chalta* were many domestic cattle and domestic buffalo, some reaching camera traps embedded quite far into the jungle. In fact, after elephants, it was domestic animals that ate the greatest amount of *chalta*. I would eventually find something similar for *lator* and *kumbhi* fruit that fell from the canopy—domestic bovids, Rhesus macaques, and elephants were the biggest consumers of wild fruit in Buxa Tiger Reserve.

And then, one day, a camera placed in a dry, sandy creek bed in the core area of Buxa to photograph tigers caught the jungle's most voracious predator. A series of photos showed three men who had unwittingly passed the camera earlier on the morning we retrieved it.

They had deeply tanned skin with sleek, knotted muscles. They walked barefoot, one carrying his slippers in his hand. 'To keep from making noise and scaring animals,' Akshu explained. One carried a full bag, with animal or plant matter one could only guess. And the leader carried a gun—a rifle whose long wooden butt looked almost toy-like.

'They have *guns*? From where?'

'They are made in some villages,' replied Akshu. 'They are very powerful. You can't even really duck effectively because these guns don't shoot one bullet. Instead, they shoot a spray of metal that goes every which way. They can even wound an elephant so badly that it could die.'

Thidey heard our exclamations and came to see the photos. 'Where did you put the camera?' he asked.

'You know the last bridge before the 23-mile tower heading east on the 23-mile road?' I responded. 'In that creek.'

Thidey clicked his tongue and shook his head. 'That is the very heart of Buxa. The poachers even go there these days?'

Over time, it would become clear this wasn't a one-off occurrence. There would be photographs of hunters wielding a long bow and a quiver of arrows; a poacher with a slingshot; and an individual who had a trowel deep in the core area. And there would be many pictures of villagers with kukris and full bags—most had probably just collected non-timber forest products. But maybe others had bushmeat.

Staring at the picture of the poacher with the home-made gun, I was unsure how to handle this reality. What would I do if I ran into poachers on a forest trail? What should I say? 'Just say,' Thidey suggested, '"Ah, you've come to collect some firewood! Good, good—carry on.

We're doing research on elephants. You have to make your living, and we have to make ours."'

———————

Living in the jungle and collecting new data regularly, I had all sorts of ideas about other types of data I should collect to tell the full story of the role elephants played as seed dispersers in Buxa Tiger Reserve: more camera trap data, data on what animals removed fruit from the tree canopies before they fell, data on what per cent of seeds made it into animal dung after a fruit was eaten, data on how far animals would take the seeds, and data on whether those seeds survived into seedlings.

Collecting all this information simultaneously required even more employees, so I began hiring people for short-term work. Akshu wasn't always great at choosing the best employees; he seemed pressured to offer jobs to his middle-aged, fairly unreliable friends and relatives, so I took more initiative in finding new workers. I looked for younger people from different castes and communities and, though I still ended up with mostly Nepali employees, over time I developed a more diverse and diligent team.

There was one axis along which, though, I particularly struggled to make progress. 'Guruji,' I asked Akshu. 'Why must our workers all be men? Why can't we hire any women?'

Akshu had worked with Jilpa and other female ecologists, and I considered him progressive. He had spontaneously asked me one day why children always get their father's last name and not their mother's, and he had suggested to me once that if men went to live with their wives' families (as opposed to the other way around, which was traditional for Nepalis), that could lead to a reduction in domestic violence. But he didn't seem to think his community was ready for what I was suggesting. 'That's complicated,' Akshu said. 'One girl working with a bunch of boys—it could be dangerous.'

I assumed he meant there could be either sexual violence, social stigma, or both. But I made a specific suggestion. 'What if we hire Chameli Didi?' I asked. Chameli was my landlord Hari's daughter. She and I had lived in the same house for the better part of a year, and we had become friends in the way two amiable people who barely shared a language could. She was short and slender and hadn't much liked school, but I had watched her lift huge piles of wood on her head and skillfully chop firewood with a kukri. She spent time in the jungle collecting cooking fuel and dealt with cleaning up the cowshed all the time, so I thought she would have no trouble helping with our dung-heavy, jungle-dwelling work. Plus, she was a year or two older than me, a rare bachelorette in her late twenties—she had, I thought, the maturity to handle working with a bunch of guys. Her parents had come to trust me to be home alone with even their younger daughter, and of course they were related to and trusted Akshu. And Chameli was at an age where it was altogether appropriate for her to assert her independence.

Akshu agreed that Chameli would be a great worker, but he still hesitated. 'Let me ask her,' I said.

A couple days later, I finally found myself alone with Chameli at home. 'Didi,' I said, 'I need another man to work for me.' I—ironically—didn't yet know how to get around gendered language in Hindi; I didn't want to tell her I 'needed a woman' and be misunderstood. 'You always work very hard. Would you like to work with me in the jungle?' I explained that Akshu would always be with her in the forest. Chameli thought momentarily, then smiled endearingly, her white buck teeth contrasting with her dark brown skin. 'OK!' she said.

Before the shy Chameli had become comfortable with me, when she hadn't wanted to answer a question positively, she had just run away from me. So I took this response as a great sign—she was clearly interested.

I reported her apparent enthusiasm to Akshu. He must have passed this information on because Thidey soon brought up the subject with me. 'Brudder!' Thidey said, among the first to drop the formal 'Sir.' 'Don't hire Chameli.'

'Why not?' I asked.

'Women aren't used to jungle work,' Thidey said. 'They get scared too easily.'

'They go into the jungle all the time! To collect firewood!' I said in disbelief.

'That's different. That's near the village, in the day. It's safe then.'

'What about Jilpa?' I pointed out Thidey and Akshu's hero. Thidey had worked for her after Akshu's injury to keep income coming into the family. 'She isn't afraid.'

'That's different,' Thidey argued. 'She has lots of experience.'

'Well, how do you think she got that experience?' I retorted. 'Was she born with experience?'

Thidey ignored my response, and I ignored his advice. It was a well-known fact that Thidey was afraid of elephants in the jungle, and I suspected he just didn't want a woman showing him up. Anyway, I thought, I didn't need her cousins' approval to hire her. As long as Chameli was still interested, I figured things would work out—I was willing to burn some social capital on this. The next day, I ran into Chameli on my way in from the jungle. 'Chameli Didi!' I said excitedly. 'I need that new worker next week. Would you still like to work in the jungle with me?'

'No,' she said. And before I could ask what had changed, she ran down the stairs and disappeared.

Concerned about how I might appear agitating to hire a young woman, I let the issue go.

———

Chameli had clearly been keen to join our work and, over the next couple of months, I occasionally wondered whether someone had intervened to change her mind. It could have been her parents reflexively withholding permission, genuinely believing my work to be beyond their daughter's abilities. Someone in her family could have expressed concerns about how doing 'men's work' would affect her 'marriageability', which was already on the decline (by traditional standards) due to her ripe old age of 27. In any case, Chameli was not one to disobey her parents. If I wanted to involve her in my work, I needed to propose something more acceptable to her family.

One day, I saw an opportunity. Narad was off for the day and, as my other employees were otherwise occupied, Akshu and I were to collect the camera traps from the jungle. The day before, however, I had sprained my ankle. I told Akshu, 'I'll come with you, and I'll help with the traps near the road, but two traps are half a kilometer into the forest. We need someone else to come help with them. Maybe we can take Chameli— just today?'

Akshu smiled as though to say, 'You never let anything go, do you?' But he also seemed to think the idea was implementable. 'Chameli Didi!' he said, mocking me— for he was older than her—'Want a day's work?' Chameli turned to her mother for permission. Maili, Chameli, and Akshu had a quick conversation in Nepali—I think Akshu assured Maili he would be with Chameli at all times, and that they wouldn't go that far from the vehicle—and Maili relented.

It was a beautiful afternoon. Chameli sat between me and Akshu in the front of the jeep, and Akshu drove. The traps were scattered across Buxa Reserve, so Chameli got to see a good chunk of the park. Chameli's very presence made our daily work an adventure. In Nimati, when we saw an elephant, she leaned forward and grinned appreciatively. Even smaller animals incited her interest—peacocks, jungle fowl, hornbills all in turn made their appearance. While she was looking overhead, a barking deer dashed in front of the vehicle. 'You're good luck!' I said. 'With you here, maybe we'll even see a leopard.' Chameli, as usual, grinned.

The last trap, on Chalta Tree #50, was in the core area. When we'd first visited in late autumn, the place had seemed almost magical. Chalta #50 and the other trees were tall and spindly, presiding over a relatively open area reminiscent of a well-shaded courtyard. Hornbills, woodpeckers, and Malay giant squirrels had played and flittered about in the canopy, and footprints below had told of various animals that used the area as a thoroughfare. As the months passed, though, the area had become desolate. There were no longer any sounds of life. The leaves of the surrounding trees had browned and fallen. Not a single animal ever tripped the camera trap here, and the surrounding fruits all decayed and rotted from the absence of frugivores. On the day we visited with Chameli, somehow the open blue sky suddenly became overcast.

Akshu and Chameli walked the half-kilometer into the forest to retrieve the trap. I sat in the jeep, hoping nothing too exciting would happen during their excursion. They returned without event, and Chameli was still smiling as we started driving home.

It was dusk now, and we were still deep in the forest. We weren't far from the 23-mile watchtower at the center of the core area when a large, hulking beast gracefully slid out of the forest onto the road. Its long neck and round ears erect, it saw our vehicle and then galloped into the forest.

'What's that?' Chameli gasped in Nepali.

I thought she was kidding, or that maybe I had misunderstood her.

'It's a sambar deer,' Akshu responded. Didi still looked dazzled, and I realized she had truly never seen a sambar before.

'Seriously? How is this possible?' I asked. 'You live in Buxa Tiger Reserve!' It felt like someone from New Jersey saying they had never seen white-tailed deer.

'So?' Akshu shot back, irritated that I might be making his cousin feel ignorant. 'You know there aren't many animals left here. Chameli only enters the forest a little for firewood. And if deer come anywhere near the village during the day, they'll be killed and eaten, so they stay deep in the core area. Elephants show up in the fields at night now and then, but otherwise Chameli has no reason to be familiar with any jungle animals.'

Our vehicle flushed a few more sambar, which trotted into the vegetation quickly. Didi was still spellbound.

And suddenly, the picture of Buxa's forest I had been willing myself not to see became clear to me. The camera traps mostly captured smaller, cryptic animals—often species that even jungle-dwellers like Akshu scarcely knew existed. Sambar deer kept near the central watch tower, distant from any villages—many villagers, especially women who were seldom allowed far from the village, might never have seen them or gaur or even giant squirrels. And even to the extent that species like deer, gaur, wild pigs, and porcupines still existed in Buxa, my data suggested that the wild mammal herbivores and frugivores of the forest had been mostly ecologically replaced by cattle and buffaloes. *Domestic* animals often ate more of the forest's fruits than did wild animals. Neither I nor any of my team had seen any sign of a tiger during our work, and my neighbors in Madhubangaon hadn't seen one for decades, and this made sense since there wasn't much wild prey available. Poachers and illegal harvesters were all over the core area, and villagers were using the buffer as an open commons. The only wild animals that regularly appeared on my camera traps were elephants and macaques—both happened to be sacred to Hindus and, by many groups, seen as inedible.

This, I realized, was what was left of the jungle: a flora of British-era plantations surrounding patches of more natural forest; a fauna of diverse small species and hangers on of large, edible wild species outnumbered by monkeys and domestic animals. And, of course, elephants. Chameli's unfamiliarity with sambar deer meant that, in this major Indian reserve, even the largest deer in the tropics was functionally invisible to the people who shared the land. Conservation, I thought, couldn't be fair and effective without local awareness and buy-in, but most of the villagers in Buxa probably had no idea that they were losing so much from their jungles. And people can't possibly be expected to try to conserve something they never knew existed.

8

When he came, it was wholly night, and no one heard him coming. After this event, the villagers of Madhubangaon would start building fences around their house—not because it would have kept him out, but because he would have had to break the fence as he crossed the land, waking the neighborhood and giving them a fighting chance. What drew him would remain a mystery to the village—perhaps the Forest Department knew more, but it was unlikely their investigation was thorough enough to reveal anything. The best explanation Akshu would think of later was that perhaps he had been drawn by the scent of rice beer, which Akshu's Adivasi neighbors were known to love. If Budri Malpahadia and her companion had eased themselves into a deep sleep with rice beer, this would also explain why they didn't react quickly enough.

In any case, what the *haathi* did transformed the theoretical dangers of elephants into a hard reality for the hamlet of Malabasti. The house he attacked was, like the Atris', built by the Forest Department for the families that worked in Buxa's original plantations. This house was elevated, but only 4 feet off the ground. It was safe from the elephant's feet, but not from its trunk. The intruder broke down the wall, maybe looking for the rice beer. Some say that Budri Malpahadia was leaned up against the wall and fell out when the elephant ripped the wall open with his trunk; others say she might have been struck by a falling crossbeam when the elephant ripped the wall apart. Either way, the 55-year-old grandmother was unable to respond before the elephant wrapped her in his trunk and threw her to her death. By then, the neighborhood had been awakened by the commotion, but the elephant retreated into the starlit jungle before they could react.

When Akshu arrived the next morning and saw the corpse, he scarcely recognized her. Everything seemed to be broken from the force of the impact—her hands, her legs, her body. She had hit the ground facing forward, so her features were obscured and caked with mud. The Forest Department arrived, took the body for autopsy, and returned fairly promptly to pay the compensation owed. Officially, the matter was closed.

As Akshu and the others looked on mournfully, the deceased's daughter and other relatives bawled. While elephants had certainly killed others in and around Buxa before, this was the first time someone Akshu knew had been so affected, and he could feel a heat growing inside his chest as he swelled with a new and profound anger. This was the work of the god Ganesh? Fine, Akshu could accept that perhaps the gods would expect people, even very poor people, to share a portion of their agricultural yield with their fellow creatures—all souls, after all, belonged to God, and it was the gods that had given humankind the bounty of the Earth off which they lived. But why would Ganesh take *everything* they grew? Why would he destroy the homes they worked so hard to build? Why would he take the very life of an old woman, sleeping peacefully in her home, harming no one?

Often, the elephants came and ate peacefully and moved on when Akshu and the others yelled out,

'Ganesh Bhagwan, go away! You've had enough, go away!' Then, the elephants seemed like gods. To be near them felt thrilling; to watch them move on felt joyful; to lose some small portion of their crop to another grand soul felt reasonable. But for an elephant to kill a person in her own home—in the moment, the elephant seemed not like a god but like a demon. Akshu wanted to track down the elephant that killed his neighbor and slay him. In the moment, he even thought he could slay the other male elephants, too. If it came to this sort of violence, thought Akshu, he would choose the side of his fellow humans over that of the elephants, whether or not they were Ganesh. An unjust god was just not a god worth following.

As Akshu's mind and heart cooled over the next days, it did occur to him that, maybe, there was some karmic logic to all the elephants did. After all, the adults in the village had arguably taken more from the jungle than they perhaps should have; what did he know of Budri Malpahadia's karma? But the seed of skepticism that had always been present in Akshu had now sprouted. As far as he could tell, when it came to the sanctity of elephants, something just didn't add up.

It had been a couple of years since Akshu's first experience working for the Forest Department on the plantation when he again found work with them and, as luck would have it, he again found himself working for Manik Barman. The beat officer had been transferred around several times and arrived back just in time to preside over Akshu's term as a firewatcher. Akshu was recruited with five others, including Moksha Chatterjee, a small but strong half-Bengali, half-Rabha fellow with dark reddish-brown skin and dimples.

The firewatchers' job was fairly simple. Over their three- to four-month tenure during the dry season, they were to ride around compartment number 15, a stretch of forest running some 3 kilometers between Buxa's main Metal Road and the Bala River. If they found a fire, they were supposed to try and extinguish it, and if they couldn't, they were to ride back to the beat office in Madhubangaon immediately and ask them to send a fire wicket. Modern forest fire management, which encourages the use of controlled fires to reduce fuel load and prevent future conflagrations, hadn't made its way to Buxa, and the Forest Department was keen to prevent fires from destroying forest that might provide wildlife habitat or a source of timber. The firewatchers were to report to the office at 8 AM and again in the late afternoon, when they would end their workday. When they reported the first day, however, Manik gave them another task.

'If you see a timber smuggler,' Manik instructed them, 'chase them or come tell us. If you see any dead animals, or even if you smell one, give us that information.' Akshu and Moksha glanced at each other. That was primarily supposed to be the role of the forest guards, but Akshu and Moksha noticed they hardly went on patrol. Despite their high pay and regular salary, the beat officer and his guards were delegating their work to the firewatchers who were paid ₹900 a month. Given little option, the firewatchers agreed to provide extra eyes and ears in the forest.

Fires occurred in Buxa's forests for several reasons. Sometimes kids would light fires for fun. As the leaf litter dried and became crunchier, poachers would sometimes light fires to clear the brush so that they could sneak up on prey without being detected. In other cases, smugglers or perhaps even forest guards would carelessly toss a cigarette or bidi into the forest, starting an accidental fire. In the first month or so of work, when the forest was less hot and dry, the firewatchers found fewer fires, but soon they were battling small fires regularly. They were provided no equipment for this work—they would break off thick, green branches, bundle them together with thin climbers, and beat the fires down until they were smothered. Every now and then, a fire would pick up beyond what the firewatchers could handle with such meager tools. Once, a hot April wind blew a growing fire in Akshu and his companions' direction, heavily singing their eyebrows. Akshu raced back to the beat office, and Manik sent the fire wicket to douse the increasingly acrobatic flames. By the time the fire had been quelled, it had already destroyed several short trees.

Manik Barman had not given up his domineering style and, despite the firewatchers' diligence, he often scolded them. 'I saw this tree that was felled near the road today,' he would yell when he occasionally ventured out on patrol. 'Why did you not find it? How come you didn't report the incident?'

Akshu and the firewatchers *did* try and tell the beat officer whenever they saw evidence of timber smuggling. The young men most frequently came across remnants of felled trees, but given the growing network of smugglers in Madhubangaon, Akshu and the others would occasionally catch the thieves in the act. Upon sighting the firewatchers, the thieves generally fled, and Akshu dutifully reported them to the beat officer. 'Oh, they ran away, did they?' Manik would say, indicating that nothing more could be done. 'Good, good. I'll just tell the DFO.'

However, one group of smugglers did not react with such timidity. Akshu, Moksha, and two others were biking on the 22-mile road when they rounded a bend and saw that a group of young men had felled a huge teak tree. They were chopping it into smaller pieces to be rolled away. There were about a dozen of them, and Akshu recognized them all—they were bullish residents of the Madhubangaon bazaar and newly settled hamlets, all from families who had immigrated to Madhubangaon to start businesses. Akshu and his companions knew these men were part of a growing gang of professional timber smugglers settled within the Reserve—not the type of smuggler that was trying to repair his home or just make enough to pay for a child's wedding, but the type that made a regular habit of selling valuable woods from the forest and spending the money on drinks, gambling, and other vices. And they weren't exactly the type to be cowed by a few scrawny firewatchers.

The firewatchers stopped on the road and turned to backtrack, but it was too late—the smugglers had seen them. 'Oh, it's *these* fellas!' one of the bazaar residents said menacingly. 'Hold on just a second. Stop for just a second! You're going to inform on us, are ya? Hold up right there'—and he and the others grabbed their kukris and started running after the firewatchers. Heavily outnumbered, Akshu and the others fled, cycling hard as they were pursued on foot.

The firewatchers immediately went to the beat office and told Manik what had happened. The beat officer responded that the staff he had on hand that day were too unfit to give chase—some were too old, some had poor sight or hearing. He said he would tell the DFO and see what happened.

Akshu and Moksha left the beat office in disbelief. The Forest Department, Akshu realized, wasn't going to do anything. What if the smugglers suspected they had been reported and came to punish the firewatchers?

Moksha agreed. He had previously done some timber smuggling himself, so he knew the perpetrators fairly well. 'What are we going to do? These guys, they drink so heavily, they could do anything.'

A couple days later, Akshu and some other firewatchers were biking on the same stretch of road where they had seen the timber thieves when they saw a Forest Department truck loading pieces of teak. The smugglers had systematically cut down many trees in that area in the previous week or two, and they had yet to remove much of what they had cut. The Forest Department vehicle was loading up all that the timber thieves had left behind. The labourers, seeing the firewatchers, told the driver, 'Go fast fast fast!' Since it was on a jungle road, Akshu and his companions easily followed the lumbering vehicle on their bicycles. They assumed that the truck was taking the ill-felled timber to the Madhubangaon depot where it would be stored and then auctioned off per Forest Department protocol, the funds then used to finance the Forest Department's conservation operations. Instead, the truck drove right past the depot on the Metal Road, toward Damanpur and Alipurduar.

Akshu sped to the beat office and found Manik. He knew better than to blatantly accuse Forest Department officials of stealing lumber. Instead, he remarked, 'It looks like that truck with the teak went right past the depot.'

'There are other depots, too,' Manik replied. 'One in Checko, one in Damanpur, one in Porro...' Of course, Manik should have known exactly where the wood taken from his beat was going, but Akshu didn't push it. Perhaps Manik was getting a cut, too.

At the end of the dry season, all the firewatchers were let go. The Forest Department, Manik informed them, no longer had the funds to continue this work.

Akshu left the firewatcher job feeling vulnerable. By this time, Madhubangaon, even Malabasti, was full of thieves who stole trees from the forest, and he had just actively tried to help the Forest Department stop them. Not long after he was let go by the Forest Department, his fears were confirmed by an acquaintance who was friends with some of the smugglers he had seen. The acquaintance told Akshu that the smugglers resented him for taking a job that interfered with their own livelihood. Akshu protested that he was just trying to help his family make ends meet, but his friend said that was beside the point.

'They don't like you because you never participate in those sorts of things. You are always acting like such a straight arrow,' the go-between said. All the other firewatchers at least sometimes engaged in timber smuggling. 'They don't trust you.'

Akshu was quite afraid of what might happen to him. The smugglers targeting him lived within a kilometer of his house, and it was inevitable that they would meet again. He reasoned that the smugglers would feel less threatened by him if he, too, had something they could hold against him—so he decided to approach one of the ringleaders of the local tree smuggling ring and ask to participate.

'Ram Ram,' Akshu greeted Om Ojha, then he lowered his voice. 'Are you going to steal from the forest any time soon? I'd like to come along.' Akshu held his breath—he was a bit concerned that Om would think he was trying to act as an informant.

But Om's response was the opposite of skeptical. 'Why not? Why not!' Om excitedly noted that Akshu's brother Chander, who had been on a couple of smuggling trips already, was planning to come on the next expedition. 'Just come with Chander, we can all go together.'

So, on a pleasant morning in late May, Akshu and Chander arose, quietly packed some bread, bitter roasted rice called *chida*, biscuits, and jaggery, and headed to meet the rest of the team around 6 AM. They soon joined the gang including many of the individuals that, just weeks earlier, had chased Akshu when he caught them stealing wood. Akshu again hoped fervently that they wouldn't suspect him of being an informant; he envisioned them yelling at him, potentially even attacking him for having reported them to the Forest Department. But that's not what they did.

'*Vwa vwaaah*!' the gang cheered when they saw Akshu. 'He wants to join our team now?' They patted Akshu on the back, slung their arm around his neck jovially, thrusting snacks in his hands.

'Welcome!' they said. 'Don't worry, you have us now. If anything at all happens, we will be there to help you! We are behind you.' Akshu laughed and nodded, though he knew full well that none of these boys cared an iota about his well-being. He marveled that there was no shortage of people who delighted in corrupting him—and at the complete absence of support when he tried to do the right thing.

The team of about 20 people followed trails within the jungle until they were near the 22-mile road, where they found a *champ* tree near the Nonai creek that had fallen naturally. Akshu, Chander, and four others set to work on the *champ* while the others moved on to fell a nearby teak tree. On the first day of work, the team worked until nearly noon, breaking the trees into pieces of wood about 1.5 meters long, short enough to be dragged over jungle trails. Akshu's team sawed the *champ* tree into 10 pieces, but 7 of them were rotting inside or their shapes were not conducive for transport, so they were discarded. Some of the others stayed throughout the night to work on the teak log by firelight, but Akshu went home.

The second morning, he returned. He and Chander were assigned to one of the marketable segments of the *champ* log. They began chiseling and smoothing the wood until it was round so that it would roll easily. The teams would knock a thick, sturdy nail into either end of each piece. The result was called a *gud-gudi*. They would tie a rope to each nail such that two people pulling the ropes would roll the *gud-gudi* along. As the teams were working on their *gud-gudis*, the watchperson on the bridge near Nonai creek alerted them that someone was coming on the 22-mile road—it was a team of forest guards. The thieves quickly gathered their belongings and fled south on a jungle path back to Madhubangaon in time for lunch.

The logs that the thieves were working on sat just close enough to the road that a careful observer, peering through the trees, might see them. But this was still the age of Manik Barman, and the forest guards were not really on patrol so much as just passing the time; they either noticed nothing or said nothing. In the late afternoon, the smugglers returned and finished shaping up the *gud-gudis*. In the late evening, they began pulling the timber, including the 3 pieces of *champ* and 10–15 pieces of teak, down a jungle trail. They stashed all the pieces in a ditch near the rail line under a pile of branches, and they went home for a good night's rest.

On the third day, the job was to pull the *gud-gudis* about 8 kilometers from their hiding spot to a location outside of Buxa Tiger Reserve. For all the apparent indifference of the Forest Department, the smugglers still opted to do this sort of work after-hours. The team retrieved the *gud-gudis* a little after 5 PM and began rolling them down another jungle trail toward the national highway that formed the southern boundary of Buxa.

To Akshu's surprise, his team wasn't alone. Timber thieves from all over Madhubangaon—from the hamlet of Taazabasti, from the bazaar—joined, some pulling single-person *gud-gudis* about a meter long and others in pairs like him and Chander, until there were over 50 people dragging about 30–35 *gud-gudis*. The southbound trail was clearly a highway for the smugglers, one of the few paths negotiable for thieves dragging heavy logs. The fact that it hadn't been detected by the Forest Department spoke volumes about the forest guards' dysfunction and apathy.

Yet, Akshu found, even without much fear of detection, the job was not an easy one. It was a half-moon night, so it wasn't pitch black, but it was dark. Chander and Akshu pulled their *gud-gudi* in the middle of the pack, staying close to the people in front of them so they wouldn't get lost. Some of the smugglers had small flashlights, but Akshu had nothing but a kukri. As they proceeded south, they came to lower-elevation ground. It was muddy from the pre-monsoon rains, so there were sections where Akshu and Chander couldn't count on the *gud-gudi* to roll, and they strained to drag the 200-kilogram section of log forward. Akshu's slippers kept coming off in the mud, so he tied them around his waist. The mild night was made hotter by their exertion; Akshu removed his shirt and rolled up his pants. Leeches crawled up from the mud and took his blood, falling off fat and happy and leaving characteristic open wounds. All this made the thieves that had once threatened Akshu with their kukris even happier. If they had been concerned previously about his dedication to the work, they no longer were. 'Good, good,' they said encouragingly. 'You've really joined our team now!' Akshu smiled—his plan to ingratiate the smugglers was working but, deep in his chest, his heart felt like charcoal.

They were moving fairly quickly down a slight, non-muddy incline when someone near the front of the line hissed. '*Haathi*!' Everyone froze so suddenly that many of their *gud-gudis* continued to roll toward them. Some were able to brace themselves and stop their logs' roll, but others, like Akshu and Chander, weren't—they jumped out of the way of their hurtling *gud-gudi*, and it rolled past them and slammed into the *gud-gudi* in front of them with a ringing thump. Somehow, no one was hurt, but they all lowered their heads and peered into the dark forests to see if the elephants would react.

The elephants, perhaps accustomed now to this regular stream of traffickers, seemed unaffected; comfortable in the depths of the jungle at night, they just made their usual repertoire of sounds—*kada kuduk, pada puduk, hurrrrrrrrrrr, gadjudjudju*. Some of the smokers in the group lit matches to signal their presence and discourage the elephants from coming closer. The leaders of the group somehow persuaded the elephants near the path in front of them to move away. They turned and whispered, '*joom, joom,*' and then everyone started moving forward again. As Akshu and Chander moved past the herd, now several meters away from the jungle path, Akshu could still hear the elephants whirring, breaking branches, talking to each other.

They passed the herd without event, but the uneasiness Akshu had felt throughout the entire operation was aggravated by the fear he felt passing the giants. Everything Akshu hated about this situation flooded into his mind at once. '*Eyy Bhagwan*!' he thought to himself. 'Why did I come? Why has it come to my doing this? Why have I come to see a day like this?' He hated that his poverty had led him to steal from the forest. Sadness set into him.

Finally, not long after midnight, the group came to the national highway. Before crossing, the thieves took a snack break just inside the boundary of the jungle. Lookouts were stationed in every direction. Everyone sat together, some eating biscuits, some sipping drinks, some eating *chida*. Everyone was drenched in sweat. They were mostly quiet. The only sounds they could hear were the cicadas and other insects singing their mating songs.

They pulled the *gud-gudis* across the national highway and out of Buxa, and then another 1–1.5 kilometers until they reached the home of the merchant who peddled illegal timber. They arrived around 2 AM and hid the fragmented logs. A young man came out. 'We don't have payment for you right now,' he said. 'Stay until the day and we will pay you.' Consulting their companions, Akshu and Chander had reckoned their *gud-gudi* was worth around ₹800, maybe a bit more. This was a fraction of what the wood would ultimately be sold for; at legal auction, Akshu suspected, their piece of wood, after some more processing, would fetch about ₹19,000 and, on the black market, closer to ₹12,000. But there was only one merchant for illegal wood in those days, and he wielded his monopsony power well.

None of the villagers wanted to spend the remainder of the night there; the team agreed to a system to retrieve and distribute payment later. As Akshu and Chander walked back the way they had come, Akshu silently lamented his poverty and asked himself why all his friends were thieves.

They arrived home when the rooster was crowing, perhaps around 4:30 AM, exhausted. To avoid the scrutiny of their parents and siblings—for Motikar would have beaten them badly if he heard of this—they crawled into the tong above the cowshed. The brothers slept there until 11 AM, when they arose to begin their farm work. Somehow, they were able to avoid discovery of their illicit deeds.

When Akshu awoke, he told Chander he didn't want his share of the payment. He figured that if he didn't take the money, he would be absolved of his sin. Chander told Akshu he didn't want to go all the way down to get it, either. Akshu never found out what happened to his share. He was done with stealing wood. He had achieved his main objective, having shaken his reputation as irreproachable and the perils that came with it. And he was gratified that smuggling was so *hard*—that those robbing the jungle of its life were not leading a wholly easy or pleasurable existence themselves.

This also indicated, of course, that those smuggling timber were mostly doing so because society had failed to offer them any reasonable, legal alternatives. This was as true for Akshu as anyone. But Akshu still felt guilt and, in keeping with his deep-seated hope that karma was real and the universe was fair, some irrational fear. Every time subsequently that he spoke to a forest guard or went to the range office, he feared that one of his adversaries had ratted him out, and that some Forest Department official would ask, 'Why did you steal wood that day?'

Of course, the Forest Department under Manik Barman and his allies was utterly disinterested in enforcement. If Akshu was to experience the force of karma for his sins, it would have to be through some other of the universe's instruments.

A few years after Akshu and his family had started running a shop at the Chowpathi, a local NGO called IBRAD began hosting a new program to finance 'eco-development'. Funded by the World Bank, the program was intended to fund both community development projects and individual families: a villager who deposited a sum in the Panchayat's account would receive four times that much for their immediate use. Akshu deposited ₹3,000 and received ₹12,000. He used that to invest in a building for the Atris' store. It was made of wood on four sides, a tin roof, and a window through which they could deal with customers. They even installed a battery-operated light bulb so they could continue to sell goods throughout the evening.

Madhubangaon being full of thieves as it was, the Atris still couldn't leave the shop unoccupied with lots of supplies at night. Whenever another male relative was available, he and Akshu would spend the night sleeping in the store to guard their merchandise; otherwise, Akshu and Rukmani would sometimes take their most valuable things home. Even the possibility that people might be sleeping inside, the Atris reasoned, would deter thieves from trying to break in.

Less than two years after they had initially erected the building, Akshu and his nephew were sleeping inside one night when they awoke with a start. The shop was shaking! Akshu and his nephew yelled. Akshu reached for the light switch; by the time the light was on, the shaking had stopped. Akshu and his companion remained vigilant throughout the night. After discussion with his family, Akshu opted to no longer sleep in the store. It was too risky.

At home a couple of days later, Akshu awoke to the sound of a crash and wood breaking outside. He raced out of his house and up the dirt path with firecrackers, matches, and a torch in his hand. The store had been turned upside down by the time Akshu had gotten there. There was a full moon that night; from a distance, Akshu saw that the elephant was no longer nearby. He slowed down and approached the toppled store.

Suddenly, Akshu saw a huge shadow move under the fig tree meters away from the toppled store—and, before another thought could cross Akshu's mind, the elephant came charging toward him. Instinctively, Akshu scrambled off the path, which happened to have a small bridge over another path connecting two fields. He jumped 2 meters down, got below the bridge and stood underneath. The elephant placed one foot onto the wooden bridge and stopped—it sensed that the bridge was too weak to bear its approximately 4.5 tons—and it trumpeted as it hovered over Akshu. The tusker seemed to be weighing his options. Akshu could smell his pungent odour, and as the elephant stood there in his agitated state, a fluid dripped from his mouth and between the planks on the bridge, covering Akshu's head with the stench. Akshu looked around, trying to predict which way the elephant might try to descend— but, by now, other villagers were yelling and shouting at the elephant, and the tusker substituted flight for fight, moving west off toward the bazaar. When Akshu climbed back up to the village path, his relatives were relieved and surprised. They had assumed he had run straight into the path of the elephant and to his death.

Akshu and the others surveyed the damage that night and again the next morning. The *haathi* had thrust his tusks into the wooden wall of the store, creating two big holes. The marks on the ground and the wood of the shop suggested the elephant had then dug his tusks under the shop and flipped it over. The elephant had shattered most of the glass jars; he appeared to have eaten mostly biscuits and salt. Mustard oil had been spilled everywhere, staining many of the goods.

Akshu showed the damage to the Forest Department, who gave him a form to fill out detailing the damages. Tallying just the value of the products in the store, he calculated somewhere around ₹12,000 of damage. He submitted the form and, after some prolonged period, he received his compensation. He was dismayed: It was around ₹500.

Akshu was incensed at the incompetence of the Forest Department, but he wasn't upset at the elephant; Akshu, too, had taken something that hadn't belonged to him. This time, he could make some sense of the karma of it all.

9

Half-way through my second field season, I hit an inflection point—I started to feel I could handle myself pretty well in the village. Somehow, I stopped missing hot showers, feeling fully refreshed from bucket baths even on chilly winter nights. I learned to drive the jeep and became familiar with several of the forest's walking trails. My Hindi—peppered with a hodge-podge of Nepali and Bengali from Akshu and English when I felt myself at a loss—was now good enough to have conversations on a variety of topics with people around the village.

One day, over dinner, a devout visitor of the Atris asked me about religion in America. 'Are there Hindus in America?' he asked.

'Yes, there are some,' I explained. 'Most are like my parents, people from India who settled there and their children. There are also some Hare Krishnas and other converts. But overall, Hindus are less than 2 per cent of the US population.'

'Oh, so what is their religion, then?' he asked.

'Most people are Christian. Both Catholics and Protestant. But there are people from all over the world in the US, and there are lots of religions. There are Buddhists, Sikhs, Muslims, and also lots of Jews. There are also people who don't believe in any god.'

'Joos!' one of the other guests, who had seemed disinterested, chimed in enthusiastically. 'I know a Joo!'

'Really?' I said, surprised. I didn't think there were that many Jews in India, particularly in North Bengal. 'Where did you find this Jew?'

'In Darjeeling!' he continued.

'Darjeeling?'

'Yes! There was a lot there! They had a tiger, and a red panda, and a bear ... Many, many animals. It was a very big joo!'

I also got better at explaining why I was even in Buxa. One day, Akshu and I had brought some wild elephant dung back to the village and were pulling it apart, looking for the *chalta*'s hairy 6-millimeter seeds. Thidey wandered by. 'Brudder, explain to me again, why are you doing this? What is the purpose of your research?'

'It's to understand whether the *chalta* tree's fruits are important to elephants, right Sir?' Akshu asked.

'No, not quite,' I said. 'We're trying to understand whether the elephant is important for the trees!'

'Ohhh ... that's a much more complicated question! Why don't you ask simpler questions? If you asked whether the *chalta* were important for elephants, we could be done by now!' Akshu joked. I pointed out that if we had finished quickly, he would be unemployed. 'Oh ho ho! You're right, Sir. I'm glad you've asked a complicated question. Please, next time ask a question that will take 15 years to answer. I have two children to educate.'

Thidey shook his head. 'I don't get it,' he said. 'All the scientists and Forest Department people, they say that the forest needs elephants and talk about "ecology balance". I get why we need frogs—because they eat the insects and keep their populations low. I get why we need snakes—they eat the frogs and keep their population low. But why do we need elephants?'

'Right,' I replied, 'That's my research question. People say that every plant, every animal is important for the jungle to function, but we don't have proof for every species. So I'm seeing whether elephants are important for the jungle.'

I explained that elephants, by dispersing even the largest seeds far from the parent tree, could potentially rescue seeds from being eaten by seed predators, like rats, or funguses. And that dispersal would leave at least some seeds in places that might have more access to sun and nutrients than under the parent tree. 'If animals leave the seeds in different places, some seeds should live and grow into mango or *chalta* trees. So trees that have big fruit might rely on big animals to take their seeds to different places so their seeds can survive,' I concluded.

Thidey listened carefully. His eyes twinkled. '*That* is why you want to save the elephants?' he asked slyly. Before I could respond, he continued. 'I tell you what, Brudder,' he said playfully, 'if you can pay us a little money, we farmers can plant those seeds in the jungle for you. And then, we can get rid of the elephants. Everyone wins! The jungle will have enough fruiting trees, we make some extra money, and our farms and homes will be safe. Deal?'

I laughed. 'I agree. It's not a good enough reason to save elephants, given the damage they do.'

Thidey smiled. 'You don't think so?'

'No.'

'Then why are you doing this research?' Thidey asked.

I tried to explain that ecologists just generally wanted to understand how ecosystems work, and that the functional role of elephants in forests could be one of many reasons to conserve them. But, I told him, I was not in Buxa just for the research. I had come for the experience—to live near the jungle, near the elephants, to better understand how to make life better for local people and conserve wildlife at the same time. Then one day, I said, maybe I could help find solutions to these problems.

Thidey nodded, still grinning. 'OK. Well, you really are very strange to see. Most of us villagers think, "Ah, if I can just get a 12th grade education, I won't have to keep drowning in all this cow shit." But you—you're working on the biggest degree, a PhD, and you're from the richest country, the USA, and you're just digging through a BIGGER animal's shit!'

'Yeah,' Akshu joined in. 'Now no kid in the village will ever want an education. They'll just say, "Why should we study? Look what happened to Nitin Sir!"'

In addition to feeling more like a part of Madhubangaon's community, I also felt more comfortable in the jungle. I purchased custom-sewn khaki socks that I could tie over my jeans, and I would tuck my shirt into my pants—thus, for a leech or tick to bite me, it would have to crawl all the way up to my neck or arms without detection. As I got better at driving stick shift, I sometimes drove into the jungle without Narad or Akshu. I learned to keep my distance from wild elephants when we drove up on them, but also how to alert them to our presence and let them approach us. I still got sick a lot—diarrhea would visit me about twice a month and fever every six weeks or so. But, otherwise, my confidence was growing.

Of course, the jungle and village are infinitely complicated settings, and I mostly felt confident because I was under the watchful eye of Akshu, Narad, or some other element of my safety net. Like a teenager, I would sometimes rebel too far in my effort to demonstrate my grown-up-ness, ending up embarrassingly out of my depth. One day, I was unable to find someone to accompany me to collect movement data on a herd of jungle-dwelling cattle, including Akshu's cows. The idea was to measure how far cattle might disperse the seeds of fruits they ate. I had followed the cows with a local assistant for two days previously. It was extremely straightforward, almost boring work, so I argued to Akshu that I could handle the job alone.

Akshu resisted. 'Sir, you have to take someone with you—someone who knows the jungle.'

'The cows don't go that far, and you said yourself they avoid elephants. Besides, they're just cows! You've shown me eight-year-old boys who work as cowherds. Why wouldn't I be able to handle it?'

Akshu wasn't willing to say out loud that I might not be as qualified as an eight-year-old. It was another sunny, dusty dry-season morning when I headed out with the cattle. The herd started with just four of Akshu's cows but gradually grew as it merged with groups of other villagers' cattle. Soon, I was traveling with 30-odd bovids as they munched away at the jungle foliage. The work was very easy—except for the occasional creek or thicket, the bovids' path was not hard to follow. They never went more than 4 kilometers from the village. I took a GPS point and counted the cattle every half hour. Otherwise, I just watched birds with my binoculars, or studied the cows. Why did one cow stop and eat the dead leaves that so many other cows had just walked past? What was it like to have so many flies hovering around all the time? Were the mother cows concerned about leopards taking their calves? Overall, Buxa cattle seemed to have a pretty solid deal. They were free-roaming in a verdant jungle, with abundant and diverse food for most of the year. While devout Hindus and loving owners cared for their cattle after they were no longer productive, less devout owners would quietly sell their cattle to Muslims or Bhutanese merchants who would slaughter the animals for meat. But even if some had unpleasant deaths, most of Buxa's cattle had a shot at a fulfilling life, enjoying both much of the food security and care provided by domestication and the freedom enjoyed by wild animals, and Hindu sanctity to boot. If I had to be a cow, I thought, Buxa might very well be where I would choose to be.

Mid-afternoon, my reverie was broken. We were in a small, grassy opening between two patches of silviculture plantation a few kilometers from Madhubangaon. The herd of cattle had been gradually chomping its way north. Suddenly, the half of the herd ahead of me turned and started running in my direction. Luckily, the move did not turn into an all-out stampede, but I was alert now. What was it that had startled the cows? An elephant or snake? A leopard? Suddenly, keenly aware that I was without my safety net, I gradually moved forward, looking for an animal of interest. I stopped near the edge of the calmed herd and peered into the trees, but I did not see anything in that direction. I looked around, increasingly curious but unwilling to step far from the safety of the herd.

I was thus distracted when a large bull approached me to my left. He grunted, standing less than 5 meters away from me. I ignored him at first—just another bovid that had joined the herd, I thought. The bull huffed and grunted some more. He was angled oddly, not facing me head-on but pointed 2 meters to my left, as though he did not want to openly charge me but wanted to keep the option open. I decided to give the newcomer some space, and I moved away, putting some cows between us.

Within minutes, the bull was beside me again, this time closer. He followed me twice more, grunting maliciously, louder and longer each time. 'What *is* this?' I thought. I had never seen this sort of behavior in a bull. I wanted to ignore it—after all, it was just a big male cow—but I could not get myself to relax. The bull was menacingly close to me.

I had seen children as young as five pick up a long stick and tap their cattle on their legs and backsides, cajoling them forward. Figuring that what I needed was a good stick, I broke a branch into two and waved one of the 2-foot rods as though I was going to strike the bull. He flinched, but he didn't retreat. He stood there—huffing. I didn't want to get close enough to him to actually strike him—what if he charged? So I raised a stick and grunted and yelled as I'd learned in the village, 'Huh! Ho! *Jao*!' Again, the bull flinched, but he stood his ground. Finally, I launched one of the sticks at his neck.

The stick bounced off the bull's neck like a drinking straw. Suddenly, I realized just how big, strong, and tough the bull was. The stick, I realized, was a psychological weapon—not a physical one. The bull realized this too, and he came at me with his head down.

It must have been a half-hearted charge, for I escaped. I jumped diagonally and to the right, quickly zig-zagging among the cows until they were between me and the bull. I sighed, embarrassed, and moved a little further away to let the bull have full access to the cows on that side. But he would not leave me alone. Soon the bull was near me, again angled slightly away, again hoofing the ground and grunting. I was at a loss. I had been bullied before, but never quite so literally. I got behind a plantation tree and stood there, occasionally waving my stick at the beast when he moved a little closer. He seemed content just demonstrating his masculinity, and I felt a measure of security with the tree between us.

Our stalemate ended as the herd of cows started moving southwest, toward home. I cautiously but quickly abandoned my safe spot and hopped into the herd, putting cows between me and the bull. However, the cows stopped on the edge of the clearing to graze some more, and I again found myself next to the bull, this time angled directly toward me. Before I knew it, he charged at me again in his half-hearted way. This time, I just ran into the herd, moving my wiry body between cows in a way that I knew he could not replicate. The bull made his half-hearted charge two more times before we returned to a stalemate.

I was exhausted—for around 90 minutes I had been in this state of constant vigilance, feeling on one hand that my life was at risk, but feeling on the other hand humiliated for being unable to control a domestic animal. It would be one thing to lose my life to an elephant or a tiger, but—to a cow? The whole situation was especially exasperating because I was not sure that the bull even intended to harm me—it almost seemed like it was toying with me. But I could not check that theory without risking life and limb.

As the cow herd gradually melted into the bushes, the bull seemed to decide that it was time to reap the rewards for his fine performance against the resident primate. He moved behind the females. I was relieved, but now I worried about avoiding the bull in the bushes where he could surprise me. I steered clear of the path I thought he had taken, and before too long I was sloshing through the creek and climbing back into the village with Akshu's cows. Several villagers who had heard I was following the cows that day saw me and called out to me, 'Hey, cowherd! Did you bring my cow back?' When I replied that I didn't know which cow was theirs, they laughed merrily and teased me for being a lousy cowherd. They were delighted to see me doing a job generally consigned to children and the illiterate.

I went straight to Akshu's house. 'How was it, Sir?' he asked. I told him that a big black bull had harassed me in the forest.

'Oh, yes,' Akshu said. 'I know that bull. That's Shiva's bull.'

'Shiva? Which Shiva?'

'No, I mean, Shiva—God.'

I looked at him quizzically. Akshu explained that most households only needed two to four bulls to plow their fields, and that if a cow gave birth to an extra bull, some farmers would release the young bull into the forest as part of a puja for Shiva. Since the bulls do not spend much time with people, they don't have much fear of humans.

That seemed like a reasonable way to deal with surplus livestock. I told Akshu about the bull's persistent charging at me and asked him what I was supposed to do. 'What did you do?' he asked, laughing. He did not act like the threat I had faced was a severe one.

'I tried to strike him with a stick and scare him off, but...'

'You hit him?' Akshu interrupted me uncharacteristically, whispering incredulously. 'Sir, he is God's bull. You're not supposed to hit him.'

I looked at him in disbelief. Didn't he realize I had been concerned for my life? Akshu mistook my expression of dismay for one of guilt. 'It's OK, Sir. I won't tell anyone,' he assured me. 'It is not a sin if you did not know.'

———

Narad and Akshu and I completed our camera trapping early one afternoon, and I decided we should stop at the

23-mile watch tower to look out for wildlife. The tower was located at the center of Buxa's core area. It was surrounded by a moat and electric fence that I never saw turned on. For some 50 meters around the tower, the area was cleared of underbrush, leaving only a handful of tall trees, such that animals nearby would be visible. Since the three-story tower sat at the intersection of two straight forest roads, an observer with decent binoculars standing at the top of the tower could see considerable distances.

The tower stayed occupied by two to three forest watchmen, presumably charged with monitoring the forest for poachers, smugglers, arsonists, and illegal harvesters. The watchmen would stay for several days at a time per rotation. There was no electricity in the tower, and I imagined their lives were mostly boring, punctuated with excitement when an animal or person showed up. As I climbed the tower, one of the watchmen engaged me in conversation.

He showed me the tower logbook. In it, he and the other watchmen recorded the animals they spotted—the species, number of individuals, and the date and time of observation. The vast majority of animals listed were elephants and sambar deer; the pages he showed me listed no tigers or leopards. He had seen leopards here, he said—but no tigers.

As we were talking, I heard gunshots from the north. I immediately got excited; I was going to see Buxa's anti-poaching system in action! I looked at the watchman expectantly, and he just stared back at me. 'What was that sound?' I asked.

'Guns,' he said. 'Some villagers from Jainti have guns, and they hunt in the forest.'

I stood looking at him for a few more seconds. 'Shouldn't you do something? Shouldn't you report it?'

The watchman said that the gunshots were from the Jainti range, not the Rajabhatkhawa range for which he was responsible. I looked down the road that went north. 'Where is the Rajabhatkhawa range and where is the Jainti range?' I asked. The guard said that the forest to the left of the road was the Rajabhatkhawa range, and the forest on the right was the Jainti range. Confused, I asked the guard how he knew which range the gunshots had come from. The guard assured me that the officers from the Jainti range would do something. I asked him how he knew they weren't expecting him to act. Then he completely changed his tack.

'Actually, we're not supposed to call the anti-poaching patrol. We are supposed to inform them of what we heard when they visit the tower.'

'When will they come?'

'Probably tomorrow.'

I looked at him utterly confused. What was the point of reporting gunshots a day late, I asked—what was the point of guards working in this tower?

'There is no point in there even being a tower here, Sir,' the guard said definitively. He began to tell me about a couple of instances in which his Forest Department superiors had ignored his concerns, perhaps as evidence of the officials' apathy, or perhaps as evidence that he had no power to improve the situation.

As we drove away, I recounted the conversation to Akshu and Narad. Akshu admired the guard's openness, but my field assistants were otherwise unsurprised.

'That's why the jungle is empty,' Narad added as he drove. He said that all the top officials lived in the city far from the action, the watchtowers were far from the villages from which poachers and smugglers entered, and there was basically no patrolling in the forest.

Akshu agreed, complaining that while the watchtower guards were powerless locals at the bottom of the pyramid, the forest guards were just plain lazy. They were paid well, Akshu said—₹16,000 a month—but they had no incentive to actually work. The forest guards were from South Bengal where the jungle was already depleted—why would they patrol someone else's jungle? 'In fact, none of them are fit—some can't see, some can't hear, few can run. Some are afraid of leeches. Leeches! How can you patrol a jungle with elephants if you're afraid of leeches? Then, on their way back home, they load a truck full of wooden furniture from the jungle and take it with them!'

Akshu said he knew patrolling could save the jungle. About a decade earlier, a very active range officer named Oraon had worked very closely with local people and patrolled the jungle regularly. Poaching and timber smuggling plummeted. But when Oraon was transferred, all the thieves poured back into the forest.

We continued our conversation on the causes of Buxa's malaise in the village over the next couple of days. Akshu told me he thought Buxa's sustainability problems came from a combination of increased pressure from people in and around Buxa and reduced interest in enforcement by the authorities. When he was young, those living in villages and tea estates surrounding the tiger reserve would have been afraid to settle on land in Buxa; they would only occasionally and sneakily hunt wild animals or fell timber, fearing punishment by the Forest Department. But, by the 1990s and early 2000s, two things had changed. First, many of the nearby tea estates had gone out of business, leaving plantation workers desperate for a source of income. Second, people in the region had learned that if someone got caught while, say, poaching or collecting forest products illegally, they would often be supported by local political leaders. 'The local politicians wanted their votes, so they defended anyone who hunted in the forest, saying they were just collecting firewood. The officials didn't want to deal with the politics, so they stopped catching people.' Emboldened, families in Buxa began expanding into Forest Department land, and people started moving to Buxa from the increasingly crowded surrounding regions. 'And now, everyone comes here to Buxa. First, there were 85 houses in Madhubangaon—now there are hundreds!' Hundreds of families freely cutting timber, catching and selling fish, selling NTFPs, and taking advantage of any available government services.

'So, the poachers...' I asked, 'like the ones from the tea gardens, are they poaching because they have to? Do they have other ways to make a living?'

'No one poaches or smuggles timber for fun,' argued Thidey. He was active in local politics, and I could tell he had given this speech to someone before. 'Look, there are the snakes—the king cobras and other poisonous ones. Then there are the elephants that can easily kill you in the night. The guns themselves are dangerous, because they shoot in all directions, so your buddy could accidentally hit you and badly injure you. Smuggled logs can fall on you—one or two people have died when a *gud-gudi* they were pulling down hill went out of control. Then there are the swarms of biting midges, the leeches, the ticks, the mosquitoes, the malaria. When people poach or steal from the jungle, it's because they have to.'

Moksha, a friend of the Atris, didn't buy Thidey's theatrical production. Moksha was multi-talented; he climbed trees like a macaque, cooked like a professional chef, and—in his earlier days—he had made off like a brigand from the forest. I didn't know the last part at the time, but Moksha spoke with great authority. 'It's not like that, Sir. Actually, smuggling is very profitable. You go in once, cut down some sal and teak trees, come out, and you don't have to work again for two weeks. You have to work hard for those two days or so, but after that you can relax.' Narad agreed—the smugglers, he claimed, were hardened criminals.

Akshu took a middle path. 'The boys and men that go in,' Akshu confessed disapprovingly, 'a few do it out of need, but many just go once in two to three weeks, sell the illegal timber outside the park, and then drink away the money.' Akshu pointed out that they ignored legitimate working opportunities like the work provided under the National Rural Employment Guarantee Act for lucrative illegal ones. He said they slept all day, caused problems at night, and, when they ran out of money, went back into the jungle.

Thidey, realizing that his friends weren't trying to persuade me that villagers were forced into crime by circumstance, became more candid. 'Actually, it's really technology that is the downfall of the jungle,' he riffed. 'If one person gets a new mobile, then all his friends want the new model too. But how? They don't have money. So they go into the jungle, cut a tree, and then they have money. Computers, televisions, music players, motorcycles—the more of these that come out, the faster the jungle will disappear. Villagers can't make that kind of money from an honest day's work! The only place you can make that kind of money is from the jungle.'

What the high prevalence of poaching and smuggling seemed to boil down to was low risk of punishment—I had seen practically no enforcement—and a lack of appealing economic alternatives. Sure, some people really just *loved* being hunter-gatherers, either subsistence or commercial, and for them it was a lifestyle. But I suspected that these people were a minority, and that at least their kids could probably be diverted away from such preferences. I basically believed there were two strategies that could be deployed to try to save a place like Buxa while also serving its local people. The first was a 'positive coupling' strategy. Basically, positive coupling meant that villagers were tied to wildlife in such a way that when the wildlife thrived, villagers would benefit. Positive coupling could take many forms. On the most commercial extreme, a place like Buxa could be managed for tourism such that local people got a high percentage of the proceeds. If villagers received more from tourists that saw tigers, elephants, and sambar deer than they lost in crops and livestock to such animals, they might support actions that boosted wildlife populations in the reserve. Where tourism was undesirable or infeasible, local communities might at least be given exclusive rights to utilize forest resources. They could sell timber and non-timber forest products, graze their cattle, and perhaps even take modest amounts of fish or meat of certain species. No matter what, positive coupling required that local people had the right to exclude others from the surrounding jungle. If they could legally prevent outsiders from coming in and taking these resources, local people would have economic incentive to manage natural resources sustainably so they could benefit in the long term. If just anyone could come in and claim a share of tourism proceeds or wood sales, the incentive for sustainable management would evaporate.

The alternative to positive coupling would be a 'decoupling' strategy. For all the villagers in Madhubangaon, just about any economic advancement—or sometimes even survival—seemed to be based on the extraction of some resource from the jungle. In addition to food and firewood for subsistence, villagers relied on non-timber forest products they could sell, milk and labour from jungle-dwelling livestock, and—for those willing to break the law—poached meat and smuggled wood they could sell for a profit. A decoupling strategy would make villagers less reliant or even unreliant on the jungle for their livelihood. At its extreme, this could mean relocating villagers to a place they liked outside the jungle where they could participate in urban or large-scale agricultural labour activities, with their children going to urban schools and losing touch with the jungle. A less dramatic decoupling approach might involve educating rural children in such a way that, if they wanted a new phone, it would be easier for them to work an extra shift in an office than to dive into the jungle to hunt a muntjac.

As things stood now in Malabasti, there wasn't a concerted program of either positive coupling or decoupling. Villagers weren't legally allowed to ever knock down a teak tree and sell it for profit, and they certainly had no exclusionary rights. So what did they care if some people, from within the village or without, smuggled and sold the tree? The people of Malabasti weren't allowed to run ecotourism operations in the core area—so why would they care if all the tigers were gone? And while some villagers were working hard to educate their children, it wasn't clear to me that enough of them would gain the skills to decouple them from the jungle.

I had already learned from reading about development economics that these theories don't always play out as planned. As I learned more about conservation, I realized how much the details of implementation mattered in determining whether a decoupling or positive-coupling approach would actually help people or conservation. Nonetheless, I was really frustrated by what I saw in Buxa, and I wanted to do something—*anything*—that could help promote conservation and the quality of people's lives there.

I had some ideas on how a community-based development project ought to be executed. I told Akshu that I wanted to do something to help develop the village that was also good for the jungle, and that I had collected a few hundred dollars from uncles and aunties in the US to fund such a project. Akshu immediately had his own ideas, but I insisted, 'The money is meant for the whole village to do something with. If you and I just decide without any other input what we should do, the other villagers may not feel interested in participating.'

Akshu saw my point. He suggested I speak with the elected leaders of the government-supported Malabasti Self-Help Group, a group of women who engaged in microfinance projects. The outgoing leader was a middle-aged Adivasi woman named Susan who lived down the path from Akshu. I told Susan I thought we should have a community meeting to discuss how to invest the money I was willing to donate. She quickly grasped what I was suggesting. I immediately saw from her manner why she would win elections even in the Nepali-dominated village.

'Sir,' she said confidently, 'community members won't have the kind of ideas you are describing. Or if they do, they might not make sense. It will be better if we just come up with a project and ask the Self-Help Group and the community to help implement it.' Akshu nodded; he had said the same thing.

I was a bit surprised by this elitism. Still skeptical that there would be enough buy-in, I insisted on a meeting. 'How about we let the community at least make some suggestions, and we can choose the best ones and let them vote on them? If they have no ideas, then obviously we can decide ourselves,' I said. Susan and the other leaders collectively shrugged. We decided to hold the meeting at 1:30 PM on my day off. Akshu agreed to spread the word to other community members door-to-door.

A couple of weeks later, only a handful of people showed up to the meeting. Four women from the Self-Help Group came on time, and a couple others joined later; only much later would I realize almost all of them were Nepali Brahmins. Susan had suddenly changed jobs and, with her departure, the Adivasi contingent of the SHG had lost interest. In addition to Akshu and Narad, two Nepali men, neither familiar to me, attended. One of them came on a motorcycle, a symbol of significant wealth in this area. I was immediately suspicious of his motives.

I told those attending that my community in the US had donated ₹10,000 to fund something to help the community in Madhubangaon. I explained that I would like to hear their ideas for developing their village, and that we could as a group decide what the best idea was. I knew this wasn't much, and I said that I could raise more for a really good idea, but that we should start with the amount I had in hand.

I need not have worried about the problem of selecting the 'best' idea—there was only one. 'We want to buy a boat for the picnic spot,' one of the SHG women suggested. Akshu translated 'boat' for me.

I tried to hide my discomfort with the idea. I hated the picnics in Malabasti. Starting in late December, hundreds of people would come from all over Bengal to Buxa for 'picnics'. The villages had asked for permission to host picnics from the Forest Department, who appeared to have agreed without condition. The visitors cooked huge vats of rice and slabs of meat and drank volumes of alcohol to match, leaving a mess of plastic and paper and broken glass all over the pasture. The events were raucous—visitors would set up dueling loud speakers to blast music throughout the day, so much so that if I was at home some 150 meters away, I could hardly think. Perhaps worst of all, the picnickers were enamored with Justin Bieber, playing his songs on rotation almost hourly. All this made me cringe—I couldn't understand why the picknickers would make Buxa as unpleasant as the cities they were escaping. To me, protected areas were meant for soul-searching and communing with nature. And I knew for a fact that no one could ever find peace while listening to the song 'Baby'.

'Why do you need a boat?' I asked. Especially in the dry season, it was difficult to imagine anyone using a boat on the narrow creek next to the picnic spot. The women told me that Porro, another village in Buxa, had gotten a boat from the Forest Department. Porro's women charged ₹5 per passenger for a 10–15-minute ride. The Self-Help Group thought that if they had a boat on the creek in Malabasti, they would attract more customers to their picnic spot.

I asked why, if the Forest Department had given a boat to the village in Porro, the Department wouldn't provide the same for Malabasti. The women looked at each other for a bit. Finally, Akshu answered on their behalf, saying they were afraid to approach the Forest Department officials. I looked to the women for confirmation. They admitted they didn't know where to start.

I suggested that the Self-Help Group ask their contacts in Porro who in the Forest Department had given them the boat. I promised I would help them approach the Forest Department. The women agreed this was fair. I asked for any other ideas.

The woman leading the discussion had picked up on my disinterest in the picnic spot. 'You tell us, Sir,' she said, 'what you have in mind.'

I frowned a bit. I knew what I didn't like, but I was less clear on what would make sense. 'I don't know as much about your community as you do. I just want something good for the village and good for the jungle,' I said. With Akshu's help, I offered them an example. I told them about how libraries work in the US, and I explained to them that, growing up, I read books for fun all the time. I pointed out that I had never seen any of the village children reading for fun. 'What if we bought 50–100 books in Hindi and English?' I asked, suggesting that leisure reading could improve the children's language skills and performance in school. I figured that being better readers would help set students on a path that led away from poaching and smuggling in the jungle.

The idea was unpopular. The women asked who would monitor the library, and they claimed that children would simply take and lose the books—they would certainly not return them. I brought up the idea of imposing fines for such behavior, but the women did not seem impressed.

'They want something that will make them *money*. They want *money*,' the man with the motorcycle said with a broad smile. I studied him for the first time. He was a handsome, bronze-skinned man with an almost Central Asian look, brimming with confidence. I was caught off-guard by his style—it was like he was gently teasing the women for not understanding my priorities, and gently teasing me for not getting theirs. Daanbir Baisya, I would find out, was a local forest rights activist, conservation enthusiast, and community leader. Even as he poked fun at all of us, there was no shortage of regard for him among the others. Contrary to my initial suspicions, he wasn't there to gain control of the funds.

I asked the group if there was anything else they wanted to purchase for their picnic spot to generate income—perhaps something that no other village had, and that would set them apart. Daanbir nodded knowingly. Again, the other women and men looked at me pretty blankly.

I told the group to let me know if they thought of something else and to keep me updated on the boat, and we disbanded. I wondered if I should have run the meeting differently or put in a larger amount of money. The next day, Akshu brought up the dearth of proposals at the meeting, and he began embellishing on his original idea. 'Sir, really, we could start a computer lab! We could build a small building there, on my land,' he suggested. 'There are several young men and women who have done a computer certificate program in the city, and they could teach the classes.' Akshu pointed out that the children in the community were very taken by my laptop, and that there would certainly be demand for computer instruction.

I wasn't enamored with technology the way Akshu was, but I admitted it was the best idea I'd heard so far. Becoming comfortable with computers would improve children's job prospects and so make it less likely that they would need to look to the jungle for resources. Several parents in the village had asked me to teach their kids to use my laptop, so I was confident there was reasonable interest. 'Who would the students be?' I asked.

'We could start off with a small group of students from the Homewood School,' he said. That was the private English-medium school where his daughter Kanchi studied. I would later learn that the school was built on land that Daanbir had donated. 'We could establish a minimum age of 10, and then students could rotate through. Right now, students are afraid to even touch a computer—they shouldn't be. Computers can help them get jobs.'

I smiled. Akshu's older child was seven; he was clearly signaling that he wasn't just trying to capture the resources I was offering for his own family's gain. We discussed how it might work. Of course, the finances quickly became daunting. Two hundred dollars would, by Akshu's estimation, barely cover the building. We would then need funds for tables and chairs, electricity, and, of course, the laptops and teachers.

But ... I had an idea. 'Guruji,' I said, 'I think I might know how to raise some more money, and even find a teacher to help. But, first, we need to make sure the women in the Self-Help Group are OK with this idea.'

Akshu and I got the green light from the Self-Help Group. And when I spoke to my girlfriend the next day, I suggested to Alopa that I had an idea for how she might be able to spend the approaching monsoon with me in Buxa.

10

'I met a girl on the bus,' Chander said excitedly as he returned from visiting an uncle in Nepal. 'She said she's from Birpada. She's a Brahmin, and her family lives in this neighborhood called Sardapalli. I want to marry her—please, go find her father and ask for her hand in marriage.'

Motikar had not yet forgiven Chander for humiliating him the last time. 'I'm not going to do that again.' But Chander insisted. 'I will marry this one, definitely,' he said.

Motikar wasn't budging. Chander continued to implore his father. 'I don't care if that girl is missing an ear, or missing a hand now,' Chander promised. 'I will marry her.'

Satyavati, seeing that her stubborn husband was unmoved, finally relented on his behalf. 'Fine, then, I'll go.' When Motikar looked at her surprised, she said, 'Well, someone has to do it.' It was, Satyavati reasoned, their responsibility to marry off all their children, and she hoped with all her heart that marriage would bring out the best in her bright but temperamental son.

Satyavati found a relative to accompany her and took a bus to Birpada; together, they asked around until they found the Brahmin household that matched Chander's description. The girl's father was, as far as Nepali villagers of the region went, fairly well-to-do, having found success in selling ghee and dairy—so much so that the man was called Gheewala. The neighbors thought well of him and his family. Satyavati and her accompaniment presented themselves and explained the situation. 'My son met your daughter on a bus the other day, and he liked her,' Satyavati said. 'Are you looking to marry her off?'

Gheewala was charmed by Satyavati's plainness and humility. He could tell she wasn't wealthy, yet he sensed that she was not there because of his own family's good fortunes. 'OK,' he said, 'bring the boy here. If we like him, we'll give our daughter in marriage.'

After that, things proceeded rapidly. Satyavati took Chander to Birpada. Gheewala and his family, presented with the more subdued public version of Chander, took a liking to him and his unassuming relatives. Gheewala's daughter, a young woman named Bani, took the expected posture of respectful silence as Satyavati spoke with Bani's relatives about her qualities and expectations. Gheewala and Satyavati agreed to join their families. Motikar and Satyavati held their breaths—there was an engagement, and then plans for a wedding, and Chander remained acquiescent. Motikar invested as lavishly as his limited fortunes would allow—he sold several cattle and took substantial loans to fund his side of the wedding, perhaps in part to make sure his new daughter-in-law would not feel too heavily the transition from a well-off to a poor household, but mostly to make it impossible for Chander to complain, as he so often had, that Motikar and Satyavati had failed as his parents.

The wedding transpired successfully and uneventfully. Chander conducted himself graciously throughout the festivities. Bani moved in with her new in-laws, and Chander's family sighed in relief.

It was only much later, after Bani and Chander had been married for some time, that Chander—when Bani was absent one night—abruptly said, 'She's not the girl I saw on the bus.'

Chander's parents and siblings all looked at each other, and then at Chander. 'Meaning?' Motikar asked nervously.

'The woman I saw on the bus—she was tall, and she had a nice figure. This one is so short.'

Satyavati realized she had never actually asked Bani if she had met Chander before. Upon hearing that Chander had seen her on a bus, Bani must have assumed that Chander had just seen her from afar, asked around to figure out who she was, and sent his parents to her house. It would have been a reasonable assumption—after all, if Chander had meant to express interest in some other woman, surely he would have said so.

But he hadn't said so. Chander had never before mentioned that Bani was not the woman he had wanted to marry and, in fact, Chander never said another word about the matter. He had promised that he would marry this girl, no matter what she looked like when his parents found her. He kept that promise—even though the woman they brought him to was an altogether different one than the woman who had captured his interest.

Perhaps Chander had been drawn by the opportunity to marry into a wealthier family. Or maybe Chander had decided he did not want to humiliate his parents a second time.

————————

It was late summer of 2000, and Akshu was looking for work again. He had spent a few months as a migrant labourer in a temple across India in Chandigarh,

Punjab, but found that the political intrigue and labor conditions made living there unsustainable. Returning to Madhubangaon, the 22-year-old had resumed asking neighbors if he could help them tend their crops or harvest their yield. This provided limited employment, so Akshu wandered the area, asking for work. Eventually, he approached a friend employed by the Forest Department; he didn't want to be positioned between the timber smugglers and their product again, but perhaps there were other opportunities that lacked such moral hazards. In any case, he was desperate.

'If there's any work for the Forest Department,' Akshu said, 'please let me know.' The friend agreed and, in mid-September, he reached out.

'There are some outsiders that have come,' he told Akshu. 'Three men. Two are from South India, and they came with a Bengali man. They need a local guide.'

'A guide?' Akshu asked. 'What for?'

'I don't know,' his friend said. 'They said they need someone who knows the forest around here. They are in the guesthouse.'

The guesthouse, Akshu thought. Generally only Forest Department officials and other important people stayed there. If they were in the official guesthouse, then they probably had influence and money. This made them intimidating, but it also was what enabled them to offer him a job. Plus, Akshu's parents had told him stories of kindly, helpful South Indians who had lived in Buxa back before it was a tiger reserve, when the Indian military was stationed throughout the area. With that favorable stereotype in mind, Akshu agreed to meet the outsiders.

Later that day, he showed up at the Forest Department guesthouse, a tall wooden building with rustic hotel-like rooms, a 15-minute walk from his home. He was greeted by the three men. The Bengali man in his early twenties was named Dinesh Ganguly. Since Akshu had studied at a Bengali-medium school, Akshu was immediately most comfortable communicating with him. One of the South Indians, a man named Kalaivannan who had grown up in Delhi, was apparently the leader of the crew. He spoke to Akshu in Hindi. Akshu had learned some Hindi in school and from watching the occasional Bollywood film on a TV set at the bazaar, and he had improved his Hindi considerably in Chandigarh, but he was not fully comfortable with the language. Kalaivannan led Akshu's interview, with Dinesh chiming in in Bengali when Akshu misunderstood.

'What's your name? What's your father's name?' Kalaivannan asked kindly. He was striking—chestnut-skinned, fit, with glasses; he must have been about 10 years older than Akshu. Akshu responded.

'How much education did you get?' Kalaivannan continued.

'I studied through 8th standard.'

'Do you know about the jungle?'

'Yes, Sir.' Akshu said simply, not really knowing what to make of the question.

'Are there elephants in your jungle?'

'Yes, Sir,' Akshu said. 'There are lots of elephants.'

'Can you show them to us?' Kalaivannan asked.

'It's on your luck as to whether I can show you elephants or not,' Akshu said with his characteristic honesty, 'but there are elephants in this jungle, Sir. They even come out and damage our crops and our property.'

'OK, so where should we go to see *haathis* then?'

'Come along, please! There's a place where you have a good chance of seeing them.' Akshu headed west with the three men in tow, chatting behind him. Akshu realized that the two South Indians often spoke to Dinesh in English, but they spoke to each other in another very foreign sounding language. Each sentence seemed to boil over with syllables, carrying a cadence that reminded Akshu of Sanskrit. But he couldn't understand a word. *That must be the South Indian language*, Akshu thought.

Eventually, he brought the group to a spot along the Dima River where elephants crossed and, when water was scarce, came for a drink. But the elephants weren't there, and it was already nearly evening. 'Will you come again tomorrow?' Kalaivannan asked. Akshu agreed to return to the guest house in the morning.

Akshu was unclear what motivated the outsiders, but he sensed that his professional opportunities with them would be significantly hindered if he couldn't show them wild elephants. By the time he arrived the next day, Akshu had a plan. He knew of a place not far from Malabasti, east of the hamlet and north of where he had once herded an elephant with his cattle, that villagers considered somewhat dangerous precisely because of the wildlife there. In addition to the elephants that often congregated near the old sal tree plantation near the local creek, other species were seen there with some regularity. Akshu had once even been hissed at in a tree by the extremely rare clouded leopard, with canines as long as a tiger's, as he collected *guruja* climber there with his dad. That, he figured, was the kind of place that would prove to the outsiders that he knew the jungle.

'It's just you and me today,' Kalaivannan notified Akshu the next morning.

'OK, Sir,' Akshu said amiably. He led Kalaivannan nearly 4 kilometers by road and then by jungle trails to a stretch of forest east of Malabasti. He didn't mind that he and Kalaivannan walked mostly in silence; talkative though Akshu generally was, he was still unsure how to communicate with his well-educated companion.

Besides, silence was how Motikar had taught Akshu to avoid trouble from elephants, to make sure that they would detect elephants before elephants detected them. Akshu's head regularly pivoted in all directions, conscious that what might seem like an uninhabited forest from one angle could reveal a herd of elephants from another. His ears were alert for any of the elephant's myriad sounds, from whirring to ear flapping to cracking wood or bamboo.

Akshu soon found some elephant tracks and then elephant dung. He pointed this out to Kalaivannan, who grinned enthusiastically. Then, not far from the local stream, Akshu's eyes detected the prize. A tusker was debarking a sal tree for food. 'See that tusker, Sir?' Akshu asked.

Kalaivannan beamed, looking at the animal through his binoculars. The tusker began to move into the forest. 'Can we get closer?' he asked. Akshu nodded and led the way. The elephant moved south off the trail, walking alongside the creek. Akshu and Kalaivannan followed at a safe distance to get a closer look.

As so often happens in the jungle, the hikers' circumstances suddenly changed. The tusker they had been following disappeared, and Akshu realized that he could now hear a herd of elephants feeding both to the east of them and to the north from whence they had come. Akshu and Kalaivannan were still walking along the creek in the depression carved by the water. To the south was a steep rise of earth, muddy and cloddy, that could not easily be traversed. The herd of elephants gradually made themselves visible, and Akshu was about to point them out to Kalaivannan when Kalaivannan noticed himself, observing in awed silence. Akshu realized, though, that their situation was not ideal—they were closed in on three sides, leaving only one direction, west, to go if the herd moved toward them. Then Akshu turned west—and he saw a tusker some distance away, moving slowly but determinedly in their direction.

Akshu pointed out the approaching *haathi* to Kalaivannan, who immediately understood they were in trouble—the tusker was getting closer, and they were surrounded by elephants on three sides and a steep rise on the fourth. Akshu, always on the lookout for climbable trees, looked to the thick and sturdy tree right next to them. It was a *katoos* tree with branches low enough for even an inexperienced person to grab and pull themselves up, as well as enough branches to climb to a height out of reach of an elephant. Akshu climbed up a couple of meters, quick as a young leopard. 'Sir, please come, please come,' he whispered to Kalaivannan.

Kalaivannan looked as though he was going to try it, but then he shook his head. 'I had an operation on my knee,' he said. 'So I can't come up there.' Akshu wordlessly jumped down. The tusker was still headed toward them, but he had shown no awareness that the humans were in the creek-carved depression ahead of him. To surprise a tusker, even in the jungle away from the agricultural fields, would not likely lead to a good outcome. There was only one option left for Akshu. He told Kalaivannan to climb up the mound of dirt and mud to the south, and he showed Kalaivannan how, digging his fingers and feet into the dirt and mud, breaking one of his *chappal* along the way. Kalaivannan scrambled up behind him. They made it over the mound of earth and back to a flatter part of the old plantation. Akshu then led Kalaivannan south to a road. They were safe.

On the way back to the guest house, they arrived in Malabasti. 'This is my house, Sir,' Akshu said.

'OK,' Kalaivannan said. He asked for directions back to the guest house and then said, 'Eat some food and

get some rest, and then come to the guest house, OK?'
Akshu agreed.

When Akshu arrived at the guest house in the late
evening, a bathed Kalaivannan smelling of sandalwood
soap emerged in a sleeveless white shirt with a handful
of cash. 'This is for some new chappals for you,' he said,
handing Akshu ₹200. 'These are your wages, 200 for
your work today and 100 for yesterday,' he said. 'And
here is a tip.' He gave Akshu a smaller bill with a look
that said, 'You know, for keeping me alive.' Finally,
just as Akshu regained his ability to hide his surprise
and excitement, Kalaivannan said, 'We are all leaving
tomorrow, but we'll be back in about two months.
There will be work here. I will call on you—can you
work with us?'

Akshu was astonished. He couldn't believe how much
money he had made in a couple of days, and that too
for such easy work—why would anyone pay a person
so much just to lead him through the jungle, looking
for elephants of all things? And now he was being
offered more such work? It wasn't even labour, it was
just ... walking! But for all his unnecessary frankness,
Akshu knew not to betray these feelings; he was afraid
Kalaivannan would make the work harder or give him
less money. 'OK,' he said coolly. 'I will work with you.'

Kalaivannan looked pleased and bid Akshu farewell.
Akshu turned and walked home, unable to contain his
cross-eyed grin.

It was about this time that the market economy sent
yet another tentacle into Madhubangaon. Business
folk, with the blessing of the Forest Department, came
into Buxa Tiger Reserve and offered villagers cash in

exchange for the cow dung they used to fertilize their crops.

The Atris and their neighbors had improved the fertility of the naturally less fertile soils through the regular use of cow and buffalo dung. Now, villagers were faced with a new choice—give up the dung and get an immediate infusion of cash, or use the dung, plow the fields, sow the fields, and bank on the plants surviving crop-raiders.

Initially, those offering to buy the dung came around November to purchase fertilizer for potato crops near the border with Bangladesh. Several village families with modest-sized cattle herds reasoned that they had about one truck of cow dung available to sell. If they kept the dung, used it to fertilize their fields before the mustard season, and were able to protect the resulting crops from animals, they would make about ₹3,000 and have grown themselves some food. On the other hand, if they sold the dung outright, they would make ₹3,500! Plus, these families would have time for other activities in the winter, whether commercial, like selling NTFPs or smuggling timber, or recreational, like visiting relatives. For several families, it seemed like an easy decision.

After the first group of families made this transition, other families followed, and soon the golden carpet of mustard flowers once visible every January became a scattering of yellow patches here and there. Initially, several farmers tried to both sell the fertilizer and grow their mustard crop anyway, but that led to a poor yield of mustard and a poorer corn crop. Once more than half of the families had given up on growing mustard, matters became more difficult for those that continued to grow. Previously, farmers worked as a team to make sure no one's cattle snuck into anyone's crops to chow down on mustard leaves instead of going to the jungle. Now, the thieving cattle once distributed across the village concentrated their efforts on the few remaining mustard fields, and the cattle's owners, most of whom hadn't planted mustard themselves, were far less proactive in restraining their animals. Those trying to grow mustard and keep their land more fertile felt beaten. Gradually, they started to sell their cow dung as well. Before long, the business people could count on everyone in Madhubangaon having set aside the vast majority of their year's cow dung for annual sale. In November and December, trucks would leave piled high with cow pats for potato farms down in Cooch Behar district. In January and February, trucks would take any remaining cow dung to neighboring tea estates. Cattle were now being employed to move nutrients from a protected jungle to distant agricultural lands.

Predictably, the export of nutrients away from Madhubangaon's fields that immediately affected mustard crops began to affect the other crops as well. Soon after families began selling their cow dung, their corn crop grew shorter and went from green to yellow, and the corn kernels grew smaller than before. To adjust to the decreasing fertility of their fields, farmers started planting corn at half the density they used to. This, rather ironically, affected the farmers' cattle the most. When cow dung had been available for farming, the villagers had planted the corn at such a high density that they would have to remove every other corn plant as the stalks thickened. They would then feed the removed plants to their milk cows, who would then yield a full 3–3.5 kilograms of milk daily. Over time, as the corn grew less vigorously, villagers planted less of it; the village's cows, scrawnier without the subsidy of corn, ultimately gave half, then a third, and then a sixth as much milk as they had when they had been fed corn regularly. Finally, as the corn grew weaker, so did the vegetables like pumpkins that were grown with it. For many years, the rice crop managed to stay strong, as it required less fertilizer.

Basically, for around ₹3,500 a year per family, villagers found themselves spiraling away from their subsistence agricultural activities. But those taking this deal may not have been shortsighted. As the elephants hammered their corn crops more vigorously each year, villagers were not unreasonable in their reluctance to invest a lot in a hard-to-defend crop that so easily hid elephant marauders during stormy spring nights. Agriculture was an increasingly uncertain investment, and with so many other market opportunities, legal or illegal but uninhibited, villagers felt less and less inclined to take such risks.

Of course, the Atris, under the principled leadership of Motikar and Satyavati, were devoted to the idea of tending their land and growing their own crops, and in 2000 they were still full-fledged agriculturalists. They resisted selling their cow dung. So Akshu did what he needed to for his family's fall rice and winter mustard crop—but he quickly ran out of work. He really wanted Kalaivannan's team to return.

He knew that Kalaivannan had said that they would be back in two months, but just six weeks after Kalaivannan and his colleagues had left, Akshu began bugging his friend at the Forest Department, asking if the South Indians had come back. He worried that if he wasn't the first person Kalaivannan saw upon his return, Kalaivannan would turn to another villager who would do just as good a job executing the straightforward and lucrative work. It was best, Akshu reasoned, that his replaceability not be discovered.

Two months came and went, and then so did a third, and it was perhaps late December by the time a boy showed up at the Atri household asking for Akshu. One of the first things Kalaivannan and Dinesh told Akshu they needed was another assistant who would work as well as he did. Chander was disinterested, so Akshu asked a cousin, Danu, to try for the position. Dinesh took Danu out for a walk intended to parallel Akshu's interview with Kalaivannan.

'What compartment of the jungle are we in?' Dinesh asked Danu.

'I don't know,' he responded.

'Where do the elephants live?' Dinesh asked.

'I don't know,' Danu said.

'Do they ever eat the leaves of that type of tree over there?'

'I don't know.'

Later, Danu told Akshu how the interview had gone, and Akshu was surprised. 'If you don't know something, just figure it out!' Akshu said.

'Do you know what compartment we're in?' Danu shot back.

'Well, I didn't,' Akshu said. 'But you know those signs on the side of the main road that say "C-O-M-P"?' Akshu asked, spelling out the letters in English. 'I think they say the compartment number. So just tell them you'll figure it out, and then find the information like that.'

Danu looked at Akshu in surprise. He knew his younger cousin had only somewhat learned the English alphabet at school, and he certainly couldn't speak English. 'I'm just not as comfortable in the jungle as you,' Danu said. 'Papa didn't take me out there the way *Badabau* took you.'

In any case, Dinesh told Akshu that Danu was not qualified. Concerned that he might lose his job if he didn't find a capable companion, Akshu turned to his cousin Hari. Small and strong, Hari navigated the forest like a jackal. But he was also socially astute—having previously worked for a World Bank-funded NGO in the area, he knew what elites like the NGO employees wanted him to say when they asked him questions, and he always catered to their preferences. Akshu sensed that Hari would succeed where Danu had failed. For better or for worse, Akshu was right.

A green Mahindra jeep arrived in Buxa the first week of January carrying two other South Indians, a driver, and a scientist named Raghurajan. The village assistants drove around the forest with Kalaivannan and the other sirs. Dinesh would ask questions about where there were elephants, open spaces, bodies of water, and hills. Akshu and Hari taught them about the landscape. Akshu heard the sirs calling the exercise a 'survey', but he didn't understand why they were doing what they did. No one explained it to him or Hari, and they didn't ask, either.

After a week or two, Kalaivannan gathered everyone and started assigning tasks for what he called the 'collaring' work. This meant nothing to the villagers; initially, Akshu and Hari's understanding was that they would basically carry supplies for the sirs. As Akshu watched, Kalaivannan gathered a bewildering array of unrecognizable instruments—tools, gadgets, boxes. The most important thing appeared to be this leather object that looked something like a humongous belt. This, Akshu realized, was the 'collar'.

'Tomorrow,' Dinesh and Kalaivannan explained, 'we are going to catch an elephant and put this collar on its neck. This is what we need you to do. First, you must help us find the elephants. You must carry this case of medicines for us, because otherwise the elephant will die. We have to carry lots of water, for if the elephant overheats, we will have to cool it down by pouring water on its head. We have to make sure that the elephant's tongue doesn't slide back into its mouth, as it could suffocate...'

Akshu and Hari were utterly lost, shocked, and terrified. If Kalaivannan and Dinesh hadn't been wealthy and apparently well-educated, any villager hearing their conversation would think them insane. The Sirs expected them to somehow catch *an elephant*? And then they were supposed to hold its tongue out of its mouth? How were they supposed to even catch the creature? Elephants run away from people, or they run toward them; neither, Akshu thought, would allow them to get this 'collar' onto one.

But in addition to being totally confused, the villagers were afraid to ask questions. These men were too powerful to question—to question could be seen as a challenge, as disrespectful. Akshu and Hari both felt they should just do as they were told. Finally, though, Akshu was just too confused not to clarify the situation.

'Sir, how are we supposed to catch an elephant and put a collar on it?' Akshu asked innocently.

When the sahibs realized just how incomprehensible the situation was to the villagers, they tried earnestly to explain what was going to happen. 'No, no,' Dinesh and Kalaivannan responded. 'We'll have a team who will catch the elephant. They will bring darts. They have medicine inside them, and the medicine will put the elephant to sleep. The team will shoot the medicine at the elephant, it will fall down and sleep for maybe 45 minutes. And then, after 45 minutes, it will get up by itself. Before it wakes up, we have to put the collar on the animal.'

Despite these efforts at explanation, the gap between the worlds of the sirs and the villagers was just too wide, and the villagers were too afraid to ask questions. Akshu was still very scared. Sure, he thought, they would have medicines to bring down one elephant. But what about all the other elephants? Wouldn't the rest of the herd come after them and try and rescue their friend? How could they possibly protect themselves from an angry herd?

To top it all off, the villagers had no inkling about what the collar was for, or why the sirs wanted to put it on the elephant to begin with. Nonetheless, Akshu and Hari were committed to at least trying to do this work. It sounded to Akshu and Hari like they would be with the sirs throughout the entire process—so if the villagers' lives were at risk, the sirs would be, too. Surely the sirs wouldn't do anything to risk their own lives, would they? Plus, if Akshu and Hari declined this rare opportunity for work in their own forest, it seemed unlikely to Akshu they would get another anytime soon. So Akshu paid very close attention to everything Kalaivannan and Dinesh told them. In fact, even when Kalaivannan was explaining to Dinesh and Raghurajan what *their* responsibilities would be after the elephant fell, Akshu tried his best to understand what was being said.

After all the preparatory explanations, Dinesh and the South Indians asked Akshu and Hari to accompany them to the main forest guest house. 'This is our Sir,' Dinesh explained when they arrived. Dr L. Sivaganesan was a stately man, lean and mustached. Akshu and Hari immediately understood that this man was substantially higher in status than even the other sirs. Dinesh and Raghurajan spoke to their boss reverentially—Dinesh grinned submissively like a juvenile macaque trying to placate an alpha male.

Dr Sivaganesan nodded politely in the villagers' direction and continued his conversation with his associates. Akshu realized that Dr Sivaganesan spoke neither Bengali nor Hindi very well—he, too, was South Indian. Over the next couple of days, the villagers would hear Forest Department officials discuss quietly in Bengali just how big a deal this man was. But it would take Akshu months or even years to understand that Dr Sivaganesan was the reason for all the work he was doing, and that, without trying or even knowing it, Dr Sivaganesan would have a profound impact on his and his family's future.

———

Early the next morning, some 25 people met in Madhubangaon to tranquilize elephants. Aside from Akshu and Hari, Dr Sivaganesan and a couple of colleagues from South India were there alongside Kalaivannan, Dinesh, and Raghurajan. There were two veterinarians, two marksmen with dart guns, and one driver for each of the four vehicles. There was a range officer, an unusual man named Arjun Oraon. And the rest were Forest Department employees, either forest guards or daily labourers working under Oraon. The team also included three camp elephants tied up nearby—two females and a young tusker—and their mahouts. Akshu had previously seen these camp elephants, kept by the Forest Department in the villages of Checko and Porro, but he had never been so close to them. He eyed them warily as the others spoke.

At 6 AM, the four jeeps split up and drove into the forest, looking for elephants. Akshu and Hari sat in one, with Dr Sivaganesan riding in the passenger's seat. Their vehicle turned east onto the 23-mile road. A January morning, it was cold and gray, and visibility wasn't great, but the villagers still found elephant tracks from the vehicle. They told the driver to turn north onto a jungle road running parallel to the Bala River, and, before long, they heard the sounds of an elephant herd. The sounds were coming from a half-century old plantation of *jarul* trees. Since the team was currently without walkie talkies, Dr Sivaganesan told the driver that they should go back and tell the rest of the group they had found a herd.

Eventually, the four jeeps and three elephants were all where the wild elephants had been sighted. Two other jeeps with high-ranking Forest Department officials joined. Everyone wanted to see the first tranquilization of an elephant in Buxa Tiger Reserve.

The two adult female camp elephants were loaded up with the crucial people and supplies—the veterinarians and their medicine boxes, the marksmen, the mysterious collar and related tools, and Dr Sivaganesan all sat behind the mahouts. The third elephant, a tusker in his mid to late teens, was loaded with heavy ropes that would be used to pull the tranquilized elephant away from, say, a pool of water where it could drown. Several people told Akshu and Hari to get onto the back of the young tusker. The tusker's mahout, a straight-talking Rabha man, offered a word of caution. 'This elephant, he is young, and he is afraid of wild elephant herds. If the herd scatters, this one could get scared and run away, and then anyone sitting on top might get knocked off by tree branches as he runs. Once someone is on the ground, he could be trampled by wild elephants.

I can't guarantee anyone's life or safety, riding on this elephant,' he warned.

Akshu translated the mahout's message into Bengali for Dinesh. 'I'll just walk on the ground,' Akshu said.

'Nothing will happen,' Dinesh said confidently. He climbed onto the tusker's back. Hari, eager to demonstrate his obedience, followed. The young tusker followed the females into the forest as the marksmen tried to get close enough to one of the wild elephants to shoot. Afraid that he would be trampled if he followed the camp elephants on foot, Akshu climbed a jarul tree to get a better view of what was happening. The old plantation was fairly clear of brush for about 50 meters, but after that it was very bushy. Thick vegetation obscured Akshu's view of the action.

Although he couldn't see clearly, Akshu caught glimpses of the forest elephants and heard them breaking vegetation as they continued to feed. Then, suddenly, the earth began to shake. 'Elephants are running!' someone atop one of the camp elephants shouted in English. Akshu heard breaking branches and jolting of trees as the wild elephants frantically scattered.

As the Rabha mahout had predicted, the fleeing wild herd running in several directions frightened the young camp elephant. The little tusker immediately began to flee to the east, ignoring his mahout. The mahout pressed himself down flat onto the elephant's body as he tried to regain control. Akshu saw his cousin and boss disappear with the runaway tusker. He dropped down from the tree and got in the jeep. 'Let's follow the elephant!' he said. The jeep drove south and then east, toward the Bala River. It seemed likely the camp tusker would emerge there, out in the open. Akshu and the driver didn't find the tusker, but they did find Hari and Dinesh. The pair was bleeding all over their arms, legs, and even from a couple of places on their torsos. Just as the mahout had forecasted, the young tusker had run straight into the thorny vegetation, and Hari and Dinesh had been stuck, scratched, and stabbed by thorns. Somehow, as the tusker had fled, the two had managed to lower themselves to the ground using the ropes and jute mats on the elephant without serious injury.

The jeep returned to where the action had happened. 'An elephant has been darted,' Kalaivannan told Akshu and Hari. The teams on the camp elephants hadn't been able to locate the darted elephant after it had run off. 'We need to go find it!' The range officer Oraon and his team were beginning to fan out. Akshu and Hari grabbed their kukris and went into the forest toward where the melee had happened.

Again, the villagers were terrified. They knew they were looking for an elephant that had been drugged and immobilized, but a wild elephant was a wild elephant, and Akshu was more afraid than ever. He still worried about what might happen if the felled elephant's friends and relatives came back to protect her.

But in addition to being fearful, Akshu was curious. He wanted to see this elephant, immobilized using these so-called 'darts'. And he was excited by the prospect of the reward they might receive if he and Hari found the elephant. Maybe they'd get another large tip? Or even a steady job?

Akshu and Hari soon found an abundance of elephant tracks perhaps 100 meters from the road. The elephants had clearly fled in multiple directions, so the villagers decided to play the odds, following the largest group of elephant tracks as it wound further away from the road. Akshu had never actually followed the tracks of a fleeing elephant before, and he was surprised by how they zigged and zagged. When he was a child, Motikar had warned him never to run in a straight line from an animal—whether a wild boar, an elephant, or a tiger, he said, always keep shifting your direction. That's the only way a human can escape a jungle creature. *Maybe elephants teach their children the same thing,* Akshu thought.

Then, a little less than 200 meters from the road, Akshu and Hari found the female elephant lying unconscious on her side. 'We found her!' Akshu and Hari hollered. 'Come here, come here!' Akshu walked behind the prostrate elephant. She had fallen onto several thick plants and saplings in an uncomfortable way. Akshu and Hari used their kukris to cut some of the woody vegetation under the elephant so that she would lie more comfortably on the ground.

The veterinarians and the others arrived. They examined the elephant and asked Akshu to cut some of the sharp, woody vegetation under the elephant's tongue so it might also rest comfortably outside the elephant's mouth. Gradually, all 30 or so people surrounded the elephant, which they named Samanthagamani. About 20 of them just looked on in fascination as the others worked. The vets measured Samanthagamani's temperature and told Akshu and Hari to pour water on the elephant's head to keep her cool. Akshu was then asked to join Dinesh and Kalaivannan in taking measurements—the length of the elephant, her height at the shoulder, the circumference of her front feet, the length of her tongue, the size of her ears. Kalaivannan noted the direction of the hairs on the brush at the end of her tail, telling Akshu that some elephants had hairs on both the front and back sides of their tails, like a fish's tail fins, while others' tail hairs only went in one direction. Several people walked around photographing the elephant.

Two participants were trying to slide a wire under Samanthagamani's neck. The idea was to use the wire to pull the collar under the elephant and then clasp the collar on top. Akshu noticed that the two men were struggling with this task—the wire was just getting bent out of shape. 'Sir!' Akshu said to Kalaivannan. 'We can dig a tunnel under the elephant using our kukris. Then you can get the wire under.' Kalaivannan agreed. Akshu and Hari got on either side of the elephant and began to dig. Kukris are designed for cutting, but the villagers were so accustomed to using them for varied tasks that they expertly made them into a shovel and scoop. Akshu focused on his task, but he was still keenly aware every time Samanthagamani took a breath. Her body expanded and contracted by what seemed like the volume of his body. As soon as Akshu and Hari could see each other's hands under Samanthagamani's neck, the wire was used to drag the collar under her, and Kalaivannan and the others installed it. Once the nuts and bolts were in place, Akshu helped apply the glue to seal the collar.

Meanwhile, others had pulled out receivers with long antennae and were testing them to see whether they could detect the collar. Akshu, always fascinated by technology, had only observed this for a few moments when the veterinarians ordered everyone back to the vehicles and camp elephants.

Akshu and Hari returned to the road and waited. Soon, Akshu heard someone call out in English, 'Tongue moving.' Then, a few moments later, 'Ear moving.' Then, 'Sitting, sitting, sitting.' Dinesh explained the elephant had sat up. 'Walking, walking, walking!' And then, Akshu heard those sitting atop the camp elephants burst into applause, whooping and hollering as Samanthagamani rose to find her herd.

That evening, the NIES team joined Sivaganesan back at the guest house. '*Bahooth achchaa*,' Sivaganesan said to the villagers, using his rusty Hindi. He asked their names through Dinesh and thanked them. Kalaivannan and Dinesh echoed his sentiments, repeating their approval and gratitude. The marksman also congratulated the villagers for their contributions. Later, as Sivaganesan and some others were speaking in English, Akshu heard them mention his and Hari's names approvingly. Akshu was filled with pride and happiness.

11

My relationship with my girlfriend Alopa had frayed during my time in India, and we had all but broken up when Alopa, a college sophomore, received a fellowship to start a computer lab in Madhubangaon. She identified an NGO that provided refurbished computers to low-income children in the US. They were thrilled to have two of their laptops going abroad, and they sold me the computers for about $150 each. Alopa's funding would bring her to Buxa to be a teacher for her summer recess and help establish the lab.

Excitement had started to build in Malabasti about the potential computer lab, and Alopa and I accepted the opportunity to spend time together. Dr Sivaganesan donated the tables, chairs, and extension boxes remaining from his old field station, and as I departed to visit the US, I left ₹13,000 with Akshu and Thidey to build a one-room structure. In my absence, they built a square concrete foundation upon which sat a corrugated metal shack smaller than a dorm room.

When I returned to Buxa for my second monsoon field season, Akshu and I focused on identifying the first batch of students. Since Alopa didn't speak Hindi or the regional languages, we needed students who had some proficiency in English. The principal at the English-medium Homewood School in the village selected eight purportedly motivated students. I had asked for a diverse crew—both boys and girls, both Adivasis and

Nepalis—and that's what we got: four boys and four girls ranging from 10 to 16 years of age, including five Nepalis, two children from the local Rabha tribe (who look rather like northeastern Indians), and one Adivasi of the ebony-skinned Oraon tribe. I told the children that they were being given a once-in-a-lifetime opportunity to learn from an American computer teacher for free. 'You have to make certain commitments before you begin,' I said. 'You have to promise to come six days a week for the computer classes for the month that Alopa is here. Will you do that?' The kids looked at each other. I found that it helped to repeat myself in my juvenile Hindi—perhaps my American accent was difficult for them.

'Yes, Sir!' they said, the younger boys the loudest.

'After Alopa leaves, it is your responsibility to become teachers at the computer lab. You must teach the other children in this community how to use the computers. We are helping you for free so that you will help other students for free. Understand?' There was nodding. 'Will you help teach other students what you learn in computer class?'

'Yes, Sir!' they said. They all seemed eager, well-behaved, and a little frightened of me. I took down their families' cell phone numbers and sent them off.

Alopa's arrival must have confused many of the villagers—here was a second Indian American who, despite the abundant food and leisure available in the US, was even slenderer than the first. Since she would only be in the village for a little over a month, she wasted no time launching the computer lab. She had installed a typing program and Open Office software onto the two laptops. Then, we divided the students into two groups and told them that classes would begin with their monsoon break.

From the outset, attendance was a problem. The worst was Ujesh, a Nepali and the only older boy in the group, who, after missing several classes, came to one and then disappeared. Alopa hated confrontation, so I was tasked with all negative community interactions. Ujesh had told me that none of his relatives had a cell phone, so I sent messages to several people for Ujesh to come see me. Finally, after more than a week of absences, I took time from my packed research schedule to go where Ujesh lived in Madhubangaon with his uncle. 'Ujesh has gone home to be with his parents for the break,' his uncle said. Ujesh lived up in Buxa Fort, a village in the nearest foothills of the Himalayas. His uncle pulled out his cell phone and called Ujesh's relative to inform them that he was supposed to be coming to computer classes. So much for no one in his family having a phone. I thanked the uncle and left.

'Do you think he didn't understand me?' I asked Akshu. If Ujesh was a successful student, perhaps I was the one who had messed up.

'All the other children understood,' Akshu said. 'Ujesh wanted to go home and play football, so that's what he did.'

While the other students were not nearly as elusive as Ujesh, they also missed class for a variety of reasons. Bhakti and Sakti, the two oldest students, sometimes missed early morning class because the river flooded after heavy rains, and there was no bridge within walking distance high enough for them to cross. Gauri, a Nepali distantly related to Akshu, fell ill with malaria, so she could not come to the late morning class for a few days. And Roshni, the 14-year-old Adivasi girl, was unwilling to come without Gauri. Of the three younger boys, Ronak and Narottam, both Rabha boys, came religiously, but Bidur occasionally disappeared to go fishing or to wander the jungle. To further complicate matters, even after Gauri recovered from malaria, any of the four girls' parents would occasionally expect them to skip class and help plant rice.

'Why didn't you go talk to the parents and explain to them that they needed to come every day?' Alopa asked rather sharply during her second week.

'We asked for the best students from Homewood School, and the students all seemed so enthusiastic! I thought the students and parents would realize what a great opportunity this was,' I said defensively. Alopa had suggested that we visit the homes of each of the students on our day off so she could photograph their houses for the blog she was required to keep for her fellowship. I suggested that we combine these visits with parent–teacher conferences.

This turned out to be a brilliant idea. Alopa told all her students to come at 7 AM on Sunday to guide our jeep to their homes, early enough for the Christian students to be able to make it to church afterward. Only two students showed up for the trip—but since they knew where the others lived, that was enough. With teacher and students aboard, I drove the NIES jeep over the creek to the hamlet of Taazabasti, where most of the students lived. At each house, Alopa would have the student pose for a photo with one of the laptops. The parents were very hospitable; they seemed quite happy to have us as visitors. I would translate all the nice things Alopa had to say to the parents about their child's intelligence and their beautiful house, and then I would give a sterner message about the importance of attending all of Alopa's classes. I told them that the money lost by allowing children to skip work in the rice fields could be more than earned back if the students became qualified to take a job that involved computers.

The only place Alopa and I struggled to play our roles was at Roshni's home. The house was literally falling apart, and Roshni's very poor family was living in the elongated kitchen on their property. Roshni's family was clearly embarrassed by their living circumstances, and I could not think of anything authentic and complimentary or comforting to say about the house. I tried to very sensitively tell Roshni's tall and stately mother that learning to use the computer could help Roshni make enough money to improve their lot in the long run—a suggestion I hoped desperately to be accurate. Since the family was supporting Roshni's attendance at an English-medium private school, I figured they were far-seeing despite their dire present economic circumstances.

Few four-wheeled motor vehicles ever came down these dirt paths, so the students' neighbors gathered around and watched as we moved about the village. Our stopovers delighted the students, and every student we visited joined our expedition to the next student's house. The Christians even opted not to go to church. The trip around Taazabasti seemed to demonstrate to the students and their parents that Alopa and I were genuinely interested in them and, as we headed back over the river to Alopa's lodging, I already felt things were going to get better.

Attendance did improve markedly after the house visits. Under Alopa's patient and creative tutelage, the students made substantial progress in typing, Open Office, and using email and the Internet. Anytime there was any need for confrontation, Alopa would tell me, and I would handle the situation when I came back from the jungle.

While I was sometimes irritated that Alopa was too conflict-averse, I was certainly too conflict-prone. I couldn't understand why people—people we were trying to help—would repeatedly say they'd do one thing and then do another. I perhaps became most frustrated with Roshni. She still wasn't showing up regularly. After Roshni's third straight absence, Gauri, who had previously said Roshni was sick with stomach pain, told me candidly that she was working in the rice paddies with her parents. Had the problem been with another student, I think I just would have written them off, as I had with Ujesh. But Roshni was our only female Adivasi student and our poorest student, and I recognized that she might require more intervention. I decided to postpone work that day and go visit Roshni again.

Narad and I crossed the river to Roshni's home. I called out, but there was no response, so I went to the rice fields behind her home. There her whole family was working, bent over the cool mud in the sizzling sun. 'Roshni!' I bellowed, in a rush. 'Let's go. You're very late for computer class.'

I could see Roshni's mother waving her to go; Roshni looked more reluctant. As she made her way over, I walked through some mud to her father, whom I had not previously met. 'What is this, *Bhaia*?' I asked him. 'I've brought a teacher from America to teach your daughter to use the computer for free, and you still aren't sending her to learn? Don't you understand this is a once-in-a-lifetime opportunity? If she misses so many classes, she cannot learn properly. Today, most of the jobs that pay well require use of the computer. Don't you want your daughter to have a chance at one of those job*s*?'

'Yes, Sir—I did not know she was missing class.' Roshni's father looked like he felt bad he had disappointed me.

'Sir!' yelled a woman close by who was working with the family. 'The girl's stomach was hurting this morning. That's why we told her she need not go.'

'I am sure that even an hour of working outside under this sun is worse than two hours of working on a computer,' I said. Their reasoning didn't make sense to me. 'This is the last time I'm coming to tell you what you should do. I have my own work, my own studies. I do not have time to do this over and over.'

Roshni by this time had reached me from the paddy field. 'Let's go,' I said again.

'Sir, tomorrow,' Roshni said. Perhaps she didn't want to face the embarrassment of being late.

'No,' I said. 'Let's go today. Every day you do not come, you fall behind.'

Roshni's parents encouraged her to go, and Roshni reluctantly went to the water pump and cleaned herself off. Then she turned and looked at me brightly, 'Sir, can I change my clothes?' I nodded. Narad and I waited in the jeep as she went into her kitchen-house and emerged in clean clothes. She looked much happier now, and she and I had a pleasant conversation in the jeep. We dropped her off at her class and headed to the jungle.

When I came back from the jungle that day, Alopa asked me what had happened at Roshni's place that morning. I recounted the story, and Alopa looked concerned. 'What if she is on her period?'

I, too, got worried. 'Oh. That would explain everything, huh?'

'It fits,' Alopa said. 'I definitely don't think the girls here have pads. I wouldn't want to leave home around here, either.'

I sighed. The weight of my presumptuousness made my chest heavy. Alopa wasn't sure, but the fact that I had not even considered menstruation as a possibility was certainly a failure on my part. Unfamiliar with the local culture's euphemisms and norms for indirect communication, I was having a really hard time understanding when it was OK to pressure people for not holding up their side of the bargain.

'It's OK,' Alopa said sweetly, seeing my embarrassment. 'After class, I took Gauri and Roshni to the bazaar and bought them some chocolate. Lots of people crave chocolate during their periods.' She smiled.

As the end of Alopa's time in Buxa approached, it became clear that all her students had made incredible progress. They had essentially learned to type. They learned the basics of creating documents, spreadsheets, and presentations on Open Office. They could write, send, and open emails, as well as conduct internet searches; the teenage girls immediately began Googling their favorite actors. By now, Alopa was far more popular in the community than I was.

Akshu, Alopa, and I turned our attention now to sustainability. We decided to put together a public demonstration of the lab to generate both community support and government financial resources for the continuation of the lab after Alopa left. I personally visited Mr Petkar, the deputy field director of Buxa, and invited him to Malabasti for the demonstration, hoping he would help find funds for the lab.

In the meantime, the biggest concern was finding a teacher to replace Alopa. I thought Alopa's main students would be good assistants, but some of them were as young as 10. I didn't think they could command enough respect to be teachers. Akshu suggested we recruit some of the young men who had gotten computer certificates in Alipurduar. They were people he knew well, and he assured me they would be dedicated teachers.

Alopa agreed to meet with them and see if they were qualified. I happened to run into the two young men on their way back from visiting with her.

'So?' I asked. 'How does our class compare to what you learned in Alipur?'

'They're about the same,' one said.

I was excited. We had created a low-cost program of equal quality to those available in the city? 'So our classes are as good as yours in Alipur were?'

'Oh yes, definitely,' the other said.

I then continued on to Alopa's lodge. 'They don't know ANYTHING,' Alopa told me incredulously. 'They don't even know how to open programs. Worse, they won't admit it—they are embarrassed that little Narottam and Ronak know so much more than they do.'

I sighed. I'd had a bit too much faith in the system. 'So what do you suggest?'

'Unless you can get money from the local government to hire a pro, my students should teach the other kids,' she said simply. Maybe the community's adults would have to keep an eye on the little kids to make sure they weren't walked over, she admitted. 'But that's what makes the most sense. My students are way more qualified than anyone else here.'

We held the public demonstration of what Alopa's students had learned at the computer lab. The neighborhood kids came first and watched while Alopa's students played typing games. Adults in the neighborhood saw the crowd and came to see what the commotion was about. About half an hour in, to my complete surprise, Mr Petkar came, a rifle-toting forest guard in tow.

'It's a great privilege to have you here, Sir!' I said. I took him to the lab and had a couple of the students run typing drills for him. The kids were totally oblivious to the status of the man observing them; they were probably more nervous when their friends had come to see what they could do. 'This is Alopa. She has been teaching these students for just a month. Isn't it amazing what they have learned?'

Mr Petkar was clearly very impressed. As we stepped back out into the sun, I told him about our aspirations for the lab to serve a larger number of students. I broached the topic of funding. 'Is there any way we could get partial funding...'

'Yes, certainly. Actually, the Forest Rights Committee is designed to provide funds for just this kind of project,' Petkar interrupted me. 'I will certainly sign off on it. You can get funds for a teacher, internet, everything. Just write a proposal and have these fellows submit it to the Forest Rights Committee.' He turned to Thidey and some other villagers and confirmed that they were familiar with the process. Thidey nodded.

'That's great!' I said. 'Thank you very much. I think eventually we can get enough funds for everything except the teacher. We just need some time to build up a buffer to pay for any necessary repairs.'

'Good, yes, we can provide funding for the first two years. After that, you should make sure that it is financially self-sustaining. Otherwise, it will become a government program. And government programs always fail.' Petkar smiled. I tried to gauge whether the bureaucrat was trying to be ironic. He wasn't.

12

The elephant collaring initiated Akshu's longest period of continuous employment, lasting over five years. The job paid only about ₹1,600 a month—about as much as the Forest Department paid its labourers as daily wage and far less than Akshu had been expecting—and it involved considerable risk to life and limb and carried no additional benefits (not that Akshu could imagine what 'benefits' were). Akshu did not have the confidence to ask for more money, but as the job provided a steady stream of income, made use of his knowledge and talents, and required no illegal activity, it appealed to Akshu.

Because Akshu knew so little of the world outside Buxa and was so afraid of asking questions, he and Hari didn't understand whom they were working for or what they were doing for some time. Akshu assumed that Kalaivannan, Dinesh, and the others were just private wealthy citizens, doing what wealthy people do, which, apparently, included putting 'collars' on elephants. Not long after the first collaring, when Akshu was spending every day with Kalaivannan trying to find the elephant they had collared, Akshu's curiosity finally got the best of him. He asked Kalaivannan why they would want to put a collar on an elephant. Kalaivannan explained that the collar would allow the scientists to understand where elephants went in the region, and to understand how much area a single elephant or herd needed.

He said that while people could make educated
guesses about such things currently, no one had good
scientific data.

Ooh, haan, OK. How much an elephant travels,
Akshu thought. He had no idea why such information
might be interesting or useful, and it didn't really occur
to him to ask. Besides, he had already dared to ask one
question—another would be too much. Because he was
so untrusting of the sahibs, it took Akshu a great deal of
time to learn anything. It wasn't until perhaps 10 months
into the work that Akshu came to realize that the people
he was working for weren't there as private citizens but
as 'researchers' doing 'science' (whatever that was) for
a government (this, he understood) university called the
National Institute for Environmental Sciences (wherever
that was). Yet, despite his difficulty conceptualizing how
the people in front of him related to far-flung institutions
and their lofty objectives, Akshu could better grasp the
immediate purpose of their day-to-day work. Akshu
focused on doing his work to his employers' satisfaction
and generally ingratiating his superiors.

Initially, much of this work revolved around three
main components: the collaring of elephants, the
tracking of collared elephants, and the execution of
what the ecologists called 'transects'. All of this work
involved considerable adventure. The tranquilizations
generated the most visceral excitement. Over the course
of the first seven tranquilizations, Akshu never quite
got over the feeling of being so close to the heaving,
incapacitated bodies of the *haathis*. With the animals
prostrate before him, Akshu could (and did) examine
every part of the elephants—their trunks, their toenails,
under their tails. The animals' helplessness was
endearing. Within a week of the first tranquilization, the
team went after their first bull elephant. Once darted,

the long-tusked male didn't lay down on his side as he was supposed to; instead, he sank into a kneel, with his front legs folded but his body erect. As he sat there, unconscious, his head grew very hot. 'Pour water on his head,' said the veterinarians. 'Pour water on him or he will die!' The unconscious elephant made a *kerrrrrr* sound. How could they possibly reach his head when he was still so far above them? Akshu and Hari pulled themselves up onto the elephant using its tusks and ears, carrying full buckets and dumping them on the beast's head. The elephant *kerrrred,* something between a cat's purr and a soft snore, and Akshu felt the reverberation throughout his body. Akshu felt a closeness with the elephant as he worked to keep him alive—an intimacy with the same species, perhaps the very same individual, that he and his neighbors sometimes confronted at night with their hearts in their throats as they battled for their livelihoods.

After collaring, the elephant research team would have to repeatedly locate the collared elephants. The collars being used did not contain a GPS, so they did not collect or transmit coordinates. Instead, Akshu or Hari carried receivers with antennae and earphones and climbed trees and hills until they could detect the direction from which the collar's signal was coming. They would then return to the vehicle and repeat the procedure from another location, triangulating the location of the collared animal. Initially, when they found the collared elephants, the herds would run away. But over time, the elephants came to recognize the scientists' vehicles and just went about their business. This in itself gave Akshu a sense of ease about the elephants—that elephants and people could grow comfortable with each other. The researchers would document the location of the collared individuals using their handheld GPS and then turn to other data collection. For instance, they would note what plant species the animals were eating, identify the sex and estimate the age of the various individuals when there was a herd, and occasionally note their distinctive physical features. Akshu and the others began to recognize which female was which calf's mother; they'd get closer looks of the babies playing and adults interacting than Akshu ever had growing up in Madhubangaon. Sometimes they would see the same tusker with a herd during the day that Akshu later had to chase away from the fields at night. As Akshu saw more dimensions of the animals' personalities and lives, as they let him and the other researchers into more intimate proximity, he found himself cooling off faster after his family's crops were raided.

In addition to all the work done directly with elephants were the transects. The transect, Akshu gradually came to understand, was how ecologists got an idea of what existed across a large landscape by examining what they found from walking a line across small parts of that landscape. So, to understand the vegetation across Buxa Tiger Reserve, instead of trying to identify, count, and measure every tree in the reserve, Kalaivannan had them identify and count every tree in some 40 skinny rectangles, the 'transects', placed randomly around Buxa. These transects could take the team anywhere, including the most godforsaken parts of the reserve: steep and barely negotiable mountainsides, unforgiving patches of itching plants, the nests of swarming red ants, or the den of a disgruntled python.

Through all this, Akshu found himself increasingly drawn to Kalaivannan. The young researcher was not only friendly, principled, and resilient, but was also interested in helping Akshu advance his knowledge and skills. Akshu became increasingly comfortable asking the scientist questions. One day, waking up in a rest house near a river outside of Buxa where Akshu had never been, he was bewildered to find the sun rising in the west instead of the east. 'How can this be?' he exclaimed.

'What do you mean?' Kalaivannan replied. 'The sun always rises in the east—that there is the east.'

Akshu scratched his head and pointed to the direction from which the river was flowing. 'The river is coming from the north…'

Kalaivannan laughed amiably as he realized Akshu's confusion. 'Here, in the plains far from the hills, the river changes directions…'

'…so the river is flowing south to north? It has turned around completely?' Akshu asked. Motikar had used the hills and the flow of Buxa's major rivers—all of which ran north to south—to teach his son the cardinal directions. 'But then how does one know which way is north or south away from the hills?' Kalaivannan began teaching Akshu to use technology to solve such problems—Akshu learned to use a compass, and then a handheld GPS. Kalaivannan also showed Akshu how he entered the GPS data from the elephants on his computer and the maps he could produce using such information.

All this expanded Akshu's world, but at least as important as the hard skills Akshu was learning were the soft skills. Kalaivannan encouraged Akshu to be more unabashedly himself—in addition to Akshu's curiosity, Kalaivannan celebrated Akshu's tendency to be honest about what he knew and what he didn't. He told Akshu not to fear anyone, ever. And Kalaivannan served as a good counterexample to the few other relatively well-off and powerful people Akshu had met, from the moneylenders in the village to the beat officers.

Kalaivannan was considerate and compassionate to human and animal alike. He spoke to Akshu's values; he (and the thrill of being near elephants) made Akshu quite happy to go to work every day.

As Kalaivannan observed Akshu's affinity for field research and heard more about the hardships Akshu faced at home, he foreshadowed Akshu's career and gave him advice. 'Akshu,' Kalaivannan said, 'I'm only going to be here for a year, and then I'll have the signature I need from Dr Sivaganesan to move on. But you should remember this: no matter how much you fight with whoever follows me in this work, stick with it. Find a way to make this work for you. One day, this work will lift you from your obscurity; you will be recognized, you will be known.'

Of course, Kalaivannan was learning from Akshu, too. He became better at seeing, hearing, and smelling elephants—or finding their footprints and feeding signs. He learned that if he saw a herd of female elephants from what he thought was a safe vantage point, he had better look around for the bull elephant likely to be with them or looking for the females in the herd. He emulated how the villagers scanned for snakes and wasps' nests, and how they reacted when they saw gaur or wild boar. And he learned how to deal with the most dangerous inhabitant of the forest. One day, while the team was doing a transect, they suddenly came upon a group of men with a wheelbarrow piled high with freshly cut wood; just as the two groups saw each other, the wheelbarrow became stuck in some mud. The men had long kukris, some in hand, others tied to their waists. Before Kalaivannan could say anything, Akshu made the first move. 'Are you taking this for your home? You must be,' Akshu said suggestively. 'Here, let us help you.' He and Hari helped them push the wheelbarrow out of the mud and saw them on their way. Kalaivannan looked on in silence, helplessly. 'The deed was already done, Sir,' Akshu whispered after the smugglers were gone. 'They were well-armed, and I don't know how they would have reacted to you.' Kalaivannan nodded wordlessly, and they continued their work.

———

Incidentally, about the time that Kalaivannan and Dinesh were establishing the NIES's field station in North Bengal, Arjun Oraon was beginning his five-year reign as range officer in Buxa Tiger Reserve. In charge of the 'Research Range', Oraon had a responsibility to go anywhere there was wildlife—especially the core area of Buxa—in search of poachers and other threats to animal conservation. Many Forest Department officials, disinterested in combatting the social and political resistance they now faced when they made arrests, preferred to claim that potential crimes were outside, not inside, of their jurisdiction. But Oraon was different both in his motivations and his abilities. Unlike many Forest Department officials who hailed far from any forest, Oraon was an Adivasi born and raised in Satali, a village next to a jungle in North Bengal. Wild elephants and leopards had wandered right up to his house, where a young Oraon had observed them empathetically. He saw the animals as just doing what all animals do— moving around, searching to fulfill their needs—and that any anger toward animals was misplaced. Animals just have to move, Oraon thought. If they killed a person or took some of their crops, it was generally without malice. In contrast, he felt that wildlife and their habitat needed protection from people. Oraon's upbringing also endowed him with skills that, ideally, every forest ranger should have. He was unafraid to move about the jungle, having learned from his family how to do so safely. He understood which forest paths locals and poachers and smugglers might use, what tracks they would leave behind, what forest goods they might try to take from the jungle. And he could relate to the villagers who lived in North Bengal's forests in a way that made them more likely to divulge information to him.

Just as unconventional as Oraon's background were his methods. Akshu observed that Oraon often patrolled the forest not with forest guards, who were often older, unfit, and apathetic, but with 8 to 10 local enforcers that Oraon hired as daily labour. These young men were villagers who had grown up in the jungle and often participated in illegal activities themselves— but now as employees of the Forest Department who could be fired at any time, they were willing and, under Oraon's guidance, enthusiastic guardians of the forest. Oraon took these men everywhere, focusing on the deep forests. Unlike many other forest officials, he happily went off-road during his patrols, ditching his vehicle and taking trails that went every which way. He would enter the jungle in one beat and then emerge in another. He didn't follow some regular schedule that could be broadcasted to poachers so they could evade him. He even visited the parts of the jungle that most villagers avoided because they were full of elephants and gaur. Even Akshu, who accompanied him on a couple of patrols, found the deep forests Oraon entered in the far northern hills to be daunting. Oraon and his men chased after smugglers, making them ditch their wheelbarrows if they wanted any chance of escape. But running, too, had its risks for Oraon, as a range officer, carried a gun, and he wasn't afraid to use it. Even though many poachers also carried arms, often village-made guns,

Oraon's approach terrified them. People in the forest where they weren't supposed to be believed, perhaps with reason, that they might be shot at if they refused to surrender when confronted.

Poachers and smugglers in Madhubangaon and elsewhere looked for patterns in Oraon's behavior that could help them avoid capture, and they settled on a new strategy. Oraon's fondness for alcohol was well known, and so they waited until word trickled back from Oraon's range office that he was on a drinking binge again. Oraon would drink for days—three, four, five days at a time—and, as word spread, Akshu would hear that the poachers and smugglers stalled by Oraon's diligence were filtering back into the core area. And then, suddenly, Oraon would disappear from the range office. Before the thieves knew what hit them, a hungover but fully functional Oraon and his commando team would be chasing surprised poachers here, apprehending bewildered smugglers there. Oraon was beating the lawbreakers at their own game. He had contacts in villages everywhere. Poachers were suddenly just as unsure about whom to trust in their communities as law-abiding villagers were in the Forest Department.

Oraon was not light-handed with his power. When a dead tusker was found with a bullet in its corpse near Madhubangaon, Oraon threatened to take all the young men in Madhubangaon to jail unless the community coughed up the perpetrators—which they did. Oraon was also not opposed to physically aggressive interrogation, undermining his suspects' rights. Despite his coerciveness, Oraon was popular with those who, like Akshu, favored a forest where people obeyed the law and a jungle that would continue to harbor trees and wildlife. To village observers, Oraon's tactics appeared to work. The

political parties were often, by hook or by crook, able
to eventually free many of those captured by Oraon.
Since the rules inexplicably required Oraon, instead
of the State, to act as the plaintiff and pay many
of his own trial costs, Oraon often skipped court
altogether, instead continuing his work in the field or
(supposedly) drinking himself into a stupor. Still, the
fact that Oraon might seize illegal wares and tools or
even shoot at culprits made poaching or smuggling
in the core area far less attractive for those involved.
Rather than continue to smuggle, young men moved
off to Haryana, Chandigarh, and Delhi to work as
migrant labourers. Once Oraon had asserted his reign,
smuggling in the jungle, as the locals say, went cold.

Of course, Oraon couldn't be everywhere—he was
primarily expected to guard the core area, leaving
the buffer areas relatively safe for lawbreakers.
Additionally, like all Forest Department officers, Oraon
would eventually be rotated to another location. The
smuggling rings and political parties knew this, and
they waited. For the time being, the illicit actors focused
on smuggling timber from the forests near villages
and under the jurisdiction of less enterprising Forest
Department officials.

Chander didn't like that his younger brother now had
steady work when he didn't. Akshu's increasing financial
independence embarrassed him.

One day, Chander made an announcement to his
family. 'Let me have my *issa*,' Chander said. 'I want to
partition and live separately with my wife and son.'

The rest of the family looked at each other. 'Your
issa?' Motikar asked. 'Why would you want to leave?'

'I don't like living under all these loans,' Chander declared, 'having to work to feed all these people. I never asked for this. Give me my *issa*, and I will live separately. Let's split the land in half.'

Satyavati balked. 'In half? You have two brothers, and one sister yet to be married. How will we care for everyone?'

'Look, here's how much remains of the loans we took for your wedding and your sisters' weddings,' Motikar tried to reason with Chander. 'Let's all work together to repay it, and then you can separate.'

'No, no, no!' Chander yelled. 'That's your responsibility. You married us off, your son and your daughters. I don't need to be involved. Why did you give birth to children that you can't even marry off properly?'

'If you want your *issa*, you can have some land and some cattle, but you also get a percentage of the loans.'

'No, no, I won't take the loan. Just give me the land and the cattle.'

Akshu looked at his sister-in-law, Bani, hoping she would be the balancing force that they had all hoped she would be for Chander. '*Bhabi*—what do you say?' he asked. He wanted her to say she wanted to live with Mummy and Papa, with him and Thidey and Rukmani.

But she was silent. That meant that she, too, wanted to separate.

Given Chander's volatility, Motikar and Satyavati decided to involve their community as witnesses in the separation. The other village elders got together to write the agreement and heard Chander's demands. 'No, son,' they said forcefully. 'You have two brothers and a sister who need to be married, and aren't there all these loans to be repaid? You can't have half the land—this can't happen.'

'The loans aren't my problem. I didn't take the loans,' Chander said. 'I'm the oldest, and I have my own family to support now. I need the cattle, the land, and the *supadi* plantation. I need half.' The dismayed villagers tried to reason some more with Chander. Motikar and Satyavati were more and more hurt as Chander repeated his arguments. They were stunned by their son's sheer indifference to his family's well-being.

Akshu found the whole thing humiliating. It was one thing for Chander to throw his tantrums in private, but to expose this family fight to the world, to show everyone the dysfunction and the pain—it was too much. As so often happened when Akshu's passions arose, his pride and moral indignation commandeered his tongue. 'Leave it, Papa,' he said to his father. 'Leave it. As long as our arms and legs are functioning, if Bhagwan wishes it, we'll be OK. We can even pay the loan ourselves. Leave it.'

Motikar, utterly deflated by the callousness of his eldest son, looked at Akshu quietly. 'So we should give him the two bulls, and that young cow…'

'And the land! Including the *supadi* trees,' Chander said, eyes gleaming. He could sense he was about to win once more. The other villagers tried to intervene, but Akshu cut short the argument.

'I don't want land! It's fine, let him have my share. My sisters and my brother need it. I don't need it.' Akshu looked at Chander knowingly. 'He's asking for more— more land, more paddy fields to work, more corn crops to maintain, more elephants to fight against. Fine! Give it to him! I want him to be well—I want my nephew to grow up well, I want my *bhabi* to prosper. But if he's getting that land, he is going to have to work to support his family.'

Chander smiled, perhaps reveling that his family could not withstand the force of his arguments and personality. Or perhaps he was already imagining the wealth he believed he could now attain. Akshu saw his brother's look of triumph, and he wanted to make this the end of all the family struggles—to finally make Chander's shadow over the otherwise loving family go away. Half sneering, half pleading, Akshu said, 'Take half—but work. Work to support yourself and your family. You have everything you need now. Just … work.'

It was a rainy June night in 2001 when a herd of elephants, females and their calves, snuck out of the forest near the railway tracks in southern Madhubangaon. The herd was crop-raiding for corn. The villagers who had planted these fields were sleeping in *tongs* to watch for crop-raiders and, as soon as they awoke and realized their fields were under attack, they began making noise to shoo the elephants away. Unlike male elephants that might resist being chased from their favored meal, the females were pretty easy to scare off, especially since their calves were among them. The herd crossed the tracks back toward the forest they had come from. Suddenly, a loud horn blasted—a train from Siliguri was speeding down the tracks toward Alipurduar, blaring the horn all the while. The farmers looking on saw one of the calves panic and—perhaps confused where its mother was—run back across the tracks toward the farm field. The calf's mother, however, had actually been with the calf on the forest side, and now she tried to sprint back across the tracks before the train separated her from her calf. She didn't make it. The train collided with her, hitting her hind quarters.

Kalaivannan got a call from the Forest Department about the accident, and he rushed to the scene. The injured female was lying in a muddy ditch by the tracks. As she had struggled with her front legs, the ditch had gotten deeper. The monsoon rain filling the ditch threatened to drown the elephant as she lay there. By the time Akshu and his friends arrived, Kalaivannan was covered in mud, bailing out the ditch with a borrowed bucket.

Akshu immediately grabbed a bucket and tried to help Kalaivannan bail out the ditch. Whenever a human approached, the elephant would weakly raise her trunk toward the stranger. The crowd grew as more villagers, Forest Department officials, and even reporters joined. Villagers spoke sympathetically about how the mother had tried to double back to save her calf. Noises from the forest demonstrated that the herd of elephants were still nearby, perhaps less than 100 meters, perhaps unclear as to what to do about their fallen comrade since she was surrounded by humans. They *kerrrred, kow-kowed,* and broke plants, eating as they waited.

Other nearby villagers and Forest Department officials joined Akshu and his friends in helping Kalaivannan scoop water from the ditch. Once the water had mostly been removed, Kalaivannan said he thought that the elephant's back legs were broken. He administered a saline drip to the elephant and tried to give it medicines intravenously as well. Only now, watching how comfortably Kalaivannan dealt with these treatments, did Akshu begin to realize what he would confirm later: that Kalaivannan was himself a veterinarian.

Working close to the elephant, Akshu quickly saw that she was in great pain. She flapped her free ear helplessly; water dripped from her eyes like tears, and she sounded to Akshu as though she was quietly sobbing. The slow, belaboured suffering of the elephant elicited a sympathy he had never before experienced. He had never seen any animal suffer this sort of extended anguish. Then, Akshu discovered there was milk dribbling from her nipples—milk, he realized, that a poor young calf was now unable to get. He felt sad that this elephant had been hurt trying to save her calf in a time of panic, that her act of maternal love had caused her such pain.

When farmers like Akshu defended their crops on foot, the elephants seemed like immensely powerful beings. It was almost impossible to think of them as being weaker, of somehow being the underdogs in the fight for survival. But now Akshu could see the weakness and vulnerability not just of this elephant but of all elephants in the face of humankind. Humans could do anything they wanted with elephants. The train had tossed this elephant to the side like a rag doll; during tranquilizations, the researchers and veterinarians had brought even bull elephants to their knees as though they were playthings. Humans were so powerful that they could destroy elephants not just through malice, with guns and bombs, but even through pure indifference, just by accident! It hit home for Akshu that it was people that ultimately held all the power. It wasn't fair that so many poor villagers suffered from the depredations of these elephants without compensation—but it *also* wasn't fair that these elephants' forests could be stripped bare, that their lives could be taken so haphazardly in their own jungle home by a locomotive pilot driving faster than he should have been in a protected forest.

As the day stretched into the afternoon, the crowd thinned. Soon, aside from villagers occasionally coming by to see the accident victim, the only ones watching the elephant were a couple of forest guards left in charge of guarding her. By late afternoon, more rain had again collected in the ditch. Kalaivannan—perhaps afraid that a large group of onlookers just stressed out his patient—returned quietly by himself and again bailed out the pit and administered treatment to the mother elephant.

Akshu visited again the next day. Kalaivannan was, again, already on site to do what he could for the elephant. Akshu watched his boss admiringly. No one else present, including those working for the Forest Department, seemed nearly as concerned or as dedicated as Kalaivannan. Akshu assisted in bailing some water out of the pit, but there was not much more he could do. More sounds came from the forest—the herd was still nearby.

'They came out last night,' one of the forest guards reported to Kalaivannan and Akshu. 'They came and checked on their friend. And the baby came to drink her mother's milk.'

Kalaivannan's efforts, however valiant, were not sufficient to save the injured elephant. She died a couple of days later. For Akshu, who thought sadly about the fate of the calf without its mother's milk or protection, the whole episode was a turning point. He began to feel very poignantly that every tree, every animal in Buxa—every bulbul, every python, every monkey, every elephant—was at the mercy of humankind. A chamber of Akshu's heart opened up. His beliefs about the relationship between humans and the jungle were changing.

13

When Alopa and I left Madhubangaon in the August of 2011, Akshu took charge of expanding computer lab access to the community. He immediately faced trouble. The first reason, as usual, was the elephants. Most of the children interested in the lab attended public school in town, so Akshu scheduled the computer lab classes in the late afternoon. But for the seven teachers, Alopa's former students, this made attending the classes unfeasible: the 11–17-year-olds all lived in Taazabasti, the hamlet across the village from the lab, and their parents worried that they would risk encountering elephants on their 45-minute walk home in the evening. So Akshu ended up supervising and teaching all the weekday computer classes, even though he was unqualified to do so. Furthermore, Akshu could not impose order on the whole endeavor—he didn't organize the 40 or so interested kids into classes, and he would not turn away children who failed to pay the nominal fee for instruction. He also could not get other parents in the community to take turns supervising the lab with him. 'The other parents,' Akshu explained, 'they think I'm being paid to look after the lab! They don't believe me when I say I'm just doing it for the good of the community, for our children's future.' Parents also informed Akshu that—even though they knew the laptops provided a genuine opportunity for their children to learn—they weren't as interested since the lab, unlike government centers in town, didn't issue certificates of completion that they believed could help their children attain jobs.

Akshu's unstructured classes came to an abrupt hiatus in early October with the arrival of Durga Puja, followed shortly by Kali Puja. Each of these Hindu celebrations wiped out at least a week of productivity, which, combined with the other problems, made the time leading up to my return a dead month for the computer lab.

I came back to Buxa in early November for a six-month field season with two more refurbished computers for the lab. I saw that Akshu's way of running the lab wasn't working. So Akshu and I spread the word to the teachers and students that, on a mid-December day after the students' autumn exams were finished, I would give a presentation on how students could earn a certificate from the computer lab. I showed a PowerPoint explaining why learning to use the computer was valuable and what the students would have to do to get a certificate: type over 20 words per minute, create an Open Office document, create a shopping list and do summations in an Open Office spreadsheet, create a short autobiographical slideshow, answer a question using Google search, and send and receive emails. The certificate would contain my signature and contact information so that potential employers could email or call me in the US to verify its authenticity. I showed them example certificates to whet their appetites. Then, finally, I tried to talk them out of their lengthy vacations. 'You cannot celebrate holidays for an entire week. You can have one or two days off for Christmas or Saraswati Puja, but if you take a whole week off for every holiday, you will never learn properly!' Before the students left, I called each one up to enter their name, phone number, and the class times they would be available over the next three months into a spreadsheet. Two classes met on Saturday and Sunday afternoons, and the others at 2–4 PM during the week. Furthermore, I told the teachers to come at 6–8 AM on Fridays so I could lead an example class for the following week. Ultimately, all 34 interested children filled out the spreadsheet.

Akshu marveled at how I organized everything. 'Everything can be done on Excel, huh?' he said admiringly. I smiled, feeling accomplished.

After days full of driving or walking around the jungle or digging through elephant or cow or monkey poop—and sometimes teaching kids to use laptops—I generally spent some time entering data. After that, there was an infinite amount that I ought to have done—I should have read scientific papers or books on the history of North Bengal, or, better still, worked on my Hindi or even learned Nepali. But, instead, usually hungry to hear something in English, I would rewatch one of the episodes of *Glee* saved on my computer. No one, I figured, would ever know.

One night in November, I summoned the energy to open a different file: 'Management Effectiveness Evaluation (MEE) of tiger reserves in India: process and outcomes. 2010–2011.' The government document had been published a few months earlier by the National Tiger Conservation Authority with the support of the Wildlife Institute of India, two institutions that had been critical for preventing the extinction of wild tigers in India. The report included assessments of the state of every Indian tiger reserve, rating them each as 'poor', 'satisfactory', 'good', or 'very good'. I eagerly scanned the report, looking for Buxa. The 'very good' category included legendary tiger reserves—places like Kaziranga, Mudumalai, and the Sunderbans; there turned out to be only one tiger reserve rated as 'poor', a place named Satkosia in Odisha that I'd never heard of. Then there was Buxa.

Buxa was rated as 'good'. It was in the same category as several world-renowned protected areas, including Corbett and Ranthambore. Tadoba-Andhari, the only place I had ever had the fortune of seeing wild tigers—four times in two weeks—was also classified as 'good'.

How is that possible? I thought in disbelief. As far as I could tell, Buxa was dominated by domestic animals and poachers. I read on. The report summarized Buxa's strengths in six bullets, including its contiguity with protected forests in Bhutan and the state of Assam and 'financial support from the State Government: Buxa Tiger Reserve receives more than 80 per cent of its total budgetary requirement from the State Government ... which allows park authorities to take required management actions on time.' The weaknesses were summarized in eight longer bullets, with the longest faithfully describing the human pressures on the reserve: 'There are about 30 forest villages inside the Reserve ... Large human population for resource dependence and associated cattle grazing have cumulatively enhanced degradation of forests.' It continued, 'Notwithstanding the fact that some promising income generation programmes ... have been successfully demonstrated ... [the] primary problem of resource use by proximate societies have not been tackled effectively.'[1]

---

1   Mathur, V.B., R. Gopal, S.P. Yadav, and P.R. Sinha. 2011. 'Management Effectiveness Evaluation (MEE) of Tiger Reserves in India: Process and Outcomes'. *National Tiger Conservation Authority*, Government of India, pp. 97.

The bullet-by-bullet description of Buxa matched what I had seen, but there was one critically relevant omission: it didn't say anything about the number of tigers in Buxa. I found that estimate a few weeks later in a newspaper. An article in *The Hindu* reported that 'an analysis of tiger scat samples collected from January to May this year at the Buxa Tiger Reserve in North Bengal has revealed the presence of 20 tigers in the reserve forest.'[2] I was stunned. I searched online and found that a similar exercise a year earlier had found at least 15 tigers in Buxa.

I told Akshu and Thidey about the report. Akshu laughed cynically. 'Twenty? There isn't even one tiger in Buxa,' he said emphatically. 'I've been working all over the reserve so many years now. I haven't seen any tiger scat, any scratch marks on trees, any pugmarks, any photos. We send all these cattle into the forest, but we've haven't seen even one killed by a tiger in decades. And I never see any tigers. And no one I work with has seen one.'

I nodded. 'But what about in the north, on the border with Bhutan…'

Akshu shrugged. 'Maybe a tiger could cross over from there now and then, but then what would it eat? There are so few wild animals left in the forest. Humans have eaten them all.'

'But then how did the Forest Department get all these scat samples…'

'I don't know, Sir. But I think they must have gone to some zoos or circuses and gotten the samples from there,' Akshu speculated.

---

2   Singh, Shiv Sahay. 2011. '20 Tigers in Buxa Reserve Forest, Reveals Scat Analysis.' *The Hindu*. Available at: https://www.thehindu.com/todays-paper/tp-national/tp-otherstates/20-tigers-in-buxa-reserve-forest-reveals-scat-analysis/article2737176.ece (Accessed on 20 October 2021).

'Brudder,' asked Thidey, 'does the Forest Department in Buxa Reserve get more money if it says it has tigers?'

A tiger reserve without tigers did stand to lose funding, but I didn't know that at the time. What I did know was that in the previous decade, it had become publicly known that in two Indian tiger reserves—Sariska in Rajasthan and Panna in Madhya Pradesh—no tigers remained, likely due to poaching. The ensuing fallout had been dramatic—the stories had taken off in the international press, leading to widespread outrage and consternation. In addition to any financial incentive, I figured there must be a very strong political incentive to pretend there were tigers in Buxa. Being in charge of a tigerless tiger reserve was just plain embarrassing.

When Dr Sivaganesan, my NIES mentor, made a rare visit to Buxa, I shared my suspicions. 'Sir, I've been in Buxa for some time now, and I haven't seen any sign of a tiger—no kills or footprints too large for a leopard, no potential tiger scat, and certainly no actual tiger. My camera traps have caught leopards and leopard cats and fishing cats and ferret badgers and three species of civets, but not a tiger...'

Dr Sivaganesan interrupted me in his quiet but authoritative way. He pointed out that I had only seven camera traps, and that I mostly placed them facing down toward fruit. 'You can't expect that they will necessarily find a tiger. You're not even really looking for them.' He told me that for three months during his early research on elephants in Mudumalai, he not once saw a tiger. Tigers, he reminded me, were a cryptic predator evolved to be as hard to find as possible, at least for 500-pound cats. Even though he hadn't seen them, he said, there were still tigers in Mudumalai.

I nodded. 'Yes, there certainly are, but that's the thing, sir. Not only have *I* not seen a tiger—no one else has, either. Ask Akshu or Hari or Dinesh—they've spent years in every corner of this reserve. None of the villagers I've spoken to has seen a tiger for decades.'

Dr Sivaganesan was silent for a moment. 'You know,' he said, his tone still critical, 'you're not the first person to say that there aren't any tigers left here.'

I felt whiplashed. Was Dr Sivaganesan's position that there could very well be tigers here or that it was obvious there weren't? 'Yes, Sir, I know…'

'So maybe there aren't any tigers here. But my point is that you don't have the evidence necessary to make an assertion.'

I nodded, about to argue that it wasn't as though I was completely without evidence—but I held back. The subtext of his message was clear: you have to pick your battles in this world. Keep your head down. You have a job to do, and it has nothing to do with tigers.

And he didn't have to remind me of a fact that rested in the back of every scientist's mind who yearned to be near wildlife in India. I was in Buxa doing my doctoral work because the Forest Department had let me in. And the same government that had let me in could also lock me out.

I was almost persuaded to let the whole tiger thing go, but then we found the *tela* road. Akshu, Narad, and I were visiting Chalta #50, a tree deep in the core area, when we found it. Usually, my village assistants had to point the signs of poaching and smuggling out to me—the makeshift bed in a tree, or the remnants of a fire scattered in the dirt. This time it was obvious. The smugglers had transformed the forest trail we used to get to Chalta #50 into a road for wheelbarrows.

The 2-foot-wide path was now 6 feet wide in places; all the smaller trees and plants that we had ducked and dodged while navigating the route had been sliced to 6-inch stumps. The exposed dirt was laden with fresh tracks of wheelbarrows. The road continued north to our tree, 500 meters from the 23-mile road, and well beyond. Akshu said that it probably continued to the patch of sal trees yet another kilometer into the jungle. We realized soon after that the road also went south, possibly straight to the culprits' village. 'They've built such a nice road,' Akshu commented. 'They'll be back.'

'They come at 11 PM or midnight, work during the night, and leave by 6 AM,' Narad offered.

I looked at him funny. 'How do you know?'

'We know how these thieves work. They're in our villages, too,' Narad said. Akshu nodded.

The felling of trees so deep in the core area bothered me a lot. I had to report this. Less than 20 minutes later, we came across some forest guards in a jeep on the 23-mile road. I waved them down, and Akshu and I reported the trail. 'It's right after where the road turns and crosses the creek, about 3 kilometers down the road,' Akshu told them.

'Please tell the range officer at Jainti,' I told the forest guards. They nodded obligingly.

The next day, when we revisited the camera trap, we saw fresh wheelbarrow tracks on the road—it didn't seem like the Forest Department had taken any action yet. On the third day, when we were taking the camera trap down from the tree, we actually heard wood being chopped down the smuggler's path. 'They're here!' I said incredulously. 'In the middle of the day!'

The smugglers would be easy to catch if they were so cocky, I thought. The next day, on our way into the jungle, we stopped at the range office in Jainti. Akshu and I walked in and saw four or five men. 'Where is the Bada Bo?' I asked, referring to the range officer.

'He's on patrol,' one of the men said.

'Well, we want to report something,' I told him. 'We found a smuggler's road several days ago, and yesterday when we were there, we heard them chopping wood.'

'Where?'

Akshu described the location.

'Oh, we were in that area yesterday,' he said dismissively. Then he paused. 'What time?'

'10:30,' I said.

'We were there at 10:30 yesterday,' the man said.

I grew angry. I caught myself before I said, 'Oh, so you were the ones felling trees in the core area?' I knew better than to make haphazard accusations against the Forest Department. But I was incensed by the pure indifference of this man, in whose care was entrusted one of the last wild homes of the Asian elephant and, supposedly, the Bengal tiger, and I couldn't hide my anger.

'Listen, it's my dharma to report to you when I find something like this in the jungle, true or false?'

'True true true,' the officer said, retreating a bit.

'OK. Well, I have done my duty. Now whether you want to do something or not is up to you. Tell the range officer,' I said. 'Let's go, Guruji.' I stomped out.

'It's a very good thing you've done!' the man called out after me.

I got into the jeep cursing angrily in English. Narad and Akshu blinked at me. I switched back to Hindi. 'They didn't even act as though they would do something.'

'That's the way this place is,' Narad said.

But my ire was fully stoked now. I had met people in the Forest Department who cared and tried, but many in Buxa showed no interest in protecting the wildlife sanctuary. At the end of the day, Buxa was being hollowed out by a metastasized tumor. It seemed that just meters from every road on any given day there was a poacher or a smuggler. And if people like me ignored the cancer, how could we claim to be conservationists? I might only be a student, but if I just sat by and watched this happen, how could I live with myself?

Something, I thought, had to be done.

14

Not long after Chander, Bani, and their toddler son moved out of the Atris' house, Motikar began to feel unwell. His eyes became blurry, his hearing began to decline, and his mouth felt dry. Akshu and his siblings accompanied Motikar to the hospital in Alipurduar repeatedly that year. After about ₹10,000 of tests and scans, the doctors told the Atris that they didn't know what was wrong with Motikar. Before long, the septuagenarian stopped walking.

Akshu, still in his mid-20s, was now the oldest able male in the family *and* the only person with regular employment, so he became the nominal head of the household. Akshu immediately began losing sleep under the weight of his responsibilities. He realized he would have no peace until he extinguished a loan that his father had taken for his sister Hemkala's wedding. The terms of the loan were predictably appalling: Motikar had borrowed ₹3,000 with an interest rate of 10 pe rcent per month. Over the course of a year, a loan with such terms would have grown to about ₹9,415—an effective annual interest rate of about 214 per cent. If Akshu didn't squelch this debt soon, the lender, a rich Nepali businessman living in the bazaar, would be able to claim much of the Atris' meager belongings.

Akshu's new financial responsibilities were one of the main reasons he tolerated the increasingly hostile environment he faced at work. As promised,

Kalaivannan had left around a year after they had started the elephant collaring work, and it quickly became clear that he had been a check preventing other more hierarchical researchers from exploiting the villagers. Akshu faced the biggest shock when Kalaivannan was replaced with a Marathi fellow named Dukhad. Dukhad took over transect work and took Akshu and Hari to reserves all around North Bengal. Unlike Kalaivannan, Dukhad was imperious and almost oppressive. He took the village assistants to do transects in tall grasslands filled with dangerous animals like gaur and one-horned rhinos, but he himself would sit safely atop a camp elephant while forcing Akshu and Hari into even the most dangerous situations. Where Dukhad stayed in neat rooms and Forest Department lodges, he left Akshu and Hari to spend the night in abandoned, rotting sheds that hadn't been used for a decade. The sheds had been reclaimed by arthropod ecosystems, with hundreds of spider webs. The villagers, exhausted from a day of labour, would clean out the sheds in the dark, spread their bedding on the floor, and pray they would wake up without a snakebite. When they were working in the field, Dukhad refused Akshu's request to pack something other than *chida* for lunch. Since the bitter rice didn't agree with Akshu's stomach, Akshu was forced to fast from breakfast to dinner, despite working all day in the jungle.

Finally, one day, Akshu found the courage to say something to Dukhad. 'Sir, we work very hard in the field, taking all this risk. Then we eat food in unsanitary places. And then we can't sleep properly because insects bite us the whole night in the rotting houses you make us stay in. This is a big problem. Please, Sir, come up with a better system.'

'*Haraami*,' Dukhad cursed through his thick beard, his thick belly shaking with indignation. 'Sometimes one has to do these things; sometimes, one has to live like that.' And since Akshu was afraid of being fired, that ended the discussion.

Akshu gritted his teeth and persevered the two or three months until Dukhad left; he had survived the worst. With transects and collaring completed, Akshu and Hari would now join Dinesh and Raghurajan for two other types of field work. First, they would attempt to identify elephant corridors, paths for wildlife between protected areas, by tracking the collared elephants and seeing how they moved between North Bengal's various sanctuaries and forests. Second, they would tackle a topic near and dear to the Atris' hearts: human–elephant conflict in the villages across North Bengal. The researchers wanted to know how much damage elephants were doing to the crops planted across the region. To do this, they began working in 19 villages. For the next three years, they visited each village every two weeks. In each community, the researchers hired a local to write down every family whose crops were raided each night. During their biweekly visits, the team would collect these reports and measure the area of crops damaged in each family's farm.

Unfortunately for Akshu, his working conditions did not improve as much with Dukhad's departure as he had hoped. While working with the Tamilian scientist Raghurajan was easy enough, the initially congenial Dinesh proved to be an incapable manager. Dinesh was allergic to initiating confrontation and utterly incapable of responding constructively to criticism. Worst of all, Dinesh was easily manipulated by flattery, meaning that skilled sycophants who had secured places on the NIES team soon heavily influenced operations. Hari was one of these sycophants. Hari was a diligent worker when his bosses' eyes were upon him, but Akshu realized that he became very lazy when left without supervision. Akshu would try and measure the total area of a field raided by elephants, and Hari would refuse to hold on to his side of the tape measure. 'Uhhh … it looks like 75 meters. Seventy-five meters long and 20 meters wide. Write that.' Soon, Hari would be lounging and socializing with friends in the village until the jeep came to retrieve them.

Akshu, scared that this data falsification would be discovered, looked for a way to free himself of Hari. When Dinesh and Raghurajan realized that they would need more employees to collect both tracking and crop-damage data, Akshu offered to find other villagers to supplement the teams, ensuring that he and Hari would no longer be left alone to work. Akshu recruited his friend Moksha, who was dependable and fun to work with.

While Akshu had freed himself of one sycophant, he could not fully disentangle himself from another. Dinesh had recently hired a local truck driver named Bhuday to drive the main NIES vehicle. The two quickly developed a strong bond. Although Akshu spent most of the day driving around with Raghurajan and his driver, at the end of each workday, Bhuday would drive any remaining villagers from Alipurduar, where the NIES researchers stayed, back to Madhubangaon. Hari generally found a way to get let off early, leaving Akshu and sometimes Moksha to ride back with Bhuday. Unfortunately, Bhuday's drinking habit meant that, without consulting his boss or his passengers, he would often stop at a bar in Damanpur, a town half-way back to the village. Akshu asked Bhuday not to stop—he wanted to get home to his family—but Bhuday ignored him and continued to stop for drinks most nights, bringing Akshu home as late as 8 or 9 PM. On the worst day, Bhuday got completely hammered, only leaving the bar at 12:30 AM. Akshu braced himself as the inebriated driver made sound effects, swerving the vehicle every which way on the dark jungle roads. Akshu was already furious when he arrived home at 1 AM; he was angrier still after his parents yelled at him. So Akshu finally went above Bhuday's head to Dinesh and told him what was happening.

Dinesh seemed unperturbed. He replied that Bhuday was able to get the vehicle safely home every night even while drunk, so why should he be bothered? Akshu gulped, and he worked up the courage to say, 'Do something or I will tell Sivaganesan Sir.'

Dinesh was shocked. Akshu had always been less accommodating than the rest of the villagers. He seemed to think that just because Kalaivannan had selected him first, he was something special. But even for Akshu, this was a presumptuous move—it was a bold and serious threat. Or was it? Dinesh squinted and called Bhuday over. 'From now on, don't do that,' Dinesh said simply.

'Oh, OK, sir. Yes, Sir!' Bhuday responded. Akshu sighed in relief—now maybe he could finally get home on time, without fear of an accident.

But after a short reprieve, Bhuday returned to his dangerous ways. Akshu backed down, unable to muster up the courage to call the esteemed professor in South India. He had no reason to believe Dr Sivaganesan would care about his safety, and he simply couldn't afford to be fired.

———

For all these challenges, working for NIES on elephant conservation still had its benefits for Akshu.

For over a century, the tea industry had been a fixture of North Bengal. During colonial times, the British recruited far and wide for employees to work the land. In addition to Nepalis and some local indigenous peoples, the British estate owners brought Adivasi workers from Bihar and other parts of Central India to work on the plantations. These tea plantations largely passed into the hands of Indian owners after Independence and, despite ups and downs in the market, tea estates still occupied much of North Bengal at the turn of the 21st century, including parts of the elephant corridors between Buxa and the neighboring forests. So when Akshu was trying to hone in on collared elephants with a VHF receiver or measuring crop damage, he often ended up spending time in the tea monocultures where hundreds of workers plucked leaves and dropped them into large bags and baskets that were strapped to their foreheads and rested on their backs, the bottoms of the baskets reaching to their hips.

One day, in mid-2002, Akshu and two others were trying to find the signal for a collared elephant in the village of Dalsingpara when they passed a tea estate. One of Akshu's companions was a young man named Shiv who lived in Dalsingpara. Shiv had gone to Chandigarh with Akshu, and the two worked well together. As they were passing the estate, Shiv recognized two of the women working in the estate and greeted them.

'Where are y'all going?' the women asked in Nepali.

Shiv told them they were working, and he stopped to exchange pleasantries. Akshu studied the women carefully. They looked quite similar, and he knew they must be sisters, one just a little taller and older. They were light-skinned but tanned from their labour, giving them the hue of golden wheat. The smock-like uniforms they wore, made of plastic, covered much of them, but their slim arms with slender muscles showed, as did the feminine curves of their bodies. Sweat poured down their faces. They smiled charmingly at Shiv, the grinning, round-faced elder sister vaguely resembling a red panda.

Shiv finished chatting, and the three young men moved on. Akshu didn't waste much time before asking, 'Where are those girls from?'

'They're from here,' Shiv said. He explained that his sister had married their older brother. 'Why?'

'I liked them a lot!' Akshu confessed eagerly.

Shiv smiled, and then something dawned on him—he remembered a conversation he had with Akshu some time ago when they were working together in Chandigarh. 'Akshu Daju,' he said, 'remember how you were depressed and telling me that you wanted to marry someone named 'Kusum'? And I told you I knew several Kusums? Well, that is one of them! The older one is named Kusum!'

Akshu was hooked. A pretty, hard-working Nepali woman who also had the name Kusum? Since this Kusum's brother had married into Shiv's family, he reasoned she must be a Brahmin—so he knew their union would be socially acceptable. Plus, Kusum was the older one, so she would have to be married off first. He was in luck as far as his timing was concerned.

Akshu was staying at his aunt's place in Dalsingpada that night, and he asked his *mami* whether she knew the family. She did. In fact, she was friends with Kusum's mother, and Akshu's uncle was friends with Kusum's father. 'They're very poor,' Mami told him. She explained that, for many years, Kusum's father had been absent from the family, having gone to Nepal for work and gotten lost in local politics. Kusum's mother Deepika had then had to support the family herself, working very hard in the tea estates to raise her five children. Deepika's husband had only recently returned. 'Why do you ask?' Mami inquired.

'Oh … I like the older one. Kusum,' Akshu said. He was utterly disinterested in keeping this to himself.

'Is there a reason you're interested in this particular girl?' Mami asked curiously.

Akshu shrugged. 'I just like her,' he responded.

Mami must not have found that explanation compelling. Despite Akshu's frequent requests whenever he happened by Dalsingpada for work, his aunt did not report any progress on broaching the topic of potential marriage with Kusum's parents. Akshu, in the meantime, couldn't keep his mouth shut. He told every one of his friends that he had taken a liking to this Kusum from Dalsingpada. It was true that they had never spoken, but that didn't bother Akshu. What he knew was enough for him. He was attracted to humble, hard-working women, which, by Shiv's and his aunt's account, Kusum was. In Akshu's daydreams about his brief encounter with Kusum, it was the sweat pouring down her face as she plucked tea and the lack of self-importance in her voice that he dwelled on. The key to a happy marriage, he thought, was to marry someone who was not so egotistical that she couldn't be reasoned with. He also didn't want to marry a wealthy woman who would find his family's circumstances to be a burden. Instead, he had wanted to marry someone for whom even his tenuous economic assets would be a boon. He had often thought about marrying a young widow, of which there were quite a few, but someone very poor like Kusum would also do. And, finally, the fact that he had been drawn to someone named Kusum didn't seem like a coincidence—he just *felt* that he was supposed to be with someone named Kusum.

That, somehow, would help him achieve an element of his dharma that remained unfulfilled.

All in all, Akshu, like all young people smitten by prematurely deep attraction, had his own explanations for the pull he felt toward a woman he had scarcely met. And, like a true romantic, he didn't mind that his reasons were under-substantiated, incomplete, and, in some ways, startlingly illogical.

Daanbir Baisya's father had been a very honest man, and he had been exploited by the unscrupulous members of the broader Madhubangaon community. Daanbir, realizing his father's powerlessness, had resolved to become politically influential—not just to protect himself from the avarice of his neighbors, but also to promote broader justice in the jungle. Daanbir's grandfather had been a forest guard at a time when forest guards were still effective and respected, and Daanbir had inherited a reverence for nature.

So, in the early 1990s, when Daanbir was in his early twenties, he joined the leftist Forward Bloc Party. He believed that leadership in a political organization would give him the influence he sought. Charismatic and focused, Daanbir was soon delivering busloads of participants from the rural areas to join protests in the city. But he gradually realized that the political parties cared primarily about serving the needs of urban voters, who far outnumbered the forest villagers. Daanbir stopped participating in city protests unless they served his community's needs. By now, Daanbir was widely respected in the forest villages—local leaders would not dare to bully him as they had his father—but he was not having the effect he was hoping to on forest management.

Despite their urban focus, political parties did help spur the establishment of Forest Protection Committees that Daanbir was initially optimistic about. These committees were to be partnerships between the Forest Department and forest and outside villages that ensured locals benefited from sustainable use of forest products, including timber. But soon, Daanbir realized that these committees were horribly ineffective. The Forest Department continued to urge villagers to patrol for smugglers and promised them all sorts of benefits in return, including funds from timber sales and the tiger conservation funds sent by the central government, but these benefits never materialized. Despite the villagers' participation in patrols, the Department would sell the confiscated wood and keep the money. Gradually, honest villagers dropped out of the patrols, and local smugglers participated in them to familiarize themselves with the patrol operations and the best trees to cut down. Then they would return when they knew the Forest Protection Committee patrol would be elsewhere, cut down some trees, and go sell the timber. The thieves had infiltrated the FPCs. Daanbir watched all this with dissatisfaction, trying to figure out how to better protect the forest and serve honest forest villagers.

In mid-2002, Daanbir saw an opportunity to galvanize action. Several families in Madhubangaon discovered that their teenage sons were no longer attending school as they were supposed to. The boys would don their uniforms, put their books in their backpacks, and leave for school—but then they would reroute to their friends' houses, change their clothes, and go into the buffer zone of the forest to make money smuggling. Daanbir went around Madhubangaon lamenting this. 'The system is broken,' he said. 'Our aspirations are in trouble. It's bad enough if the smugglers are destroying our jungle, but by diverting our children from an education, they are ruining their future. If the kids are studying, at least there is hope that our community will improve—we need to stop the smuggling around our forest.' Daanbir was persuasive, and about a dozen young men, including Akshu and Hari, joined his cause.

Perhaps inspired by Arjun Oraon's work in the core area, Daanbir made his followers into a special enforcement unit. Instead of patrolling randomly, they systematically sought out tips from the village community on where smuggling was likely to happen on a given night. As such, the work was sporadic and dangerous. Soon after they began, a man they were chasing threw a kukri at Daanbir, barely missing his mark. On another occasion, someone in the group heard about a smuggling effort in the forest west of Madhubangaon near the old logging road. The 12 patrollers searched the various paths in the area, and they eventually found a muddy trail with two wheelbarrow tracks. It was already evening; Daanbir suggested they hide on either side of the trail and then ambush the smugglers as they emerged from the forest. They waited for hours—and when the smugglers finally emerged in the dead of night, the group was much larger than they had thought. Though the patrollers couldn't count perfectly in the dark, some three dozen people appeared to accompany seven wheelbarrows weighed down with heavy timber. The smugglers, not anticipating any resistance that night, wheeled down the path right between the ambushers.

'Attack!' Daanbir shouted, and the patrollers jumped out with long wooden poles in their hands, mercilessly beating the smugglers. The confused thieves were thrashed from the left, the right, and behind. They could neither see nor count their attackers, and they fled. It was a good thing, for had they known they outnumbered the patrollers three-to-one—and that their assailants were local villagers without Forest Department support—the outcome might have been quite different. However, the patrollers had probably overcompensated for their inferior numbers—one of the smugglers near the back of the line, who happened to be one of the facilitators living in Madhubangaon, was beaten so badly that he grew ill and eventually died from his injuries.

From then on, the patrollers were taken quite seriously, and they continued to be effective. Over six months, they made nearly two dozen interceptions, seizing numerous wheelbarrows and over 50 bicycles loaded with illegal timber and turning them over to the Forest Department. However, smuggling didn't stop altogether, and Daanbir was frustrated that the Forest Department had no interest in capitalizing on their progress. When Daanbir heard tips about smuggling operations, he shared them with Forest Department officials, but they generally found some excuse or another not to confront the thieves themselves. Worse, Daanbir realized at least one person in the Forest Department was working to return the confiscated bicycles and wheelbarrows to their original owners. Daanbir once came across a smuggler pushing along the very same bicycle Daanbir and other patrollers had confiscated from him and surrendered to the Forest Department.

'How'd you get it back?' Daanbir asked in surprise.

The village smuggler shrugged. 'I gave them ₹250, and they gave it back to me.' Akshu and the others similarly noticed that they seemed to seize the same wheelbarrows more than once. Apparently, when it came to the more dedicated smugglers, the patrollers were essentially just diverting a share of their profits to unscrupulous forest guards.

Daanbir one day came across the deputy field director of Buxa's east division, and he tried to remedy the situation. He explained how Forest Department officials appeared to be aiding smugglers for their own profit. 'You might as well just set up Forest Department checkpoints at the paths used by the smugglers and charge a fee for every bicycle that goes by.'

The DFD was incensed by Daanbir's impertinence, but he instituted a new rule: all confiscated bicycles and wheelbarrows would be auctioned off, just like confiscated wood. This seemed to work briefly—but then Daanbir heard that the forest guards had started selling confiscated bicycles and wheelbarrows on the street half-way back to the station, before they even registered their confiscation. After all, forest guards wouldn't benefit personally from an auction: only the State would. The adaptability of corrupt players sometimes surprised even a seasoned political operative like Daanbir.

The patrollers could, in theory, have made it trickier for officials to sell off unregistered confiscated materials by taking them all the way to the range or beat office—but without a vehicle, that would have been a lot of work for the already overstretched volunteers. To make things worse, Daanbir started getting complaints from the shopkeepers in Madhubangaon. As villagers had accumulated more disposable income over the previous decade, many more had started opening stores in the bazaar to serve the growing consumer base.

'Why are you hurting us?' the shopkeepers asked Daanbir. 'We're not getting any sales anymore.'

'What do your sales problems have to do with me?' Daanbir asked.

'Ever since you started your patrols, no one has money to buy our stuff,' the shopkeepers said. 'You're not helping the village.'

Daanbir sighed. Without some benefit to replace the influx of money from smuggling, he knew the success of his patrols would harm the economy of his village. Ideally, villagers should have been rewarded with proceeds from sustainable sales of timber from the jungle, but the Forest Department had shown no interest in helping the villagers create such a system. Daanbir's men were exhausted, and they were demoralized that the government would not likely help make their efforts sustainable. Daanbir told the team that he would try another strategy to save the forest, and the group disbanded.

Months had passed since Akshu had first asked his *mami* to speak to Kusum's family, and no progress had been made. Finally, Akshu received news of a development, though it wasn't exactly what he had been hoping for.

One of the many friends Akshu had told about his new obsession was Chander's brother-in-law. Bani's brother, Batsal, still lived in his father's house in Birpada, not far from Dalsingpada. Batsal, too, was on the hunt for a wife but, unlike Akshu, he was following tradition, visiting a series of Nepali Brahmin households with eligible daughters in the region. Eventually, Batsal's search had taken him to Dalsingpada, where his local contacts took him to visit a home with two unmarried daughters who worked in a tea estate and a mother who, despite the father's presence, clearly acted as the head of household.

Batsal's wealthy father was one of the first to acquire a landline phone, so not long after Batsal's third or so visit to Dalsingpada, Batsal used it to call the landline in the bazaar in Madhubangaon. The operator there summoned Akshu.

'*Daju*,' Batsal said. 'I'm engaged.'

Akshu was confused by the tone of Batsal's voice. He sounded ... sad, almost apologetic. 'That's great!' Akshu responded enthusiastically. 'Who's the girl? Where's she from?'

'She's from Dalsingpada,' Batsal said.

Akshu's heart sunk. He knew exactly why Batsal sounded apologetic. 'What's her name?'

'I visited so many homes, but this is the one where I found someone that matched me,' Batsal explained. 'She was pretty, she liked me, and our parents got along fine, and our *kundalis* matched,' he said, referring to the Hindu astrological charts used in Nepali communities. 'I hope you'll understand...'

The feeling that had sunk to the bottom of Akshu's intestine burst, and heat rose into his chest. '*Aare!* I told you ... we've talked so much ... couldn't you find another woman?! Why did you go to that house?'

Batsal's tone changed. 'I know. I know there might be women in other places, but this is where I found someone I wanted to marry.' Now he sounded almost gleeful.

It felt so cruel; Akshu wanted to cry. Had Batsal been in front of him, Akshu might have hit him. 'I told you...' Akshu gasped. 'I told you ... I wanted to marry Kusum ...'

'Yes, yes, I know,' Batsal replied.

'And now you've taken her!'

'No,' Batsal said. 'I haven't.'

Akshu heard Batsal laughing. 'I thought you just said you were promised to Kusum...' Akshu said, confused.

Batsal laughed even harder. 'No, no, no—I left yours for you. I went lower down. After all, you're older than me.'

Akshu was still bewildered. 'But Kusum is older, how did Auntie let you skip her?'

'Mercifully, our *kundalis* didn't match,' Batsal said. 'I wanted to marry the younger one, and her mother didn't care about breaking order. So it's fixed.'

After Akshu congratulated Batsal for his excellent prank, Batsal said, 'Now that I'm in, Akshu, I will speak for you. This is good news.'

Akshu saw that it was, but the pain he had felt when he thought he had lost the Dalsingpada Kusum felt like a lesson to him. He had been sitting idly for nearly eight months, hoping that his aunt would initiate marital negotiations but as far as he knew, she had made no progress at all. He had to do something.

One of Akshu's friends had suggested that he send Kusum a greeting card. The Western New Year was approaching, and the custom of sending New Year's cards to friends had taken root in North Bengal. When Akshu was in Alipurduar one day, he visited a shop selling cards. He found one whose cover featured a lotus and the English words 'Happy New Year', written in glitter.

The card was blank inside, leaving Akshu the problem of filling it. Sitting in the Alipurduar field station while his bosses entered data, Akshu filed through his mind, trying to think of a classy way to express his inexplicable affection. Suddenly, the calendar on the desk caught his eye. It was written in English, and each month featured a quote or saying. While Akshu could read many of the words, he couldn't really understand them. But, he thought, how great would it be if he wrote a note in English? He flipped through the months. He found one slogan with nine words, all of which he thought he recognized, including 'dreams' and 'day', which seemed innocuous enough. This seemed like it could work!

Akshu carefully copied down the saying onto the card. He was about to seal the envelope when he worried that maybe the saying in English, whatever it meant, might be *too* subtle. Mulling it over, he decided to add a drawing. His name meant 'eyes'; Kusum's name meant 'flower'. So he drew a pair of eyes looking at a flower.

The next time Akshu happened through Dalsingpada for work, he gave the card to his cousin, a boy under 10. 'Go give this to that girl Kusum who lives over there!' he instructed. The boy ran off, presumably making the delivery.

Several days after he got back home, when he had heard no response from Dalsingpada, he suddenly realized that he wasn't that sure of the meaning of what he had written in the card—that in English, as in all languages, words often had second and third meanings in addition to the most obvious one. Kusum's first impression of him could be something entirely inappropriate! Worse, what if she showed it to her mother, and Deepika Auntie took a disliking to him? Akshu fought hard not to become despondent, but he had that sinking feeling again. He was sure that he had blown it.

15

Unsurprisingly, Madhubangaon's children ignored my advice about taking only a couple of days off for holidays. Whether or not they were Christian, they took a whole week off for Christmas. That led straight into the Gregorian New Year, which was not to go unheralded. A couple of weeks after that came Saraswati Puja, a celebration of the goddess of knowledge, and, beautifully but frustratingly, the Christian children joined the Hindus in skipping their computer classes.

I was flabbergasted by this extensive holidaying. Most of the students bunking their lab classes did not cross paths with me on a day-to-day basis but Champa, my landlord's daughter, did. Champa had been very eager to learn to use the computer but recently, as the lessons felt more like work and less like games, her interest had flagged. Akshu and I had given her a stern talking to, and she had attended a couple classes after New Year's. But now, a few days before Saraswati Puja, I again caught her skipping. That night, I saw her in the kitchen as I was heating water on the fire for a bath.

'Don't say anything,' Champa pleaded.

I stayed silent for all of 10 seconds. 'Champa, why didn't you go to the computer lab today?'

'I had to sell tickets to the Saraswati Puja,' she said. Every year, the children in Madhubangaon held a puja for the goddess of knowledge, science, music, and art in which they would sing and dance. The children would fund the talent show-slash-party with donations large and small from everyone they met. They even blocked off the main road, only allowing cars to pass if the drivers donated for the puja.

'So...you skipped a computer class to raise money for the goddess of education?' I asked.

The irony was lost on Champa. 'We still had a lot of tickets to sell!'

'Champa, what does Saraswati want from you?' I asked. 'What does she need? Does she need money from you?'

'No,' Champa said wearily, as though providing a rote response. 'She wants my faith.'

'No!' I said, realizing that my effort to speak in religious metaphor was failing. 'Saraswati does not need your faith, either. She will be fine without your faith. She is God, after all. What she wants is for you to learn. She wants you to understand the world. When you go to computer class and learn to use the computer, you are worshipping Saraswati. Then, Saraswati is happy.'

Champa may not have processed what I was saying. 'I'm the youngest in the family, and you're supposed to scold the youngest the least. Instead, you scold me the most,' she complained.

'Stop making the same mistake over and over again, and I'll stop scolding you,' I said unsentimentally. I walked out for my bucket bath, wondering if Saraswati's net effect on kids' education was positive or negative.

A month after I had restructured the classes, the multicultural holiday season came to a close. On weekends, many of the computer lab's students began showing up more regularly. But the classes that met on weekday afternoons were practically empty—often only the two 11-year-old Rabha boys who taught the class showed up, happy to have the computers to themselves.

I decided to try and understand why about 20 of the students who had signed up for the computer lab in December had failed to show up for a single class. On a day off in late January, I borrowed a bicycle to travel the three sprawling village hamlets and find as many students as I could. Akshu made me a map to locate their houses, and I left after lunch.

At each home, I would explain to the child's parents that their child was not showing up for the classes they had signed up for. Some of the parents whose children had signed up for weekend classes knew their child had been skipping classes, others didn't. Some cited the holidays, others logistics.

'Well, if your child keeps skipping classes, she won't learn. It's that simple,' I would say. Where I could find a logistical fix, I would offer one but point out, 'You should have come to tell me there was a problem. From now on, it is your responsibility to tell me if there is an issue.'

The parents whose children were supposed to be attending the weekday classes all had a straightforward answer. 'The class is from 2 PM to 4 PM, but our child does not get back from school or tuition classes until after 3:30 PM.'

I was perplexed. Back at the December informational meeting, I had asked every child to check the spreadsheet to indicate when they were available for class, and I had designed the schedule around this. I managed to ask a few of the children why they had signed up for a class time they could not attend. One student said that she had just not thought ahead to school—she had been thinking about when she would be available during the break (not that she actually attended classes during her break). The others looked as confused about why they had done this as I was. In any case, even though they had voluntarily signed up for the class, these students and their parents had never come to me to ask for a different class time.

Realizing the scheduling problem affected so many people, I said, 'I will send one of the teachers to your house to tell you what your kid's new class time will be, OK?'

Having accepted and then refused many a cup of tea, I started back toward Malabasti a little after 6 PM with the luminescent moon as my guard against elephants.

———————

The remaining challenge, then, was to rearrange the classes so that everyone could attend them. I was able to squeeze most classes into the weekend, but two classes still needed to be taught during the week at 4–6 PM. I filled these classes with students from Malabasti so that they wouldn't have to walk far to get home. That left just one problem: the three boys who taught the weekday classes had to somehow get to their homes in Taazabasti in the evenings without meeting elephants on their road back.

'Guruji, Thidey Bhaia,' I asked, 'can we find two people in the village who have motorbikes to take the teachers back? One on Tuesday, one on Thursday?'

Akshu and Thidey came up with a couple of ideas. One was Daanbir Baisya, the farmer-political leader, who had a motorbike. Daanbir's daughter was also one of the students attending the computer lab. He agreed to help when he could but made clear he wouldn't always be available. Thidey pointed out that one of the Rabha teachers had a cousin about my age with a motorbike.

We asked him to come take the young Rabha boys back once a week—he agreed but then, instead of coming himself, he sent his uncle on bicycle. The middle-aged man came to get his son and the other teacher, but he told Akshu, 'This is a little risky, going back home on bicycle at this time.'

I had one other idea. 'What about Tia Bhaia?' I asked Akshu. Tia was Hari's Bengali friend who lived in the bazaar, and he visited the house I was staying in most evenings to watch TV with Hari. When he came, he would park his motorbike out front. He, like Daanbir, was clearly better off than most of his neighbors. 'I've seen him in the lab with his son once. Maybe he would be willing to help out?'

'You can try,' Akshu said. It was his way of saying it wouldn't work. But out of other ideas, I asked Tia at Hari's house the next day if he could take the two young teachers back to Taazabasti once a week.

'That would be unsafe,' Tia said. 'There could be elephants on the road at that time.' He said they could topple his motorbike.

I knew then that the conversation was a lost cause—but I kept going anyway.

'I've never seen elephants anywhere near the village at 6,' I said. 'You could leave at 5:50, and then be back by 6:30. The risk for you would be tiny, and definitely safer than the children walking or cycling home by themselves and only getting there by 7.'

'What day of the week?' Tia asked.

'Whatever day works for you,' I said.

'My kid has tuition classes in Alipur twice a week,' Tia said. 'They end at 7 PM.'

'That's fine. That leaves three other days. Whatever day of the week you are free, we can move the class to that day,' I said.

Realizing he had picked the wrong line of excuses, Tia retreated to his original position. 'It isn't safe.'

'Tia,' I said sourly. 'How come you'll spend 40 minutes on the road after 7 PM twice a week coming back from Alipur, but you're telling me it's too dangerous to drive to Taazabasti and back before 7 PM?' Sitting beside him, Tia's friend snickered.

'I like what you are trying to do, but you do not understand what life is like here,' Tia Bhaia said. 'People don't have time, they are so busy here.'

I said sharply, 'You have time to come here and watch two hours of TV every day before I have even taken a bath. And you're saying you don't have 40 minutes to help the community once a week?'

Tia looked at me discontentedly, and I stared back. Tia agreed to try dropping the kids off a couple of times. I told him to come at 5:50 PM on Tuesday. Instead, he avoided coming to Malabasti at all that evening—not even to watch TV.

I let go. The young teachers and their parents adapted on their own. The teachers generally left half an hour early; Daanbir showed up when he could; the parents sometimes picked up their children by bicycle. Attendance and payments were still spotty, with new children appearing and disappearing at whim, and many wealthier families continued pouring their money into completely ineffective computer classes in the city so their children could get government certificates. Thanks to Thidey's efforts, the Forest Rights Committee approved a resolution requesting funds for the computer lab, but it got lost somewhere between the committee and the deputy field director's office. There was no outcry from the community about what had happened to their computer lab funding. The computer lab, instead of becoming a sustainable community institution, sputtered and operated in fits and starts.

I did observe one thing improve over the rest of my field season: as the winter subsided and the days lengthened, elephants emerged from the forests later, and the teachers missed less and less of their classes.

—————

While I was willing to confront my neighbors directly, I took a more circuitous route dealing with Buxa's governance. For a few months, I decided to document everything I could to demonstrate Buxa was not a 'good' tiger reserve. On the 67 days I collected data, I documented 29 instances of illegal activity. Most of the infractions involved felling trees or collecting firewood from the core area, but we also documented the collection of forest products by people from outside the reserve, three poachers with hunting dogs in the core area, and teams of villagers from Madhubangaon smuggling *narial* leaves and *narkale* fruit from the core. Once, we even documented a forest guard openly pushing a wheelbarrow full of wood out of the core area to the village of Jainti.

While seeing all of this saddened me, it no longer surprised me. Only one thing we found truly shocked me. One day, we took a shortcut we had never used, and we came across what could be best described as a makeshift timber mill in the middle of the core area, right next to the small road we had come on. An area the width of three or four bowling lanes had been cleared. There were dozens of wooden planks strewn on the ground. Most remarkable was the big rectangular pit at the end of the cleared space. The pit was about 3 meters long, 1.5 meters wide, and over a meter deep. I asked

Akshu what it was for. 'Some of the trees they felled were too big to carry out,' Akshu said. 'They would lay a tree across this pit and take a long [two-handed] saw. Three men would stand underneath and one man would stand on top, and they would cut planks from the wood that way.' Sawing the log perpendicular to the ground, he said, was more efficient than trying to cut the log parallel to it.

In addition to documenting these activities, I began systematically searching for evidence of tigers in Buxa. Not using camera traps—Dr Sivaganesan was right that I didn't have enough to do anything thorough—but through interviews. I basically asked as many people as I could—villagers, contractors, forest guards—whether they had seen a leopard or a tiger in Buxa and, if so, when and where. I never asked anyone's name or village, but I did take their GPS locations. I figured that I could ultimately use the responses to build a model that—based on information from other forests about tiger and leopard territorial sizes and ranging behavior and detectability—showed the probability of tigers actually existing in Buxa.

The results were amusing. Of 165 people asked about leopards, 66 said they had seen one, with six claiming they had seen one in the last day. In contrast, of the 174 people I asked about tigers, 165 said they had never seen a tiger in Buxa. Of the remaining nine, one older man said he had had a run in with a tiger in the 1980s, four said they had seen a tiger in the last year, three in about the last month, and one in the last week. And the handful of people who claimed to have seen a tiger recently— well, most of them acted kind of funny. In two separate cases, one person in a group of three claimed that all three of them had seen a tiger, only to be contradicted by his two companions. Two government contractors claimed together that they had seen a tiger twice within the last year in two totally different parts of Buxa. In contrast with these very lucky individuals, 52 of the 54 forest guards and tower watchmen we asked said they had never seen a tiger. This meant these government employees whose work required them to walk and cycle around the forest or sit in a tower in search of wildlife basically never saw these massive predators. And perhaps because the forest guards spent so much time in Buxa, they were also the most categorical with their answers.

'There aren't any tigers in Buxa,' one said with certitude.

'I've never seen a tiger or even heard a tiger's roar,' said another.

'How could tigers possibly be here?' a third asked, gesturing at the degraded forest around him.

Others were a bit more careful. 'We haven't seen any tigers,' one said snidely, 'but we will find them during the census.'

We gave a ride to a forest guard who told me in Hindi, 'No, I haven't seen a tiger, but we have found tiger scat before.' Then, he turned to Akshu in the back of the jeep and whispered in another language, 'There isn't a single tiger in Buxa—the scat we find are these little things, not from a tiger. But how can I tell Sir this?'

Perhaps most heartbreaking was how many forest guards held out hope that it was just their part of the forest that had lost its charismatic apex predator. In the core area, the watchmen at the 23-mile tower said there weren't any tigers there anymore but that they still lived in the forests north of Jainti. In Jainti, they said tigers had disappeared locally, but they heard they were still east in Rydak. In Rydak, they said the nearby forest was too degraded for tigers, but they heard there were still tigers in the core area. And everyone believed that there were still tigers in Jaldapara, the neighboring national park.

One day, Akshu and I visited Jaldapara to see if we could expand our study to include the national park. As per Jaldapara's rules, an armed forest guard accompanied us to keep us safe from rhinos and elephants. Early on, Akshu casually asked the guard if he had ever seen a tiger in the forests or grasslands of Jaldapara.

'No, there aren't any tigers left here,' the guard said. 'No one has seen them here for years. But I hear there are tigers in the forests east of here.'

'The forests east of here?' Akshu asked.

'Yes,' he said. 'In Buxa.'

Akshu nodded acceptingly. Then he turned to me, flashed his cross-eyed grin, and winked.

Armed with a plethora of circumstantial evidence demonstrating the absence of tigers in Buxa, I still didn't have a clear plan for what to do with it. I could go to Dr Sivaganesan, the Forest Department, or even the press—I wasn't sure what would be the best way to promote effective action to shape Buxa up into a real tiger reserve, or at least stop funding for Buxa that could be better spent elsewhere. What I did know was that I had no intention of sharing this information before my PhD was over. I wanted to maintain good relationships with everyone in the region's institutions for as long as possible. Plus, I hoped fervently that, by the time I finished, the Forest Department would reveal Buxa's status themselves, and I would be spared the awkwardness of trying to reveal—without conclusive evidence—an open secret.

If I *had* wanted to share the data I had collected with the Forest Department, I had plenty of opportunity. Now and then, I would meet with Deputy Field Director Petkar in Alipurduar or during his visits to Madhubangaon. Petkar wasn't shy with me about the problems of governance in Buxa. Once, I asked him about the widow who had lost a goat to a leopard during my first field season. She still hadn't received payment. 'I'm curious, how do you calculate the compensation for that? I suppose it takes time to do the investigation?'

'Yes, we don't have time for such investigations,' Petkar said. He gestured to the ludicrous pile of files on this desk. 'We are heavily understaffed. So what we ultimately do is take all the money allocated for human–wildlife conflict and'—he made a chopping motion with his hand—'just divide it by the number of requests!' He smiled at the absurdity of the process. When I told Akshu this later, he fumed—no wonder people who had really suffered depredations got so little. All the fraudsters were getting a cut, too!

One March day, I met Petkar to update him on my research. He was pleasant and charming as always, interested in my visit despite the mounds of files on his desk. His job seemed to run 24-7—his phone was always ringing, likely late into the evenings. I myself had called him once after sunset to report that my jeep had broken down in the forest, and he had quickly dispatched some men to tow us back to the village.

I was showing Petkar pictures of animals from my camera traps when, unexpectedly, Petkar said, 'I have a question for you ... you study ecology, so perhaps you will have an idea. When our men are patrolling, just by chance every year we find about three leopard carcasses in the jungle. We know from our census that there are about three times as many leopards as there are tigers.

That means that in one year we should be finding at least one tiger carcass a year. But we never find even one in a year. Do you have any idea why?'

I was startled. We both knew neither of us had ever seen a tiger in Buxa. We probably each suspected that the other suspected there were no tigers in Buxa. But aware of the risks of opposing the government's official line, neither of us had shared our suspicions. It seemed like Petkar was trying to create an opening for frank discussion…

I decided not to risk it. I shook my head dismissively, as though the question were no mystery at all. 'Animals do such strange things when they are dying,' I said. 'Most animals die quietly in obscure places. Perhaps leopards are just more likely to die somewhere accessible to people.'

Petkar studied my reaction thoughtfully. 'Well, what I thought was that … there are so many people in Buxa all the time. Maybe other people find the tiger corpses and take the skin and parts to sell them before our forest guards have a chance to find them.'

I stared at Petkar for another moment, and then I began nodding slowly, trying to hide my bewilderment. Here was a deputy field director of Buxa Tiger Reserve who admitted he had never seen a live tiger in the park. Furthermore, he admitted that while his employees occasionally found dead leopards, they never found *dead* tigers, either. He admitted that the borders of Buxa were not secure, and that people were omnipresent in the park. He observed that these trespassers would find it profitable to sell tiger parts, and even that they would be able to escape the forest with these parts in tow without being detected. Was he trying to draw me into an open discussion?

My own reticence surprised me—I was so willing to speak directly with villagers, and though I thought

I believed in treating everyone equally, here I was, exceedingly reluctant to speak my mind. This man was friendly, and we had rapport. He worked hard and seemed to want to do his job well. As an individual, I had no quarrel with him. But a part of me was unwilling to challenge the power hierarchy Petkar represented. 'Yes,' I said finally. 'I suppose that is possible, too.'

Petkar, perhaps sensing I would go no further, changed his approach. 'You know, I've worked in many places, many forests, and Buxa is a very difficult place. You live with Nepalis—you are lucky, for their food isn't so spicy, and their village is neat and organized. But the tea gardens are a different matter. All these people have come from Bihar and Jharkhand and Assam, and they put a great deal of pressure on the forest, you know? They hunt and chop trees and collect all these NTFPs. Especially with the tea business struggling, the workers look to the forest for resources, and they are difficult to control.'

I murmured something, trying to be agreeable without reinforcing ethnic stereotypes.

'And then, there's the forest guards. They're all over 50 years old! And most are very unfit. None of them can run a kilometer after a poacher.'

Finally, my curiosity surmounted my caution. 'So why don't you replace them with younger, fitter guards? If they're not able to do their job, shouldn't they be replaced?'

Petkar replied with a smile of one whose exasperation had matured into bemusement. 'It's impossible to fire any of them! The forest guards have a very strong union with strong support from the government, so we can't even replace the bad ones. And we can't afford to hire more able staff while maintaining the older ones. We IFS [Indian Forestry Service] officers have to somehow make a difference with all these sickly and aged staff—and that too, within two to three years, because after that, we'll be transferred.'

'I didn't realize that's why the forest guards are so old,' I said finally. 'There should be some way to change that and hire young local people to chase out the poachers.'

Petkar smiled at my idealism. 'Yes. But that will be difficult.'

I understood what Petkar was trying to communicate. Maybe the problems in Buxa weren't because of any one person's mismanagement or some giant conspiracy to keep capturing funds for tiger conservation; maybe it was just a series of structural problems generated by complicated politics. Perhaps the Forest Department was tired of being the butt of everyone's blame for the natural consequences of extractive colonial policies and tumultuous postcolonial democracy.

But still—a tiger reserve without tigers!? Was there any surer sign that something needed to be done? And shouldn't I be doing something? I left Mr Petkar, uncertain about whether my reticence to speak truth was prudent or cowardly, and what if anything could salvage what was left of Buxa's jungles.

16

When Raghurajan and Akshu arrived at the scene of destruction in the corn season of 2003, they didn't say a word. It was horrible to see. An elephant had attacked a hut built on the ground in Taazabasti, the hamlet across the bazaar from Akshu's home. He had broken the bamboo-mud-dung wall of the house and trampled both a father and his 10-year-old son while the older son, about 15, managed to escape. The thatched roof had collapsed onto the victims. Presumably after the trampling, the elephant had eaten some rice and taken salty ashes from the hearth. Neighbors had emerged to see a peculiar-looking tusker—with one tusk bent toward the sky (*akash*) and the other toward the underworld (*patal*)—fleeing the area.

The neighboring villagers had recovered the bodies. Akshu saw the father's face, flattened like a roti. Brain was oozing from his head. It was the worst corpse he had ever seen, but it was when he saw the dead child that his heart broke.

The Taazabasti villagers watched as the elephant researchers looked around in silence until one of them, an Adivasi like the victims, began to yell. 'Here are the elephant people! *Sala*!' he said, his voice quivering with anger. 'They go into the jungle, the elephants' home, and they put collars on them—they disturb the elephants, and now we have more problems with elephants than ever before!'

Some of the others agreed. 'Before you started working here, things weren't as bad—now they're killing more people, they're damaging more crops—it's your fault!'

The villagers were speaking in local languages, and Raghurajan, a Tamilian, may not have really understood what was being said. But others saw Akshu and recognized that he must be suffering from the same growing alarm as them.

'Things are getting worse,' they said. 'An elephant killed two of your Nepali people in Malabasti, and another woman was killed in Baamnibasti, just in the last months. They have never been this violent before. You work with elephants,' they said, implying he worked with the elites. 'Please tell the government to do something. Our situation has become very difficult.'

More combative individuals in the crowd shouted, 'If we see an elephant, we will shoot it! They are killing us!'

Akshu looked again at the slain child, and he felt the anger, sorrow, and fear of the other villagers. While he found it plausible that there might be karmic justice in an adult facing death at the hands of an elephant, he did not believe any child could deserve such a violent and untimely end. This kid was not old enough to have gone to the jungle to steal wood or the foods eaten by elephants—what justification could any god have for his killing? Akshu also felt for the boy who had survived, who would now be orphaned and brotherless, who would have to depend on the unreliable sympathy of others to make it through his youth. The destruction wrought by the elephant was completely unnecessary; if Akash Patal had just eaten some crops and left, the villagers might even have done a puja in the elephant's honor and made a religious offering of the loss. Now, even the most devout in the community seemed to sense the deep injustice this elephant had bestowed.

This elephant, Akshu felt, needed to be pursued and beaten badly—it should be half-killed. It had to be punished for killing people, including an innocent child, so it would be less likely to repeat its crime.

Yet, despite Akshu's distress at the injustice, he couldn't muster the same kind of anger toward all elephants, or even all male elephants, that he had felt when he was younger. He remembered watching elephant calves playing in the forest, and how one young calf would run at the vehicle trumpeting and waving its ears, realize it was still afraid of the stationary vehicle, turn dramatically, and run back to its mother. He recalled standing on a debilitated tusker that was at his mercy, pouring buckets of water on the magnificent creature to keep it alive. He remembered the mother elephant that died trying to save her child from a train, and how the calf returned to its dying mother for milk—and that he and all the villagers around him were constantly taking things from the jungle, things that the elephants needed to eat and to live...

Although Akshu wanted something done to the perpetrator, he wanted a balanced approach—but the decision to lobby the Forest Department to do something was Raghurajan's to make. The researcher did not seem to be egging them into action. Raghurajan instructed Akshu to measure the elephant's footprints where the ground was soft, and the team left.

But then the horrible event repeated itself in Taazabasti. A tusker again toppled the home of an Adivasi family built on the ground. This time, the father escaped as his wife and children were smothered. Nearby villagers quickly responded and yelled and went to get weapons—the tusker calmly rummaged through what was left of the house and then escaped into the darkness. Again, the villagers reported that the tusker had a tusk pointing upwards and one facing downwards. Akshu's measurements of the elephant's front footprints matched those of the prior attacker.

This time, the villagers pled directly with Forest Department officers for help. When this didn't yield results, the villagers went to the Forest Department range office and protested. 'Do something!' they demanded. 'Stop this from happening again! This elephant has gone crazy!' These protestors now blamed the problem not on elephants in general, but on a particular individual: Akash Patal.

The Forest Department's ears finally stood up. They decided to track this so-called Akash Patal and see if he caused any more trouble. The Forest Department summoned Arjun Oraon to lead the search. In addition, the Forest Department informed Raghurajan that the NIES research team was to accompany them to collar the suspected elephant. Within the day, the NIES team received word that an elephant had killed someone in Nimati, and they were asked to help the Forest Department identify the elephant.

The NIES team arrived in Nimati as evening fell. Akshu and Raghurajan measured the footprint, and they interviewed the villagers who had seen the destruction of the hut, which again rested on the ground. The villagers again reported tusks pointing to the sky and to the ground; again, the footprint measurements matched the prior attacker's.

The string of deaths by elephant continued, first in Chuapara and then in Gopal Bahadur Basti, some 15 kilometers from Nimati. Oraon's team, now including four Forest Department vehicles and the NIES jeep, drove to the site of each attack. In each site, the measurements and the descriptions matched those of Akash Patal, and Oraon made a startling observation:

the elephant's footprints suggested that he had knocked down the wall on one side of the house and then moved to the side with an exit, intercepting the occupants as they fled. Perhaps, Oraon thought, this was the serial killer's method.

This elephant, Akshu mused, did not seem to distinguish night from day—he covered great distances, he did not seem to sleep. In contrast, the Forest Department took long meals and lots of cigarette and bidi breaks. They joked and laughed, exhibiting a laziness Akshu had long associated with the Forest Department. The Department had not authorized the use of captive elephants for the operation, so the team couldn't even track Akash Patal off-road. The officials didn't exactly move as though they were in charge of finding a potential serial killer. Akshu thought that Oraon, whom he admired, must be stifled by his less motivated colleagues. For his part, Oraon felt they needed incontrovertible evidence before he would consider appealing for lethal action against an elephant. He had spent his whole life trying to save wildlife—he was terrified of killing an innocent elephant, including one that might have killed a human by accident.

Suddenly, the tenor of the search changed. The elephant made the mistake of killing a politically influential man in Madharihat. His followers were furious, and they held a protest. The Forest Department, feeling the pressure, authorized Oraon's team to use two captive elephants to track the murderer off road.

Meanwhile, the next elephant attack was in Dalmore, over 50 kilometers away from Madhubangaon. The caravan—which now included around 10 vehicles—went to that area and, finally, they found fresh tracks of the right size and fresh dung just outside a forest patch where the alleged murderer was likely sheltering. The Forest Department called for captive elephants, but Akash Patal left the area before they arrived. A witness saw Akash Patal heading through the tea gardens toward Moraghat. The caravan arrived to find another person had been killed— this time, the elephant had yanked someone from the second-floor porch where he had been sleeping. The Forest Department's higher-ups finally gave Oraon permission to kill the elephant, assuming Oraon could determine beyond a shadow of a doubt that the elephant he was killing was the murderer. Jeeps were sent to Chalsa to pick up a marksman, revealing that the caravan of 10 forest vehicles didn't already include someone with that skill.

Oraon and the NIES team reviewed the evidence that a single elephant, one with tusks pointing to heaven and hell, was responsible for all the killings. Everyone was nervous. What if, after killing Akash Patal, the killings of villagers continued? What if they killed an innocent elephant *and* failed to stop the slaughter?

But it was too late to try and take conservative action. If Akash Patal was found but allowed to live another day, the next killing would certainly be seen as the responsibility of the government.

With the jeeps driving along on the nearest roads, Oraon led the captive elephants after the murderer. Soon, Oraon found an elephant with tusks askew on a dirt road. The marksman loaded his gun and waited for Oraon to give the order. 'Is this the elephant to be shot, Sir?' an officer asked. Oraon, tears streaming down his face, prayed that he was shooting the right elephant. The officer asked two more times before, finally, Oraon responded. 'Yes. This is him.' The marksman fired. Akash Patal fell right away, but he stood back up, swaying. Oraon worried he would charge. The marksman fired once more. Akash Patal, hit again, tried to walk off the road. The marksman fired a third time. And Akash Patal fell, never to rise again.

To Oraon's great relief, the stream of villager killings at the trunks and feet of elephants ceased. At first, Akshu was also relieved—he would not be associated with the unjust execution of an elephant. But over time, Akshu grew angry at the government. He realized that, even before the killings in Taazabasti and the following killings to the west, there had been a slate of elephant attacks east of his village in Sankosh, Newlands, Dhoulajoda, Jainti Tea Estate—and that it was quite likely that these killings, too, were by Akash Patal. But the Forest Department hadn't launched an investigation then. It wasn't until the Forest Department faced political protests that they took action. Some 10 villagers' lives were lost before the Forest Department provided the resources and attention necessary to deal with the problem.

If only, Akshu thought, the Forest Department took villagers seriously. And not just the value of their lives. If the Forest Department officials had asked him for suggestions on how to save people while protecting innocent elephants, he would have given them good ideas, Akshu could have encouraged them to provide the captive elephants as soon as possible, to begin tracking the killer elephant off-road from Nimati onwards. But he knew that wasn't what they wanted from him. They wanted him to go when they said go; sleep when they said sleep; eat when they said eat. The Forest Department's people seemed to think that low-class people had only low-class minds, and Akshu had felt no power to influence the outcome.

It was around Western New Year's Day, 2003, when a neighborhood boy in Dalsingpara ran up to Kusum. 'Kusum Didi!' he said. 'Take this card!'

'How cute,' Kusum thought. Her little neighbor was giving her a card. Then it occurred to her that the kid probably didn't have the money to purchase such a gift. '*Bhai*, who is this from?'

'Akshu Daju!' chirped the boy, and he ran off, gleeful at having completed his task.

Kusum was shocked. She had heard from several friends that this Akshu fellow, the goofy-looking guy whom she had seen first at the tea plantation, was interested in her, but this was a very unorthodox move. What would the neighbors say? She was afraid of gossip that might suggest she was in some sort of clandestine romance. Such a rumor could damage her family's reputation and ruin her chances at an honorable marriage.

She thought about returning the card ... but ... maybe he was just giving it as a friend, after all? Kusum was too curious to send the card back. She opened the envelope. The card inside contained a hand-written note in English. Kusum didn't know a lick of English. She'd have to get it translated. But she also saw the drawing—a picture of two eyes looking at a flower. That message was less ambiguous.

'Ma.' She found her mother in the kitchen with her sister and cousin. 'This boy sent me a card.'

Deepika took the card, and the others gathered around. Soon, everyone was laughing.

'Looks like this boy can't get his eyes off this flower!' Kusum's cousin laughed heartily.

Kusum felt embarrassed. 'What kind of boy goes around handing cards out on the street?' she asked.

'Well, obviously, he likes you,' Deepika said. She had heard from Akshu's *mami* that he was interested in Kusum, and she was rather charmed by Akshu's effort. 'That's why he gave it to you.'

Kusum's interest was effectively piqued, but she didn't want to give the impression that a silly card had won her over. 'Well, he's a Brahmin, and we're Brahmins,' Kusum said. 'Why didn't he have the guts to just come to our house and express interest in the normal way?'

As news of Kusum's card spread through the community and more people were laughing about Akshu's gimmick, Deepika also began to get nervous that the gossip could turn malicious. She visited Akshu's *mama* and *mami* to ask that Akshu make a formal expression of interest.

As her mother worked to diffuse the risk of rumors, Kusum became more curious about what was written in the card. She got a cousin who knew some English to translate it for her. 'Hold on to your dreams,' he said, 'your day will come.'

Kusum decided that she liked the card, and she kept it. As far as her dreams were concerned, they were fairly straightforward—she'd been working in the tea gardens since she was a child, and she wanted out. No more picking little leaves in the blistering mid-day sun; no more inhaling the pesticides sprayed and the dust blown off the dirt paths in the dry seasons. It was tedious work, and she was sick of it. The one marriage proposal she'd received so far was from a man who lived alongside a tea garden, so she'd turned that down.

Kusum's feelings toward this Akshu fellow were fairly neutral. When she had seen the lanky, cross-eyed fellow approach with Shiv some eight months ago, she had not felt the instant attraction he had—in fact, when her friends began talking about his interest, she had initially laughed at the idea of marrying him. But Kusum's friend from Madhubangaon urged her to consider him. 'He's a good boy,' she told Kusum. 'Marry him, it'll be good for you.' Kusum knew that

Akshu's family lived nowhere near the tea estates, so she decided to keep an open mind.

Some time later, Kusum attended a wedding in Taazabasti, not far from Akshu's home. Sure enough, he was there, too. She noticed him put himself into conversations where she could hear him without directly speaking with him. He didn't stare at her; he was at ease in conversation. Initially, she was relieved at how considerate he was—that he was not too forward. But then he surprised her.

'When'd you get here?' he asked her directly.

'Today,' she said simply.

'Oh...' he said, 'so, I'm taking your sister and Batsal to Cooch Behar. We're going to just wander around there. You should come too!'

Kusum looked beside her—sure enough, her sister Rupa and her new husband Batsal stood there, smiling. Akshu's move was clever; having her sister with them would likely prevent criticism or rumors of promiscuity, and it would give her and Akshu some opportunity to get to know each other. But Kusum was unconvinced. Too many people knew he was interested in her. It could still be seen as a romantic premarital date. 'No,' Kusum said. 'I'll go home instead.'

Akshu was disappointed, but he understood that Kusum might just be of the cautious variety. He appreciated her seriousness, and he knew all was not lost. He spent the day with Batsal and Rupa.

When Rupa went home, she launched a full-throated endorsement of Akshu. 'He's a very good boy, Ma!' she told her mother. 'I've asked several people who know him well. He doesn't do drugs. He doesn't even drink alcohol. They say he would never beat his wife—he is kind and gentle. His family is nice, his house is OK. He looks after his father and respects his mother. He spoke very nicely with me. Batsal likes him.' She turned to Kusum. 'You should marry him.'

Kusum smirked, 'Don't worry, I'm already considering him because he doesn't live near any tea.'

Their mother took the endorsement more seriously. She had Akshu's *mami* over and they discussed the kind of life Kusum would have if she lived in Madhubangaon. Deepika learned about Akshu's temporary position as a research assistant and his eighth standard education. 'They have land, and they have cattle,' Mami told Deepika. 'So Kusum would have to plant rice and corn and collect cow dung. She'll always have enough to eat, but she'll have to work. Could she do that kind of work?'

'Yes, my daughter can do that kind of work,' Deepika said proudly.

Soon, Deepika heard that Akshu had been invited to a wedding she was attending in Dalsingpara in March. She took the opportunity to meet Akshu. He was with Moksha and a couple other friends. 'Akshu,' she said.

'Yes, Auntie?' Akshu responded respectfully.

'Why did you send that card? It isn't proper, you know.'

Akshu apologized. 'I'm sorry, I didn't mean it that way.'

'Are you interested in marrying my daughter?'

'Yes, Auntie,' Akshu said. 'I'm sincerely interested.'

From Kusum's perspective, things then proceeded rapidly. Kusum's mother asked her if she would be willing to marry him. 'If your *kundalis* match,' Deepika said, 'and you agree, I'll marry you to him.'

Kusum felt truly ambivalent—everyone had told her just how nice and responsible and wonderful this guy was, but she didn't feel any passion for him. She'd scarcely exchanged a dozen words with him. But she was willing to let the chips fall as they may.

The two *kundalis* were a match. Deepika declared that if Akshu could bring his parents to the engagement, she would marry her daughter off to this lively and popular young man.

———

The wedding took place quickly, at Deepika's request—Akshu and Kusum were married on 6 July 2003. As was customary, they held the first part of the wedding at the bride's home in Dalsingpara, drawing some 200 guests from the tea estates. Then, they migrated to Madhubangaon for the rest of the ceremony, where the Atris' neighbors joined in. To pay for his family's share of the wedding, Akshu took a loan of around ₹3,500, again at 10 per cent interest per month. Overall, the Atris' side of the wedding cost ₹12,000 to ₹13,000, equivalent of about five months of Akshu's salary. Akshu's family, Chander excepted, all pitched in. The Atris fed around 200 guests with paneer, dals, chutneys, and popadam. No animals were killed for fear that it would taint the auspicious occasion.

If Satyavati, Motikar, and Deepika were looking for a sign that they had successfully fulfilled their duty as parents, they got it. For months, the Public Works Department had been stringing poles and power lines around the village. Thidey excitedly bought light bulbs and fixtures and installed them around the house. The PWD activated the connection the very day of Akshu and Kusum's wedding, catapulting the community to within reach of the 21st century; magical glass bulbs illuminated the evening events of Kusum's first night in Madhubangaon. Kusum, whose home in Dalsingpada hadn't had any electricity, was enthralled. Wedding guests cautioned the Atris that using so much power would cost them handsomely, but the Atris couldn't resist the beauty of the symbolism—the lights shined on. Ultimately, the electricity cost the Atris no more than operating their kerosene lamps.

'I have something I want to tell you,' Akshu told Kusum not long after the wedding. Then he told her about his childhood friend Kusum, how her mother had yelled at him, and how she had been taken away and married off. He confessed he had liked her in the past, but that now they only spoke briefly, as friends, if ever they met at all. And he showed her the picture he had of Malabasti Kusum. 'She gave me this picture back when she was still living here. Would you prefer that I get rid of it?'

Kusum said it was up to him. Akshu tore up the photo up in front of her and threw it away. 'From today, it's just you,' he said. And if it is in fact possible to fully let go of an unresolved past romantic interest, from that day onward, Akshu showed every sign of having done so.

17

With less than six months of field work left in Buxa, I turned my attention away from the socioeconomic issues of the village and the political intrigues of the tiger reserve. I felt overwhelmed by everything that seemed broken in Buxa and flustered by my inability to understand what my village neighbors really wanted or how I could help.

So I decided to focus fully on my research. I reasoned that I was employing local people in ways that didn't hurt the jungle and learning skills I could use to promote conservation in the future. People who participated in local conservation projects or ecological research often became champions for wildlife. I thought that might best explain why Akshu, whose life, livelihood, and property were still threatened by wildlife, seemed to advocate for other species to be protected. Obviously, Akshu and his neighbors had an affinity for wildlife and intact ecosystems that had nothing to do with outsiders, but they were probably more likely to act on that affinity once liberated from economic distress.

The last big component of my fieldwork provided plenty of opportunity to employ people. My team's observations in the forest had determined that elephants, Rhesus macaques, and domestic cattle and buffaloes ate most of the fruit of the tree species we were studying, and we had collected movement data on these animals. Now, I needed to learn what happened to seeds eaten by elephants. Primarily, I needed to measure what per cent of seeds made it past an elephant's teeth and ultimately into its dung, as well as how long elephants carried the seeds they ate.

The best way to get these data was through feeding trials. The Forest Department gave us permission to feed fruits to captive elephants throughout Buxa. We would then collect every dung pile from those elephants and search for seeds until none appeared for at least 36 hours. By ensuring the elephants didn't eat any *chalta* fruits before or after the feeding, we could estimate how long seeds took to make it through an elephant's gut and what proportion of seeds survived the journey.

All this was easy to understand but hard to do. The elephants had to take long walks at least every other day to collect some of the hundreds of kilograms of food they needed daily. After we fed them the *chalta* fruit, we had to follow them wherever they went and collect their sizeable poop. Digging out all the seeds in all the dung produced by two elephants each day was tough. Finding the *chalta*'s little 6-millimeter seeds could easily take a couple of people an hour per dung pile. And each of the captive elephants in Buxa produced several kilograms of dung between 7 and 14 times a day.

So once we had fed *chalta* fruit to two elephants, Joda and Sanjushri, in the village of Malangi, I had to employ about 20 people: mahouts to manage the elephants, my field assistants to collect and label the dung, and a team of part-time dung openers led by Akshu. Except for a brief period around dinner time, I and my regular assistants were essentially on the job around the clock, even spending our nights with the elephants so we could retrieve dung before they stepped on it.

I missed being in the jungle, but I was glad to be near elephants. Sanjushri was an old, almost toothless female with the sweet disposition of a contented grandmother. Sometimes, I would stroke the soft, wrinkled skin on her cheek or trunk; she would lift her trunk and beg for food. When she carefully lowered her trunk and pressed it against my hand, I realized just how effortlessly she could snap my arm in two. But the mahouts were completely unconcerned that Sanjushri might be violent.

Joda was another matter. The tusker, though only about 20 years old, was bigger than his elderly companion, and had apparently at the age of 8 knocked down and injured a mahout. As a result, except for the two to four hours every two days when Joda was taken out to bathe in the river or collect food, Joda's back legs were bound together by chains to prevent him from kicking or moving suddenly. Instead of simply walking, he had to hop-shimmy. Aside from when the mahouts fed or bathed Joda, it was hard to see much joy in his life. An elephant's natural prerogative—to explore the world, to have a vibrant social life—was out of his reach.

Dismayed, I gently broached the topic with the mahouts. They shrugged. The Forest Department never paid for their injuries, they said, and they had been given scarcely any training or facilities to care for the elephants. 'We still get paid only ₹3,000 a month,' said Vinod, an engaging Bengali man with a round face. 'It's nothing. We have to look after the elephants 24 hours a day, seven days a week. There are no holidays. The prices of some foodstuffs have doubled. The salaries of all government employees are supposed to have increased, but ours have not. The Forest Department is eating our salaries. Instead of fixing the toilets in our government housing, they'll put on a fifth new layer of paint on their own houses. We have to collect the leaking waste in buckets.'

I realized that I'd been naive. On some level, I had assumed that villagers became mahouts because they loved animals, like many American zookeepers. Some mahouts I would meet matched that description. But as Vinod spoke, it dawned on me that most of the mahouts had taken this job because it was all they could get. They had been forced by poverty and circumstance into dealing hands-on with deadly, four-ton creatures day-in, day-out, with insufficient equipment, little pay, and no insurance.

A week of collecting and digging through Joda's and Sanjushri's dung for *chalta* seeds passed. While I was monitoring the elephants on Saturday afternoon, Narad called to inform me that there had been no seeds in the elephants' dung for over 36 hours. The trial was finally over! All we had to do was open any dung backlogged from earlier in the feeding trial, and we would have all our data. Feeling liberated, I decided to join Joda and Sanjushri for their bath in the river, about 1.5 kilometers from Malangi.

At the river, the mahouts rechained Joda's back feet and prodded him toward the water with bull hooks. As I watched, I noticed two mahouts, Saurav and Anoop, on their knees next to a fresh pile of Joda's dung. They started to open it, looking for *chalta* seeds. 'No need to do that,' I told them. 'The work is over. The seeds are finished.'

'But here's a seed!' Anoop said a minute later. I looked at him, confused, and went over. Before my eyes, Anoop and Saurav each salvaged another seed from Joda's dung. I held the three pale, hairy seeds in my hand. My head spun. 'How could seeds suddenly appear after almost two days of absence?' I thought. The literature-recommended 36 hours had passed since the last seed had been found in Joda's dung, which meant he should be harboring no more seeds in his gut. I tried to come up with excuses to dismiss these seeds. 'They look different,' I said. 'They're white.'

'They're definitely *chalta* seeds,' Saurav said. This was true. I looked at the mahouts in suspicion. Could they have planted the seeds? The mahouts were paid by the day. They had an incentive to extend the trial, which was well-paying and easy work for them. All they were expected to do was keep the elephants from eating more fruit and keep us safe as we retrieved the dung. But I didn't have any evidence they had broken our agreement. I snuck off to the side and called Akshu on the Blackcherry cell phone he had lent me.

'Bring the seeds here,' he said calmly. 'Let me see them.'

I told the mahouts that I had to run home to prepare for another day of work given their recent finding. I told them that I would be back for the night.

As I loaded the bags of dung from the morning, I saw the mahouts Rohan and Vinod. I told them what had happened.

Then, I looked at them confidingly. 'Did someone feed the elephants another *chalta* fruit?'

'No, no. You've entrusted us with this work. Why would we betray that trust?' Vinod asked. He looked so earnest. I wanted to believe him. I got in the vehicle and drove to Madhubangaon.

'These seeds are fresh-fresh,' Akshu told me. Thidey and I leaned over his extended hand. 'On the first day or two after we fed the elephants, the seeds we retrieved from the dung looked like this, white-white. After several days in the elephant's gut, the seeds look dark red or black.'

'Maybe Joda found a fruit on the path and gobbled it up before the mahouts saw it. Or the mahouts saw it but didn't report it out of fear of upsetting you,' Thidey suggested. Akshu, our elephant dung forensic expert, observed that there was no evidence of the actual fruit remains in the dung. The chalta fruit has three layers—a tough outer peel that Akshu had taken to calling the fruit's 'bark', a crunchy pulp beneath that, and a gooey mass of seed pods at the core. The bark showed up in elephant dung within a day or two after the fruit was eaten. The bark would then stop appearing while the seeds continued to surface.

'They must have fed the elephant only the seeds. They probably mixed the seeds in with the elephants' evening meal,' Narad asserted. I worried that the mahouts had done this multiple times previously—and that my data were altogether useless.

'Why are you paying them by the day, instead of giving a flat payment?' Thidey asked.

'Well, we weren't sure how long the trial would last, and I wanted them to stay interested the whole trial. And since we are with them most of the time, I thought they would cooperate.' We had also worked with these mahouts once the previous year, and I had come to trust that they weren't the type to sabotage the trial and jeopardize our relationship.

'How about Narad and I go over there and talk to them,' suggested Akshu. 'We'll ask them to tell us what happened. They may open up to us, since we too are villagers and they've known us for longer. We'll promise they won't be punished if they tell the truth.' I agreed.

I was eating dinner at Akshu's when he and Narad returned. Akshu laughed when I asked him what happened at Malangi. 'They fed the elephants the seeds,' he said confidently. I asked if they had admitted it.

'As soon as we got there, we met two of the mahouts. We explained to them that we had found seeds in the elephant dung, and that maybe someone had fed the elephants a fruit. Right away, they said, 'No, but you didn't find any of the *chalta*'s bark, right? If the elephant had eaten the fruit, you would have found bark in the dung!'

I laughed. 'That was some fast thinking!'

Akshu nodded, 'Exactly. I then explained to them that while seeds that came out a day or two after an elephant had been fed are white, older seeds are dark, and I showed them some example seeds. At this point, Rohan looked up and said, "Aaah, yes, there must have been some sort of cheating here."'

Rohan, the only ethnic Rabha of the six mahouts, was rather the outcast of the group. I also felt he was honest. 'What did the others say?' I asked.

'They were silent for a bit. Then one of them suggested that perhaps some of the lads in the village had been eating *chalta* with salt near where Joda was tied up. He suggested that the lads had just thrown the seed mass onto the ground—and that maybe Joda had sucked up the seed mass while no one was looking. But then such people would have dropped the bark there, and we searched but couldn't find any *chalta* bark anywhere. Still, the mahouts stuck to their story.'

I sighed, beginning to feel heavy. 'So, we don't know exactly what happened.'

'No,' Akshu said, digging into his food. 'But I think they fed Joda those seeds. They mixed the seeds in with his rice to extend the trial. I'm pretty sure of it.'

Initially, I was very clear-minded about my priorities in this situation: I had invested hundreds of dollars and great effort into this feeding trial, and I needed to know if the data were usable. If Joda had been fed additional fruits just once shortly before we found an unexpected resurgence of seeds in his dung, then that would suggest that Joda's gut had been emptied of the seeds from the feeding trial, and we could basically ignore the seeds we had found on Saturday. On the other hand, if the mahouts had fed the elephants *chalta* seeds multiple times, then the data would be unsalvageable—it would be impossible to distinguish the seeds from the feeding trial from the seeds the mahouts had been surreptitiously feeding Joda and Sanjushri.

I was unclear on whether I should pay the mahouts. On the one hand, I sympathized with them: the Forest Department gave them little pay and less respect for the dangerous and never-ending work of caring for shackled elephants. Despite our late nights together and heart-to-heart conversations—and despite the generous pay I offered—they surely saw me as just another elite with resources to spare. I, of course, felt a little betrayed, but I wanted to be sensitive to the realities the mahouts faced: it was unfair to expect them to be strait-laced in a world that was obviously unfair to them.

On the other hand, one or more of the mahouts had deliberately done the exact opposite of what I was paying them to do. For me to pretend they were incapable of moral action just because they were poor—wouldn't that be the most patronizing, disrespectful thing I could do? Shouldn't I treat them just as I would anyone else who agreed to do a job and deliberately botched it?

The day after the seeds were found, I asked Akshu what the norms were in such a situation. Akshu didn't see poverty as a good reason for dishonesty. 'Sir, here you are not obligated to give them anything after such cheating,' he said.

Of course, there were six mahouts, and it would be unfair for me to withhold payment from those who hadn't participated in the illicit feeding. How could I find out if my data were salvageable? And how would I figure out which of the mahouts had broken our agreement?

Suddenly, it hit me. In my first college biology course, my professor had explained the prisoner's dilemma, a game theory scenario meant to help scientists understand whether people and other animals would cooperate with each other. In the scenario, two criminals suspected of breaking the law are questioned in separate rooms by the police. The suspects (who are guilty) have two choices: to 'cooperate' with each other and lie to the police, or to 'defect' and sell their partner out to the police for leniency. If both suspects cooperate with each other, the police won't have enough evidence to really punish them. But if one defects, the defector will get off and the cooperator will be severely punished. If both criminals defect, they will still be punished but not as severely (since they agreed to help the police). Researchers wanted to know whether the suspects were likely to cooperate with each other. After numerous models and experiments, game theorists concluded that defection was the more rational strategy. As long as each suspect didn't know what the other was up to, their fear that their partner would defect would cause them to defect themselves.

Maybe, I thought, if I questioned each person individually and offered to reward honesty, I could triangulate the testimonies and figure out what happened.

Two days after we discovered the illicit seeds, I and several assistants appeared in Malangi around sunset, unannounced. The mahouts were asked to come meet me. Anoop was already there—so I asked him to climb into the jeep's back seat. 'Can't we wait for the others?' he asked nervously.

'I'm going to talk to each of you alone,' I assured him. 'You might as well be first.' Narad sat in the front. Akshu sat in the back with Anoop and me, ready to provide translation if my Hindi got choppy. I sent a third assistant to sit with the other mahouts near the fire and make sure they didn't agree to a common story while I conducted other interviews.

I began each interrogation by presenting the evidence that Joda had been deliberately fed seeds from a *chalta* fruit—the 50-hour gap between seeds, their white color, the lack of a believable alternative explanation. I told them that the flagrant violation of our agreement meant I was not obligated to pay them for their work.

'But I need to know exactly when and how the elephants were fed to correct my data. So here's what I will do. I'm going to ask you five questions. If you answer them honestly, I will give you your full pay. If you lie, and we figure that out from the other interviews, you will not receive your pay. I don't care if you are the one who fed the elephants the seeds—as long as you tell me the truth now, you will still get your full week's pay.'

I had Akshu make sure Anoop understood, and I asked the first question. 'Whose idea was it to feed the elephants the seeds?' Anoop gawked and said he didn't know that the elephants had even been fed seeds to. I pressed on. 'Which elephants did you all feed the seeds?'

Anoop began to shake his head. Then, suddenly, he cracked. 'Joda,' he said. 'They fed Joda.' His whole body slumped, and he stopped his slight trembling.

'Not Sanjushri?' I asked eagerly.

'No, just Joda. Listen, don't tell anyone I said this,' he pleaded.

'I won't. Everything you say here will be kept secret,' I assured him, making a mental note to add that to my speech. The mahouts were prone to drunken brawls, and I certainly didn't want truth-tellers to be punished for their honesty. 'Now, whose idea was it to feed the elephants seeds?'

'Someone in Joda's team,' he said. 'Kiran or Saurav. They did it.'

'How many times did they feed Joda extra seeds?'

'Oh,' he said, 'Just once. The last evening, during the mealtime.' Akshu looked at me knowingly.

'How many seeds did they feed the elephant?'

'The seeds from one fruit.'

'How was Joda fed the seeds?'

'They were mixed in with his rice and banana leaves.'

'How do you know all this?'

'Rohan told me on Friday evening.'

I assured Anoop he would get his payment in secret and asked him to send in Vinod next.

If Anoop had raised my hopes that this would be resolved cleanly, Vinod and Kiran dashed those hopes. My speech did not impress them. Kiran insisted that some local fellow eating a *chalta* had discarded the seeds near Joda, who had just sucked them up. He also said he had not seen this happen, as failing to stop such a feeding would have made it his fault. Vinod just said he couldn't report on something he hadn't seen. Lokhan, the fourth mahout, pointed out that he had not been in town the day of the scandal, but he offered to call if he heard anything.

During all these interviews, Rohan had been hovering nervously around the vehicle, just out of earshot.

I called him in and gave him a modified speech. 'Look, I know you're a hard worker,' I said. 'And I know that since you are Rabha and not Bengali or Adivasi, you face difficulties here. Would you be in danger if you told the truth?'

Rohan eagerly answered. 'The other day, when you asked if someone had fed Joda the seeds, my heart ached because I wanted to tell you the truth—but I couldn't, because others were right there. But I have to tell the truth...'

'We'll do whatever we can to protect you,' I assured him. 'Whatever you say will be kept secret...'

'Secret or not, it is fine,' he said. 'Kiran and Saurav fed Joda at a little after 4 PM, after you left that Friday. I heard them talking about it that evening. They only fed Joda, and they mixed the seeds in with his rice and leaves.' He told me that to his knowledge, it had only been once—but he couldn't know for sure what had been done previously.

I thanked Rohan and sent him out, asking for Saurav. I really wanted a confession from this last mahout. Both Rohan and Anoop had said he was directly involved in illicitly feeding Joda. If he admitted it, I could feel sure about what I knew.

'Whose idea was it to feed the elephants those *chalta* seeds?' I asked him.

'I don't know of anyone having done that. No one fed them seeds. Sometimes boys around here eat *chalta*. They must have thrown the seed mass next to Joda.'

'Did you see them do this?'

'No, no I didn't see this.'

'So, on Saturday, you didn't know that Joda had eaten seeds on Friday?'

'No.'

'Then why did you open Joda's dung on Saturday? I told you that the trial was over, but you still pulled apart his dung looking for seeds.'

He was clearly startled. 'Just like that.'

'"Just like that?" How come you never helped us open dung before?'

Saurav looked at the floor of the jeep.

'Sir is just a student, little brother,' Akshu weighed in. 'Look how much he invested in this experiment. Sixteen employees. Tens of thousands of rupees. And if his data are bad, his research, his degree—his whole life could be ruined! Don't worry, this isn't a murder mystery! If you tell him what happened, you will get your salary.'

Saurav looked like he was ready to break. His eyes shifted from the villagers to the floor. He sat thinking for almost two minutes.

'No,' he said decidedly. 'No, I didn't see anything. I don't know of anyone feeding the elephants *chalta* seeds.'

I thought that Saurav had every incentive now to tell the truth. But our construct didn't quite match the prisoner's dilemma's theoretical conditions. The game assumes that the prisoners trust the interrogator's offer— and that they can relate to the concept of amnesty for a transgression in return for the truth. And that they face no risk of retaliation from co-conspirators for confiding in the interrogators. Saurav stuck to his incoherent story, and I told him we were finished.

Lokhan, the mahout who had been absent the day of the illicit feeding, called me the next afternoon. 'Saurav and Kiran fed Joda one fruit's seeds,' Lokhan reported. He said that, as far as he knew, it had only been once.

When I asked how he knew, he said, 'Saurav told me. He was really stressed about the whole ordeal.'

It seemed clear that Saurav and Kiran were the culprits, and that Vinod was covering for them. I was less sure about whether I could still trust my data. For now, I turned my attention to the question of paying the mahouts for their work. I worried that if I failed to pay the culprits their salaries, they would attack Rohan— and that Anoop and Lokhan would simply step aside and watch. Hearing of my dilemma, Narad said just to dock the liars' salary by ₹200—that this level of punishment would be tolerable to the mahouts and protect Rohan. I found myself, however, trapped by my own principles and promises. I wanted to pay each mahout what I had told him I would based on his response. It did not seem fair that I should pay three employees who had broken their contract. It was not my duty to coddle them. Buxa, I felt, was falling apart at the seams in part because of an unwillingness to adhere to principle.

I decided finally that I was worrying too much about unforeseeable consequences. I put Rohan's, Lokhan's, and Anoop's full payments—between ₹600 and ₹900—in envelopes. I put small notes as low as ₹10 in Vinod's, Kiran's, and Saurav's envelopes, just so they wouldn't appear empty on that sunny day. I figured it shouldn't be easy to distinguish those paid from those unpaid.

When I got to Malangi, I found Vinod first. I gave him one more chance to tell the truth. 'How can I tell you something that I didn't see?' he responded.

'Well, you could tell me what you heard, Vinod.'

Vinod looked at the ground. I found each mahout and distributed the envelopes, whispering to Rohan and Anoop not to reveal how much they had received, and telling Rohan to call me if he was in any danger.

I gave Saurav his envelope last. He was short with sinewy muscles, beautiful dark skin, and a strong jaw. Yet, as he approached me, he looked meek.

'I told you that if you told the truth, you would get your full payment. That if you lied, you would get nothing. You lied. Here is nothing.'

Suddenly, as I handed Saurav his envelope, I realized something was amiss. Until that moment, I had earnestly seen myself as a person who had been wronged, the victim of a broken contract scrambling to pick up the pieces. But as soon as the words left my mouth, I suddenly saw my actions as something else: an expression of power. An unearned power, a power of a type I had always disdained and never asked for, but that now, as I exercised it, I could not deny I had. And as I turned and walked to the vehicle, I knew I had gone too far.

18

By 2005, Motikar and Satyavati Atri were finally able to look upon what they had achieved for their family with some satisfaction. The Atris no longer experienced intermittent food insufficiency. All but their youngest surviving child, 21-year-old Thidey, had been married off. Akshu and Kusum had had their first baby, a girl named Kanchi. With Akshu's consistent income, they had their loan payments under control. There was also significant material progress. During their travels, migrant labourers from the village had seen the benefits of owning a latrine, so the more well-off individuals in Malabasti began building outhouses near their homes. Before Akshu and Kusum's wedding, the Atris had become the third family in the hamlet to make this investment, which required a substantial 21 bags of cement. At first, Akshu and his family had struggled to get accustomed to using a toilet—in the jungle, no one could hear their bodily noises, but sounds from the latrine were easily audible to those nearby. As they realized that everyone had the same problem, embarrassment abated. Not long afterward, the Gram Panchayat funded latrines throughout Madhubangaon, and all but the most resistant families soon had toilets they could use at night without worrying as much about elephants interrupting them.

The Atris had also replaced the thatched roof of their kitchen with clay tiles and three of the kitchen's four mud-and-bamboo walls, which periodically rotted, with wood. They also procured their first pressure cooker. And they no longer used dried fruit or ashes for soap. They now bought soap for both bathing and laundry.

Then, there were electronics. Motikar, who could no longer spend his days wandering the jungle, badly wanted a color TV to watch the *Mahabharata* and the *Ramayana* serials that played on basic cable. The government, ever-more interested in the votes of poor farmers, had begun a program that provided old farmers about ₹400 a month. In 2005, Akshu took the money Motikar had assiduously saved from this pension and procured a ₹7,800 color TV and a dish that played free channels for the Atri household. Meanwhile, Thidey had started doing work for various companies in the region, and he needed a way they could contact him. So, Thidey was the second person in all of Malabasti to buy a cell phone. It was a hefty Tata Motorola set, a noisy thing that cost Thidey ₹3,200. The Atris were very excited to have a phone, and once they had circulated their phone number, they sat staring at the phone wistfully, hoping someone would call them. It was a problem that would soon be unrelatable.

All this would have been of limited solace to Motikar if he had remained entirely bedridden, but there too was progress. Not long after Akshu and Kusum's wedding, two friends came from Alipurduar to check on Motikar. They asked about the medical tests he had undergone.

'Maybe they didn't do a sugar test at the right time,' one of the visitors said, referring to a test to diagnose diabetes.

'The right time?' Akshu asked.

'Yes—the test has to be done an hour after he has eaten. One of our friends had diabetes, but they first tested him before he ate, and the doctors didn't detect it,' the visitor explained.

When the Atris had Motikar's blood glucose levels tested both before and after eating, it became obvious that Motikar had type-II diabetes. Akshu was both relieved and furious—why were the doctors in Alipur so incompetent? Why was there no quality control? They took poor people's money and provided no real service in return!

Once Motikar was put on insulin, he slowly improved. He began roaming around the village. Then, he started going into the forest plantations to collect grass for their village-bound livestock. Then, he began to participate again in farm work, harvesting maize and milking cattle as much as he could. Now about 70 years old, Motikar would never again be a far-wandering jungle strider but, thanks to his insulin injections, he was able to rejoin the family workforce and partake in the joys of jungle village life.

Although the Atris had arguably escaped the throes of extreme poverty, they were still poor—none of them held a 'permanent' job, and malaria continued to regularly hit the family. Across the community, agriculture had become an increasingly unreliable source of income as villagers continued to sell their cow dung instead of applying it to their fields. Worse, with elephants engaging more and more in crop-raiding, many farmers had begun to stop planting corn altogether, unwilling to battle the giants in the 9-foot-tall maize.

Akshu resisted this trend. He was convinced that elephants were taking more maize because the people of his village were getting lazier, resorting to less lucrative (or less legal) types of work. He urged everyone to plant corn. 'Before, when we all stayed in the *tongs* and kept watch through the night, we were able to protect the crops. Why wouldn't that work now? If we all plant corn, we can work together to protect it. It will benefit all of us.' Hari's family felt similarly, so both Hari's and Akshu's families continued to plant corn, but no one else heeded Akshu's exhortations and, by 2003, they were nearly the last families in Malabasti still doing so.

Each year, the Atris planted about five well-fertilized blocks of their land with corn. For the first two years, leery that elephants would be drawn to their land, the Atris cut the plants before they had fully matured and fed them to their cattle as fodder. But after growing beautiful corn the first two years, the Atris grew ambitious. In 2005, the Atris built a fence around their crops strong enough to keep out almost all barking deer and wild pigs. Beginning in late March, Akshu, Hari, and their male relatives took turns guarding the half-meter-tall corn at night. They slept in a *tong* built in a *sirish* tree next to their cowshed, facing the forest. The nights were chilly, but sleeping in the tree house was comfortable and even invigorating, with the cool spring air blowing under the starry skies. Occasionally, brief storms animated the heavens overhanging the forest. As the weather warmed through the spring, the night filled with insect calls. And through this all, the corn grew.

One night, Akshu was guarding crops in the *tong* with his *badabau*, Hari's father. Akshu was exhausted from his day of research work and dozed off quickly once they spread their bedding.

A little before midnight, a loud crack awoke Akshu's *badabau*. He shook Akshu. 'A *haathi* has come.' Akshu reluctantly turned over, shone his flashlight in the direction of the sound, and saw the elephant that had broken their fence.

Twenty years earlier, just flashing the light at the elephant would have been sufficient to drive the invader away. Ten years earlier, the elephant might have resisted a bit before leaving this bountiful food source, forcing the villagers to holler or approach it to scare it off. Five years earlier, perhaps the elephant would have ignored the villagers until there was some other escalation, like a firecracker or projectiles. But now, this elephant actually turned *toward* the light and took a couple of steps closer to Akshu and his *badabau*. The two men yelled with deep voices, '*Huit, huit, huit!*' Immediately, the elephant turned toward a sturdy, half-meter wide *kamari* tree beside him—stronger than the tree that sheltered Akshu and his *badabau*—and wrapped his trunk around it. He broke the tree in two, throwing the shattered log to the side. The elephant was one of the largest Akshu had ever seen, and the message was clear: *Look at me! Look at how strong I am! Do you really want to challenge me?* And then, the tusker started marching toward them.

'*Badabau*,' Akshu whispered, 'turn off the light and be quiet.' His uncle obeyed. They couldn't see much in the starlight. They listened helplessly to the elephant munching their corn.

Having heard Akshu and his *badabau*'s yells, a group of village men had alerted the new Forest Department-funded 'Elephant Force'. These daily-wage employees, armed with powerful flashlights and guns that fired blanks, arrived to chase the tusker away from the Atris' corn. They climbed onto Hari's deck and the neighboring school, shining bright lights and firing blanks at the elephant. He stopped eating and charged toward the light, trampling more of the Atris' crops underfoot. He was nearly within reach of the school when the forest guards shut off their light. When the elephant backed off and returned to the crops, the Elephant Force retreated to Hari's house for safety.

Triumphant, the elephant spent nearly an hour in Akshu's and Hari's fields, eating luxuriously. Then, he climbed out of the corn field, probably en route to another village.

Night after night, as the Atris listened helplessly, the same tusker appeared, eating more of the crop. Finally, the last night, the villagers saw a different elephant, a *makhna*, come to finish off the Atris' corn.

Akshu responded to the 'I told you so's with defiance. 'If we villagers hadn't ever stopped defending our crops, the elephants wouldn't have become so used to freely eating all our crops! Once an animal is used to something, it's hard to take it away from it. Instead of working, everyone wants to sleep with his wife.'

There might have been something to this claim, but the changing landscape meant there was much more at play than just how villagers defended their crops. In any case, after that year, the Atris' land, too, would remain barren until it was time to plant rice.

———

While the crop-raiding elephants disheartened Akshu, the most persistent storm cloud in his life was still Chander. As Akshu had predicted, Chander had no interest in actually working the land his parents had given him. Chander sold his bull and all the areca nuts from his trees and left, moving around with Bani until they landed back at her parents' house in Birpada. Bani's father Gheewala, clearly fond of his daughter, built them a house right next to his own.

Then, one day in early 2006, Chander returned to Malabasti. Bani had been forcing him to work, and he had grown bored of it—so he reappeared at his parents' house and just stayed. Soon, he started scolding his

father and mother again. 'Why did you give birth to me?
I'm so poor! Why did you leave Madharihat and come
here?'

Akshu was out working during much of this verbal
abuse, but when he heard of it, he laid down the law.
About 28 years old, having held down a job longer
than anyone in his family, with a wife and child of his
own, the lean young man was indisputably the head
of the household now. 'You have no right to say these
things to our parents,' he said angrily. 'You don't give
them anything to eat or drink. I am the one struggling
to feed this family. But even though I feed them, I
respect them. If I hear any more from you, I'll break
your mouth.'

After a few more altercations, Chander fell into his
dark silence. He would just sit, staring hatefully at his
brother. Kusum, who would serve everyone at meals,
gawked at him. 'He's my elder brother,' Akshu said
resolutely. 'Give him food.' Afraid it would hurt their
parents to see their sons in such conflict, he didn't want
to push Chander out of the home. As long as Chander
didn't say or do anything harmful, Akshu would let
him stay. One day, Akshu hoped, he would come to his
senses and start working for himself.

Meanwhile, the National Institute for Environmental
Sciences continued their study on crop-raiding by wild
animals around North Bengal. In every village where
the NIES collected crop-damage data, they hired one
or two local people to write down the families whose
fields were raided by elephants and estimate how much
damage was done. When Akshu and Moksha or Hari's
team showed up, the local scouts would hand over the

list of raided fields, and the NIES team would make measurements there.

For this modest part-time monitoring work, the local hires received ₹300 a month. For several years, this system worked well, and everyone was happy. Then, around 2005, Dinesh told Akshu, 'We are out of funds, but I'm going to South India to meet Dr Sivaganesan. Then, I can quickly get the funds and distribute them to everyone.

'When you meet the local hires,' Dinesh continued, 'ask them to sign this bill saying that I've paid them. Then I can submit these bills, and NIES will give me the money to pay them.' Dinesh made a chart showing how many months' payment was owed to each local hire, calculating the amount to write on each villager's bill.

For all his complaints against Dinesh, Akshu hadn't had any trouble with the lead researcher when it came to salary payment, so he obediently collected the signatures of all the local hires during their next round of visits, explaining that if they signed this document, they would receive the pay they were owed for the last three or four months of work. They all trustingly gave their signatures.

Dinesh went to South India, and he returned—but he didn't distribute the funds to the local hires. Either unable or afraid to approach Dinesh directly, the local hires tracked down the Atris' phone number and began calling Akshu incessantly. 'What kind of people are you?' they would ask. 'Didn't we earn that money long ago?'

Akshu had little control over the situation, but he still felt guilty. He repeatedly conveyed these pleas to Dinesh. Initially, Dinesh responded, 'The remaining money is yet to come. It'll come.' Then, after several months, Dinesh suddenly changed his response entirely. 'Payment for what?'

'Payment for what...' Akshu repeated, stunned.

'They already gave their signatures saying they've been paid,' Dinesh said.

Akshu was stuck. The swindled villagers kept calling and showing up at Akshu's and Hari's and Moksha's homes, asking what happened to their payments. Akshu, again too afraid to call Dr Sivaganesan, said he didn't know why Dinesh hadn't paid yet and that he would remind him again.

In mid-2006, Akshu saw a new opportunity to plead the local hires' case. A new NIES researcher arrived in Buxa, and Akshu quickly became hopeful that he would have the kind of easy friendship with her that he'd once had with Kalaivannan. Jilpa Thurairaja, the second female researcher Akshu had ever met, was a Tamilian like Kalaivannan. She had curly, jet-black hair and ebony-chocolate skin, large eyes and a broad, pearly-white smile. She laughed frequently and oozed friendliness. She had just started learning Hindi less than a year before, but Akshu quickly saw that she possessed an effortless, consistent kindness. Jilpa never segregated herself from the village assistants—she ate with them whenever she could and, instead of living in the field station in Alipurduar, she rented a place in Madhubangaon, more interested in village life than the material conveniences of the large town.

Sensing her openness, Akshu asked Jilpa lots of questions, both about her and her project. Jilpa explained that she had moved out of India in her early twenties. She had been a white-water-rafting software engineer in the US for several years until, on her 29th birthday, she realized she didn't want that sterile life serving corporate interests anymore. She returned to India, where she worked at a school for the blind in Sikkim, and then she convinced Dr Sivaganesan to employ her doing elephant research.

Jilpa's project was to see whether chili pepper fences could prevent elephants from crop raiding. Since elephants have very sensitive trunks and a distaste for spicy chili peppers, some thought that painting fences with chili pepper paste might serve as a low-cost crop raiding deterrent. Jilpa's project was straightforward—to help construct such chili fences and see if they worked to keep elephants away.

Even the nature of the project—which aimed to directly help people—gave Akshu confidence in this woman, who, just four years older than him, immediately felt sisterly. So, one day, Akshu broached the subject of the unpaid wages from the crop-raiding study.

Observing the phone calls he was receiving, Jilpa was quickly convinced that Akshu was being truthful. She confronted Dinesh.

'No, no,' Dinesh said. 'I gave the money already. Who told you otherwise?'

'If you gave the money already,' Jilpa responded, 'why are all these villagers still calling?' They argued back and forth until Jilpa threatened to report Dinesh's embezzlement to NIES. Dinesh capitulated—sort of. He went to each village and handed out funds, but essentially docked each person about ₹300, or one month's payment. That was, in essence, the minimum fee for being foolish enough to trust Dinesh Ganguly.

It was late June, and Jilpa had given Akshu the weekend off, which felt like a great blessing. Akshu was sick. As he climbed out of bed sniffling and feverish, he remembered that the Forest Protection Committee was meeting a couple of kilometers away in Taazabasti.

All the young men and boys of Malabasti were going. Akshu saw his friend Bharat passing by his house and called out. 'Bharat Daju—take Chander with you. Maybe it will engage him a bit. He just spends the whole day at home.'

'Chander Daju, *joom*!' Bharat called.

'Sure, I'll come after a while,' Chander called down.

Motikar went to visit a plot he had planted while Akshu, Kusum, and Satyavati sat down to eat, Akshu sniffling pitifully with his back to the open door of the kitchen.

'*Daju*,' Akshu called out to Chander. 'If you're not going, come and eat.'

'No, I won't eat,' he called back. 'I just ate some corn.'

Kusum had just served Akshu rice and was sitting down when—'*Maaraaa!*'—Satyavati let loose a bloodcurdling scream.

Akshu turned just as Chander brought the kukri down on him.

Akshu tried to dodge him. Kusum sprang up and grabbed Chander from behind, bear-hugging him to hold down the arm with the kukri. Chander was a strong man; his limbs had been honed by decades of labour in the jungle and the field. But Kusum was strong, too and, for a few moments, she held on as Chander struggled to throw her to the ground. Satyavati ran out the door stammering, calling for help.

As Chander grew more frantic and forceful, Akshu saw Kusum growing nervous and looking to run away. Akshu tried to stand—but he couldn't. Perplexed—for he felt no pain—he looked down and saw his kneecap hanging from his left leg. So Akshu grabbed the *gamcha* wrapped around Chander's waist and pulled his attacker toward him. Akshu grabbed the kukri by its blade, and Kusum released Chander and ran away, screaming for help. Akshu and Chander struggled over the kukri, pulling Akshu up onto his good leg. The kukri was cutting up Akshu's fingers and hands. He managed to shift his grip to the handle, and, holding it tight, he dropped his butt to the ground, sitting with such force that he pulled the kukri blade through Chander's hands, slicing the webbing between his brother's pointer and middle finger.

Chander tried to grab the kukri back, but Akshu started swinging at him desperately, yelling and screaming madly. Chander ran out of the kitchen and behind the outhouse. Akshu crawled out of the kitchen, leg trailing and kukri in hand, so that Chander couldn't ambush him again. Chander watched him from behind the bathroom. He ran to a pile of bricks left from constructing the outhouse and began pelting them at Akshu. Akshu crawled behind the palm tree next to the kitchen for shelter, still clinging to the kukri.

It was then that a neighbor, having heard Kusum's cries for help, came running. 'Chander Daju!' he yelled. 'Why are you doing this? Don't do it, it's wrong!'

Chander pivoted and threw a brick at the neighbor, who dodged it adroitly.

Other villagers arrived, and they quickly apprehended Chander. Akshu slumped to the ground, too shaken even to cry. He was covered in monsoon mud. He realized that the webbing between several of his own fingers, his palm, and his arm had also been sliced open as he had struggled for the kukri. He looked at his severed knee cap. Under it, clinging to the exposed flesh of his knee, were mud, rocks, and some small snails.

The villagers found a Forest Department driver at the *chowpathi,* and Hari loaded Akshu into the vehicle and accompanied him to the hospital in Alipurduar. It was the same hospital where, over a decade before, Bhagavati had died.

The doctor took one look at Akshu's leg and said he couldn't do anything to treat it—it was cut up too badly. By the time Akshu returned to the lobby, Jilpa had arrived. She began working to secure an ambulance to take Akshu to Cooch Behar, a small city about 25 kilometers away. Meanwhile, Motikar sat with Akshu, overcome with guilt and shame and confusion and sorrow. He was on the verge of a nervous breakdown. 'Papa, Papa, nothing will happen to me,' Akshu assured him. 'Only my arm and my leg were hit. Don't worry, an operation can fix it.'

But Akshu was not at all confident. He was deeply afraid. He prayed that the doctor in Cooch Behar would be competent.

The doctor in Cooch Behar didn't even administer anesthesia to Akshu; actually, the doctor didn't lay a hand on Akshu. He supervised a civil servant—presumably a nurse or other medical professional—as he sewed up Akshu's knee while Akshu screamed in pain. They sent Akshu to a recovery ward with some painkillers. There, he drifted into a fitful sleep punctuated by great pain, followed by a pill, followed by sleep. Akshu himself could not recall afterward whether he remained conscious through it all.

In the meantime, the villagers faced the problem of dealing with Chander. The men of the village put Chander, his right hand bleeding profusely, in the Atris' home, emptied it of weapons, and stood guard outside. It didn't immediately occur to them to call the police— after all, the police had never served them before—but someone eventually caught wind of the attack and the fact that the villagers were guarding Chander. Policemen from Kalchini were called to deal with the assailant.

When they arrived, some of the villagers with Chander tried to convey the story.

'Sounds like the two brothers just had a fight, maybe lost their tempers,' one policeman suggested.

Satyavati and Kusum forcefully disagreed. 'No. They never have fought this way. Akshu is not violent. Chander surprise-attacked him.'

The officers observed the large cut on Chander's hand. By now, several jars had been filled with Chander's blood. 'Oooh,' another policeman said condescendingly. 'So you only love the other boy, you don't love this one. His hand has been cut so badly, but you haven't treated him—but the other one you took to the hospital right away?' The policemen told the villagers to take Chander to the hospital—and then drove away. They had spent a total of 5 minutes at the Atris' home, and they offered no way to transport Chander.

Soon, Thidey arrived, and he organized a ride for Chander to the Alipurduar hospital. The doctor there took one look at Chander's hand and announced that he couldn't do anything to repair it—it was cut up too badly. He recommended that Chander go to Cooch Behar.

And so it was that, when Akshu awoke in his recovery ward, he realized with horror that his attacker lay in a bed in the opposite corner of the very same room. And while Akshu was helplessly immobile and in tremendous pain, the murderous Chander was, aside from his right hand, fully able-bodied.

Neither Akshu nor his family thought they could ask anyone to move Chander elsewhere. Akshu begged his family that two of his people be present in the ward at all times, one to sit by him and one to sit with Chander. Even though a series of cousins, in-laws, nephews, and neighbors came to provide supervision, sometimes only

one caretaker was present, and Akshu found himself
terrified whenever that caretaker stepped out for a
restroom break or dozed off at night. Sometimes, when
Akshu was awake, Chander would walk over and stand
close to him as other patients and their caretakers looked
on. He would take a long look at his hobbled brother.
'How are you? You, how are you?' he asked.

Akshu was loved, and his family had more resources
than ever before. But constrained by poverty and in the
care of an incompetent State, Akshu knew no way to
escape this hell on earth.

One day, Chander disappeared from the ward. The police
had obtained a witness statement from Kusum, and they
apprehended Chander for his assault. Akshu finished his
17 days in the hospital and returned home.

For five or six months after his injury, Akshu spent
most of the time sleeping. He needed help to go even
the shortest of distances. His hand and forearm cut by
the kukri were also in great pain. He peed in a bottle
and pooped over some plastic. His toddler Kanchi,
now about two years old, played near him, and Akshu
wanted badly to hold her and walk with her and sit her
on his lap—but he couldn't. He feared for her future,
wondering why the gods had let him have a child
that he wouldn't be able to raise properly. Sometimes,
Motikar came and sat close to him, and Akshu, unable
to maintain a strong front any longer, wept. He had
promised his father that he would look after him until
his end—even as a teenager, he had said that he would do
whatever it took, work any job, to make sure his parents
had a comfortable old age. Akshu had hoped he would
be able to maintain the peaceful life that Motikar, after

decades of uncertainty and illness and loss, had begun to experience. But now, Akshu himself had become the ultimate source of turmoil.

Initially, Akshu's friends and relatives would spend a lot of time sitting with him, providing him company. Over time, this diminished, and Akshu found himself lying alone. He felt helpless as others milled about the house. He worried about what he might never be able to do again. He thought about all the time he had spent in the jungle and all the work he had done. He remembered his jungle transect work, crossing rivers and climbing hills. He remembered the elephants and how close he had once gotten to them physically and emotionally. He felt sure he wouldn't ever be able to go into the jungle again. Depressed, he realized that this thing he had often taken for granted—that had often felt like a chore to him—was a critical part of who he was. Without the ability to go into the jungle, he felt something deep inside him suffocating.

Toward the end of the year, Akshu started using his crutches to slowly venture around the house and neighborhood. But when he gradually tried to shift even a little weight onto his injured leg, he felt excruciating pain.

Consulting with his family, he decided to go back to Cooch Behar to try and get physical therapy. After about a week of sessions that made Akshu cry in pain, the physical therapists called Akshu in. 'There's something wrong inside the leg. You need to see a doctor. Not a doctor here,' the therapist said with compassionate candor. 'Go see a good doctor.'

When Jilpa heard of this, she stepped in. 'Akshu, it seems that your leg is really messed up. The doctors around here say they can't treat it. As you know, my father is a doctor in the South, in Tamil Nadu. If you can make it down to Vellore, I will arrange for you to see surgeons there. Can you make it down south?'

Akshu assumed he would have to take an airplane to get to Vellore; he didn't realize that Tamil Nadu was connected to Bengal by land. Once Jilpa helped him understand where Vellore was, Akshu got support from his family and neighbors—they came up with a plan to accompany him and pay for the train travel.

Several of Akshu's Christian Adivasi neighbors realized that Akshu was traveling to a hospital that belonged to a Christian institution, the Christian Medical College. These Adivasis had a good relationship with the open-minded Akshu. When the Christians held functions at the local church, the Atris often loaned a pot or some chairs, and the Christians did the same for the Hindus. The Hindus and Christians of Malabasti had also worked together to defend their crops from elephants, repair each other's homes, and monitor their playing children. Now, several of Akshu's Christian neighbors went to their church in the nearby town of Damanpur to secure support for Akshu's trip south.

The Christians returned with a note, written in English, that they gave Akshu to take on his journey.

'To the Principle Christian Medical College in hospital, Vellore, South India: Happy Christmas and New Years.

'Subject: a prayer consideration. I thank you very much for doing great favor during last years a number of times. May I refer to your kind consideration for Mr Akshu Atri, son of Motikar Atri, of Malabasti, P.O. Madhubangaon, District Jalpaiguri, West Bengal. After the medical treatment of his knee, he is unable to walk. It seems an operation is required. He is married and has a minor daughter. The financial condition of the family is not good. He was temporarily employed in the Forest Department. No one is in any service. They depend for their living on little cultivation. They're extremely poor. They are by religion Hindu, but very good, always cooperative and helpful with Christian communities. He lives under the parish of Catholic church Damanpur. May I kindly request for concession for his treatment.

'Thanking you in anticipation, yours sincerely.' The note was signed by the reverend friar.

19

It felt like we were fleeing Malangi. A sober mood filled the jeep. Lokhan, Akshu said, had opened his envelope immediately, right in front of Vinod. It was clear that when Vinod opened his envelope and saw how much less he had received, all hell would break loose. Narad spoke out against me first. 'When I get my salary from you,' he said, 'I'm going to give those three ₹400 each. My heart aches for them. They stayed up with me all night watching elephants, and now they get just ₹10.'

Narad, I knew, wasn't prone to great acts of generosity. 'Good for you. That's up to you,' I said.

Disappointed I hadn't taken the bait, Narad got real. 'One day, we are going to be working in the jungle, and one of them is going to shoot us dead with a bow and arrow. I told you you should have just taken ₹200 off their salary! Now you are going to go off to the US, and all of us will be at risk. And poor Rohan—one day, they're just going to push him in front of one of the elephants and—finished.'

I knit my brows and looked at Akshu. He, too, clearly felt glum. He waited until he and I were alone in my room to let me know how he felt.

'It may not be likely that they will try and kill us or anything. But this does make things difficult for us.'

'Why?' I asked. 'They live 10 kilometers away. You said yourself that the Nepalis rule Madhubangaon, and that you are safe here.'

'Yes, we are safe here. But you don't seem to understand how this place works. At some point or the other, some work will take me to Malangi. Then, how can I convince the mahouts to work with me?'

'What? What job would require you to work with those elephants again?'

'What if another PhD student comes...'

I looked at him disapprovingly. 'You would take another PhD student to work with these cheats again? Are you serious?'

Akshu put his hands up defensively. 'It's my duty to tell students what these mahouts have done in the past. Then, it's their decision.'

'So you want me to pay the mahouts for terrible work now so that they can have an opportunity to screw over some other student.'

Akshu looked at me with deep sadness. 'You don't understand how this place works. You should have paid them for their first six days of good work and then just not paid them for the last day when they cheated.'

'You told me that it was normal not to pay people who cheat like that. I gave them an opportunity to come clean, but they still didn't. Before you said this would be OK, and now you are changing. Listen, if you are saying, 'Nitin, I want you to pay them to protect me and my family,' then I will pay them to protect you.'

'No, I won't ask you to pay them for me,' Akshu said. 'But what about Rohan?'

'What about him? I asked him if I was causing him any trouble by this, and he said there may be a little but that he would be able to take care of it.'

'You say you care about people...' Akshu said.

'This is such a simple matter! They broke contract, then they lied, showing absolutely no concern for my professional well-being—and I'm not paying them!

You said yourself that this isn't a murder case. Why has this suddenly become such a big deal?'

'Because we are dealing with people who drink *dharoo*,' Akshu protested. 'This isn't America, Sir. There is no justice system. You don't understand.'

I rubbed my forehead. I hated having to choose between pragmatism and principle. I hated giving in to fear of people because they lacked a conscience. I had always thought of myself as a person who would find a principled way to navigate across practical constraints, but Buxa was repeatedly assaulting my self-image. I tolerated a tiger reserve without tigers so I could keep my permissions to do research. I tolerated elephants tied to stakes their whole lives because I wanted data. And now I was being told to pay to prevent an alcohol-fueled tantrum.

'Fine, we'll do this,' I told Akshu, 'I have no problem paying you, Narad, and the other assistants for your excellent work. Here is ₹1,400, 350 for each of you. This is also the amount Narad suggested I pay Saurav, Kiran, and Vinod. If you want to pay them, then feel free to do so. But now you have to make the decision. You can either use this extra money to pay for school fees or extra books for your kids, or you can pay off the mahouts. It's your money, and it's your decision.'

Around January of 2007, Akshu's friend and cousin accompanied Akshu on his first of three trips to Vellore, Tamil Nadu, where he went for treatment for his unhealing leg. The Atris had raised enough funds for the travelers to get seats in the sleeper class—the minimum required for Akshu's unbending leg—and the train ride was far less painful than a bumpy auto rikshaw ride.

As the trains crossed various state lines and passengers swapped themselves out, people speaking in tongues less and less intelligible to Akshu gradually surrounded him, until few passengers were speaking any of the three languages he was comfortable with. When they disembarked in Vellore, it was a great comfort to all the travelers when Jilpa, who had arrived from her family's home in Madurai, greeted them.

Jilpa had arranged everything for Akshu and his companions. Within a day, she had introduced Akshu to several doctors to get second and third opinions about his treatment. The doctors, who essentially all gave Akshu the same prognosis and recommendations, tried to explain everything to Akshu. 'We can offer you two options,' the first doctor said. 'The first is that we can try our best to make your knee better.' This option, he explained, would involve temporarily affixing his leg with metal rods and plates until it healed. The doctor told Akshu that, based on the accident and his initial treatment, he probably wasn't going to be able to bend his knee again. 'But if we fix up your leg and you keep it straight, you'll be able to carry a load of 40, 50, 80 kilograms, no problem. When you're fully recovered, you'll even be able to carry 100 kilograms...'

Hope fluttered in Akshu's chest. 'Are you saying,' Akshu asked, 'that I will be able to walk in the jungle again?'

'Why not!' said the doctor with a smile. 'You'll be able to walk anywhere, but you'll be about 2 centimeters shorter. There won't be any other side effects. You'll be able to run a little bit, but not like before. Just run a little, here and there. For emergencies.'

The doctor explained that the other option was to give him an artificial knee—it would entail a longer recovery time plus other costs and risks, but he would ultimately regain full use of his leg and knee, including bending capacity. The artificial knee would cost ₹110,000—the equivalent of nearly three years' salary for Akshu at his most recent pay rate—and it would have to be replaced every ten years.

'What do you think you want?' Jilpa asked. Akshu knew she would pay for whatever surgery he desired, but he made the prudent assumption that she wouldn't necessarily be available in future decades to cover the ensuing costs of treatment. He didn't want to be dependent on her that long, anyway. And he knew that, with a child to feed and educate and no guarantee of a job, he couldn't afford to take on having to pay for a new knee every decade. Akshu decided that keeping his own leg, even if flawed, would be better than the artificial option.

The hospital set Akshu's surgery for about a month away. As Akshu left Vellore, he marveled at how different his experience with Vellore's doctors had been from those he'd had in North Bengal. This further confirmed Akshu's suspicions that most of the doctors he had seen before were either incompetent or treacherously apathetic. The doctors in Vellore were clearly there to serve their patients. For the religious Akshu, speaking with Jilpa and the Vellore doctors felt like the closest he had ever come to meeting God.

When Akshu woke up from his surgery the following month, his feelings toward North Bengal's doctors took yet another turn for the worse. The Vellore surgeon explained that he had found pieces of brick and other small debris inside Akshu's knee. The North Bengal doctors had failed to even clean his wound before suturing his leg. The foreign bodies left inside had probably been the main reason Akshu experienced excruciating pain when he shifted weight onto his leg even months after his injury. Akshu felt both fury and despondency thinking of the elitist doctors in North Bengal who grew rich on government salaries as the poor people they were supposed to help suffered from treatable ailments and preventable deaths. He simply couldn't understand what caused people, especially well-off people whose basic needs were satisfied, to have such little regard for human life.

That night, Narad, Akshu, and the others decided to go to Malangi the next morning and offer the extra money I had given them to the mahouts. They deliberated in Nepali, and I didn't know whether Akshu had to convince the others to give up their bonuses for the mahouts—but most persuasive, perhaps, was the phone call that came from Rohan that night, asking Narad to come pick him up and take him somewhere safe. Things were heating up in Malangi. The four Nepalis were ready to go intervene when another phone call from Rohan's father-in-law assured them that the violence was over for the night, and that no one was seriously hurt.

In the morning, the four took my jeep to Malangi to give the mahouts the money, telling me that would stem the conflict. But Vinod and Kiran reportedly refused the money they offered. 'Why should we take money from you, poor villagers like us? Sir is the one we worked for, and he is the one that must pay us.'

Akshu returned while I was eating breakfast. 'Things got very violent last night,' he reported. 'Kiran and Saurav were ready to beat the pulp out of Rohan, and Rohan didn't want to back down from the fight. They had all been drinking *dharoo* heavily. Rohan's wife ran in to intervene, and she was struck in the head and leg…'

'They hit his wife?' I was incredulous. I couldn't believe my actions were causing violence to spill out into the community.

Akshu shrugged. 'They were drunk. Anyway, the Forest Department's beat officer, who is in charge of the mahouts, intervened. But otherwise, they say someone could have even been killed last night. That's how bad it was.'

Thidey scolded me. 'This is terrible. Look what will happen to the National Institute for Environmental Sciences' reputation. The mahouts will tell everyone that an NIES student came, and that he took a week of work from them, and that then he didn't pay them.'

I looked at him in disbelief. 'You can't make decisions based on what liars may or may not say about you.' But, in fact, I was starting to feel responsible for what had happened. 'Can I put a stop to this?'

Akshu nodded. He thought I might need backup, so he, Narad, Thidey, Hari, and I all piled into the jeep and sped to Malangi. I went first to meet the beat officer, who was supervising the repair of a bridge leading out of the village. I met him with my hands in *namaskaram*, asking him for forgiveness. 'I didn't know it would turn out this bad,' I said.

'No reason to ask for forgiveness,' he said, 'but you cannot do this sort of thing. You can't pay six people who did the same work differently—one person 600, one 100, one 10. That's not fair.'

'Sir, if I'd known it would turn out like this, I would not have—but you have to understand. Three of these men told the truth, and three tried to cheat me. I spent nearly ₹20,000 on this experiment, and they deliberately tried to ruin it. Is it not fair to pay honest men for their work, and leave cheats out?'

'This reminds me of how the British ruled India,' the beat officer responded. 'Divide and conquer,' he said in English. 'You should pay everyone the same amount.' I thought this argument made no sense, but I figured he was just trying to act well-educated for my benefit. I apologized again and left the man that may have saved my PhD from the shadow of a murder.

I motioned to Vinod, who had been standing behind me as I spoke to the beat officer, to walk with me. 'Tell me, Vinod—what did I do wrong here? I told you straight that if you lied you would get nothing, if you told the truth you would be paid. How is what I did unfair?'

Vinod held his head up. 'Ah, fine! Three of us are honest, and three of us are liars. Yes, I am a liar! You should not pay a liar. But know this—tonight, if there is violence, if something happens to someone, it is your responsibility.'

If I knew how to curse comfortably in Hindi, I would have. Vinod realized that I was there to get the blood off my hands—and that all else was immaterial. 'Listen,' I said, 'if one of you commits a murder, it is your responsibility.'

'Still,' he threatened confidently. 'Something will happen tonight. I won't do it, but I can't stop the others.'

Soon, Kiran and Vinod and Anoop stood with me in front of the lead mahout's house, my companions from Madhubangaon flanking them, while Rohan stayed near his house, milking his cow. Lokhan had fled home to avoid the violence. Saurav would not join me. Several other villagers gathered around to see the confrontation. I started to ask something, but Kiran and Vinod began yelling.

Kiran was indignant. 'I've never lied in my life. I never lie,' he said. 'You come here, you make us work for six days, and then you give me ₹10? Ten? I am not so poor a man. I have dignity. I may not be educated, but

I am every bit as much of a man as you. You know that? Here is the money you gave me, and Saurav, and Vinod. Take it. We don't want it.' He handed me ₹120.

Vinod repeated what he had told me just before, but with a dramatic flourish to suit his new audience. 'You think we're liars? Well, then take back this money. Why should you give a "liar" even a rupee? Go on, take it. But know this—this is India. You either pay everyone, or you pay no one. None of this British system.'

I realized Vinod had overheard my conversation with the beat officer. It pained me to think that, after all my efforts, Vinod's takeaway would be that payment based on performance was a colonial scheme.

My Hindi was not up to the task of responding to all these verbal assaults. More than anything, though, I realized that I was not in a realm where my reasoning would serve any purpose. I quietly said, 'I've come to pay you.'

Continuing his Oscar-worthy performance, Vinod started to storm away. Thidey and Hari followed him and held and patted his arms, telling him to let bygones be bygones, steering him back to the group. I looked at Kiran. 'Will you take your salary?'

'Only if you pay all of us,' he said. I handed the money to Kiran, and he and the other mahouts divided everything up as originally intended. Since I had lacked exact change, the money included an extra ₹50. Vinod realized this and handed me a 50-rupee note. 'We won't take more than we agreed on either,' he said. I realized then just how much I had affronted the mahouts' dignity. Being called a liar, being treated like a liar, was an insult that felt to them disproportionate to their transgressions. It was as though Vinod believed he could restore his self-image with a small act of honesty.

After Akshu returned from his surgery in Vellore, it took several months for the pain in his knee to subside. About three and a half months later, he returned to Vellore to have the plates and rods removed from his knee. When he returned home, he kept his weight off his leg, but he began to go farther and farther with crutches. By June 2007, a year after his injury, Akshu could crutch his way to the *chowpathi*. Still, Akshu only ventured out in mornings and nights. Otherwise, he stayed at home, less confined and more hopeful but still just as worried about his family's future.

It was probably another eight months before he was able to start contributing more substantially to his family's activities. He accompanied his mother across the creek to help cut some firewood and collect fodder for the cattle and goats tied up at home. Even a full two years after his injury, Akshu was afraid to go any farther than that into the jungle. One of the Atris' calves went missing, and some villagers said they had seen it—that it had survived a leopard attack and was wandering around, disoriented and emaciated. Akshu, now able to walk in a stiff-legged sort of way, crossed the creek to look for the calf nearby, but he would not go any farther. Unable to run, he feared for his safety even in the middle of the day. If an elephant or even gaur or wild boar charged him, he would be powerless.

It was about this time that Chander once again became a matter of concern. The Atris had all testified against Chander in court. Chander had pled guilty and was led away after the trial, but the judge had not publicly pronounced a sentence. He had simply written something down, handed it around to other officials, and that was that. In 2008, without informing the Atri family, the government released Chander. The Atris were shocked when they heard this; they scrambled to figure out what he might do if he returned to Madhubangaon. Instead of returning to his childhood home, Chander ventured to his wife's place in Birpada. Hearing this, Akshu called Chander's father-in-law, Gheewala. 'Look what he already did to me,' Akshu said. 'I don't think his mind is sound. He thinks in the wrong direction, and he angers very quickly. It could affect Bhabi or their children. I'm giving you this information—it's up to you now.'

Gheewala took Akshu's warning to heart. 'He went after his own brother,' he told Bani. 'I'm not allowing him back here. Why did he do that? What reason could he possibly have?'

Bani had always been loyal, and now she chose to remain loyal to her husband. 'He's my husband! And it's my life. He wants to come live with me,' she said. And she welcomed Chander back into their home over her father's objections.

Soon, Chander began urging Bani to borrow more money from her father, but Bani was no longer amenable to this. 'We've already taken so much. How much can we take from our dad? You must work now,' she said.

One night, Bani arose from their shared bed to go to the bathroom. She returned, thinking that Chander was sound asleep. Chander, however, had used the opportunity to fetch a long piece of firewood. As Bani turned away from him to latch the door, Chander struck her savagely in the back of her head. The mother of his children yelled and fell to the floor. Chander struck her again, beating her head until her skull was bashed in and brains began to fall out.

The neighbors and relatives heard the commotion. They quickly apprehended the murderer and held him until the police arrived to take him away.

There was, of course, great sadness over Bani's murder. But there was also an element of uncertainty. The Atris didn't understand how the legal system worked, and none of the authorities took the time to explain it to them. Chander's trial was repeatedly postponed—would they release him without trial? Why did they release him the first time? Would anyone be informed? Akshu was afraid but also resolute. If Chander returned, something had to be done to keep him from harming anyone else. Akshu wondered if he might one day have to lead a group to kill his own brother.

Akshu really had little idea of how the family was making ends meet during his recovery—in fact, even his parents weren't that sure. Somehow, Akshu's younger brother Thidey was making things work. Thidey had taken over Akshu's work with NIES. He worked with Jilpa on the chili fence project until she finished in early 2007. And then, having run out of favorable employers, Thidey agreed to work for Dinesh, who was now mostly based in the town of Chalsa, some 100 kilometers west of Buxa Tiger Reserve.

By the time Akshu had improved enough to consider rejoining the workforce, Thidey had lost patience with Dinesh's managerial antics and returned home. Yet Akshu, desperate to begin earning money again after two years without work, reached out to Dinesh and offered to take over any duties he could manage with his disability. Dinesh offered Akshu ₹3,000 a month to look after the station. Akshu accepted and moved to Chalsa. The field station was rife with intrigue. Akshu discovered that the incorrigible Bhuday was fueling his drinking habit by stealing 5 liters of gas at a time from the NIES vehicle. Worse, a young Muslim maid who worked at the station tearfully told Akshu that Bhuday had laid his hands on her and refused to let go. After some sleuthing, Akshu concluded she had been raped. He reported all this to Dinesh, but the researcher did nothing. Finally, when Dinesh refused to reimburse Akshu for a 1,000-rupee purchase that he had forced Akshu to make, the Nepali left his job after less than a year and returned to Madhubangaon.

Akshu asked around desperately for employment that would not require mobility or labour. He thought about building a new shop, but he didn't have the funds necessary for the initial investment and, in any case, a store wouldn't provide enough to support a family. Opportunities for anyone living in Buxa were limited—but for an apolitical disabled man, unable to farm or carry weight or even walk far, the world seemed particularly devoid of options.

One day, feeling depressed and defeated, Akshu called Jilpa to ask for advice. He explained his situation, expressing his fears that he would never again be able to support his family. He wept over the phone. Jilpa listened fully and said, 'I'm going to start a project in Kaziranga soon. You can come with me.' Kaziranga was a famous national park in Assam, perhaps a day's travel from Buxa by train and bus. Jilpa was starting her doctoral research on elephant behavior there.

'But Madam,' Akshu cried. 'How can I work in the jungle? My leg is no longer capable...'

'It's not that kind of work!' Jilpa said reassuringly. 'Don't worry—I'm here, aren't I? Trust me, Akshu. Trust me.'

Kaziranga National Park was India's best response to Africa's savannas, hinting at the landscapes that must have existed alongside the subcontinent's grassland-dwelling rivers before *Homo sapiens* took over. Kaziranga had the world's largest population of one-horned rhinos, wild water buffaloes, and swamp deer. It had the highest population density of wild tigers of any national park. The park was home to a range of charismatic creatures—everything from pangolins to pythons to clouded leopards crept through the vegetation, while small-clawed river otters, brown tortoises, gharial, and even river dolphins swam through the park's water ways. A wide variety of large birds, from bar-headed geese to the Bengal florican to fish eagles and vultures, also graced the area. And all this was in addition to most of the species still found in Buxa.

For Jilpa, the extraordinary richness of the ecosystem was a bonus. What brought her to this naturalist's paradise was the elephants. Jilpa was curious about something considered fundamental to elephants: she wanted to know why they had tusks. Unlike African elephants, in which both males and females had tusks, only male Asian elephants had them. Females instead had slightly elongated teeth called tushes. But what fascinated Jilpa most was that, in northeastern India, about half the male elephants were tuskless. The reason for this was unknown, though many suspected the obvious: that since humans often killed elephants for their ivory, male elephants without tusks, *makhnas*, had the advantage of attracting less attention from the top primates. But, Jilpa wondered: if male elephants had evolved tusks for a reason, then were *makhnas* at some sort of disadvantage? Perhaps female elephants were more attracted to males with tusks, or perhaps tuskers tended to beat makhnas in fights over mating opportunities? So, in 2009, Jilpa set out to observe the sex lives of elephants, and to see if tusks made a difference. Akshu joined her.

Akshu's mood started to lift as they spent more time in the park. He felt like he was dreaming. He hadn't seen a wild water buffalo since he was a child exploring Buxa's forests with his father. And now, they were everywhere! And there were rhinos all over the place! Watching these giants interact with various smaller species was magical to Akshu—but, drawn to complex emotion and behavior, he again found his attention gravitating to the elephants. Unlike in Buxa's forests, Akshu could easily watch whole families of elephants as they soaked and played in the *bhils*. Whole teams of elephant calves would plop around in the water, kicking and pushing each other, using their heads to lift each other up. They would pull each other by the trunk or tail. Mothers busied themselves with eating and seemed to entrust each other with their calves—a calf from one family would run off and play in another herd farther down along the same *bhil*, reminding Akshu of how children in Malabasti visited each other's houses.

Watching this every day, Akshu completed his conversion. He was now fully in love with elephants. Akshu was both unsurprised and shocked by his evolution. On the one hand, he knew a person that spent every day with any animal, even a snake, would come to love it—such was the nature of companionship, of sharing one's limited time in this lonely world with another feeling creature. But still, for a person whose crops had been repeatedly eaten by elephants, whose shop an elephant had destroyed, whose neighbors and acquaintances elephants had killed, whose own life had been repeatedly jeopardized by elephants— for him to feel such love for these animals, as individuals and as a species, surprised him. He felt this feeling of kinship was not just because elephants helped him find employment. Akshu recognized their fundamental soulfulness. He no longer saw elephants primarily as agents of Ganesh but as independent beings—sometimes-affectionate, often-self-interested, clever but often ignorant beings like himself. They were sacred not because they were pure manifestations of God, but because they had within them both divinity and fallibility, just like people. They were less creative and had poorer eyesight, but they had better smell and stronger bodies; the same individual could be unbelievably loving or insanely malicious. To Akshu, it felt as though humans and elephants were made from the same ingredients in different ratios.

More practically consequential was the effect Jilpa's research had on Akshu's confidence. Jilpa recognized Akshu's proficiency in learning to use technology, and she made full use of his unmatchable sense of responsibility, teaching him to use a video camera and store photos and enter data on her laptop. One day, Akshu slid into the jeep's driver's seat as a joke, but both Jilpa and the driver encouraged Akshu to give driving a shot; with a little coaching, Akshu was soon a proficient backup driver. As time wore on, Akshu eventually even started accompanying Jilpa on foot in the park. 'It's not like I can outrun an elephant either,' Jilpa would joke. Kaziranga's forest guards looked on in amazement as a dark-skinned woman and a villager with a limp worked their way across a landscape full of buffaloes, rhinos, and tigers. For Akshu, Jilpa was like an antidote to elitism, classism, able-body-ism, regionalism, colorism, casteism, sexism. There could have been no better person to challenge his assumptions about what was and wasn't possible, to push him to want to be better, and to help him once

NITIN SEKAR   321

again believe that he had something to contribute to
science and society.

———————

When I got back to Madhubangaon after the
confrontation with the mahouts, I plotted the data that
we had collected from Joda and Sanjushri's feeding
trials. I found several irregularities. I would continue
telling myself for a few weeks that maybe the data were
salvageable until, finally, I would admit that I couldn't
use the data at all. The feeding trial was a waste.

Through my open window that afternoon, I saw
Akshu on his way home from the bazaar. He was all
smiles. He was the happiest that the mahouts had been
paid off.

'Guruji!' I called out. 'When we were in Malangi, did
you hear what happened to Rohan's wife last night?'

'Yes sir. She was beaten as she tried to pull Rohan
back from the fight. I told you that this morning.'

'Yes, but did you know that it was Rohan that hit
her?'

Akshu shared my surprise. 'Are you sure?'

'Yes—that's what her father told us when I went to
apologize to her. He said it right in front of Rohan. Hari
heard the same thing.'

'Well, Rohan has a real temper.'

'Yes, but still! He hit his own wife?'

'He was drunk.'

'Yes, but...' I sighed.

Akshu smiled at me, studying my naivete. 'I'm
disappointed too, but it's a good thing, what you did
today.'

'Will they really stop fighting, though? Aren't they
still going to be upset with Rohan and the others for
their betrayal?'

'Money represents forgiveness, Sir,' Akshu said. 'You have paid them in full, so all is forgiven.'

I shook my head. These rules were incomprehensible to me. 'This doesn't make sense. They were the ones who cheated me!'

'This is North Bengal,' Akshu said. 'Now you understand why this place is so slow to develop. What you did was legitimate. But people don't follow such rules here. You can't change the mindset of a person who has lied and cheated and drunk his whole life with reason. Maybe, if their kids get a good education, they will be slightly different. Things will get better, but not in five or ten years' time. In generations.'

As Akshu turned to leave, I flipped what he had said in my head: it was also true that the mahouts had been taken advantage of and given the raw deal throughout their lives, and I knew it might not be fair to expect them to act as though the world rewarded honesty and justice. But there was a problem with this explanation. There was the teenager that returned my lost phone instead of selling it; the shopkeeper that corrected me when I offered ₹60 for something that costed ₹7; the cobbler and tree-climber that refused even modest tips for exceptional work, saying they would only accept the amount we had agreed to. There was Akshu Atri.

'But Guruji,' I called after him. 'This is what I don't understand. You—you are poor too. You grew up in the same place as all these other people. How come you don't steal from me?'

Akshu smiled, shook his head, and resumed his stilt-legged limp down the dirt path to his home.

———

About nine months after Akshu joined Jilpa in Kaziranga, Jilpa came to the field station with bad news. 'Akshu,' she said, 'The Forest Department doesn't like that I have hired someone from Bengal to come work here in Assam.' The Assamese were no fonder of outsiders taking local jobs than were Nepalis.

'I'm not Bengali, though,' Akshu said. 'Did you tell them that?'

'Yes, of course,' Jilpa said. 'They have made it mandatory that I hire someone else locally. I'm so sorry, Akshu. I have learned a lot from you being here, and you've been a huge help. I owe you my life, I'm sure. But I have fought this as long as I can. It's out of my hands.'

Akshu cursed his luck, but he knew Jilpa had done everything she could for him. Soon, he returned to Buxa.

While Akshu was not completely comfortable in his disabled body, he was certainly emboldened by his experience in Kaziranga. Lots of jungle-related work, he reasoned, could be done from a vehicle, with only short and careful trips into the jungle. Especially given his improved technological skills and increasing logistical prowess, maybe he could find work again after all. What he wished most was for another researcher like Kalaivannan or Jilpa to come to Buxa who could overrule—or at least ignore—Dinesh.

In early 2010, he got a call from Jilpa offering just that. 'He's an American,' Jilpa explained. 'He is actually Indian, his parents went there, and he was born there. But he doesn't speak much Hindi—he's like I was when I came to Buxa. Maybe worse.'

'That's OK,' Akshu said. 'He'll learn.'

'Yes,' Jilpa said. 'He's actually just a child, Akshu. He's not even 25 years old.'

This surprised Akshu—he had never worked for someone younger than him.

'...but he's a good kid. You will like him. I worked with him in Mudumalai.'

'OK, Madam,' Akshu said. Her vote of confidence meant a lot. 'But do tell him that I am disabled, and that I can't walk very far…'

'He knows, he knows,' Jilpa said. 'I told him. Don't worry. Just take good care of him. Americans don't understand how things work in India. You need to look after him.'

SYNTHESIS

Satyavati was the most surprised to see me again. 'I told you I would be back!' I said.

'*Everyone* says that they will come to visit,' Satyavati complained with a big smile. 'Has Kalaivannan come back, or Jilpa? No one comes back. They rarely even call.'

'Well, they were all adults when they came here,' I said, groping for words. I hadn't spoken my mongrel Hindi for nearly two years. 'I didn't understand the jungle, or the village. How to work properly—I learned all of that from all of you, from Guruji. I grew up here.'

And I meant it. When I'd left Buxa at the end of my research, I was bitter, exasperated by the poor management of the forest and the ambivalence toward my efforts to help. But, eventually, the feelings of frustration and personal hurt melted away, replaced by an appreciation of my clearer view of how the world operated. As I walked by the patch where the computer lab—now dismantled for parts—had stood, my old expectations seemed naïve. I thought I could set up a new educational institution in my *spare time* during my PhD? I now saw how my experience captured the challenges faced by those working to address poverty and the degradation of nature. Those of us who were well-off and well-educated simply expected people to change their behavior too fast, whether the solutions we offered were valid, ill-informed, or downright hypocritical.

We expected people from a different context to play by our rules when they had no reason to believe the game we offered was fair. We didn't question enough why we, as (sometimes exceptionally young and naïve) outsiders, had ended up with the resources and power to offer a new game to begin with. An equitable model of conservation required more than good intentions in the afterhours. It took time to build relationships, learn local realities, earn trust, and create value.

As it turned out, Buxa wasn't done teaching me about conservation and development. My return to Madhubangaon in 2018, six years after I had moved away, revealed to me just how quickly India's economic tide was rising. The kinds of changes that Satyavati and Akshu had described playing out across Buxa for decades—a generally unplanned, largely unpredictable march of politics, economic development, and ecological transformation—continued to unfold across the landscape. The Metal Road that ran through Madhubangaon was now coated in black-top, no longer ridden with potholes. The main dirt path into Malabasti was now white concrete. A new temple blasted religious music through its speakers starting at 5:30 AM. Akshu's family was doing particularly well. During my PhD research, his dilapidated wooden house had truly been falling apart around his family. Now, his house would have been utterly unrecognizable to Motikar, with a sturdy concrete foundation and pillars holding up three wooden rooms, painted a calming dark blue. Akshu had added two ground-floor rooms as well, including one for Thidey and his wife and child. Now, using a government scheme for the disabled, Akshu was building a modern kitchen.

The pace of change was dizzying. When I had arrived in 2010, the only wheels the Atris had access to was a borrowed bicycle, but now they owned a gypsy jeep to take tourists into the forest and a two-wheeler they could afford to use at will. In 2002, the village didn't have electricity, but now everyone had smart phones—Akshu, Thidey, Kusum, and most of the former computer lab students each had their own Facebook page and a proclivity for taking selfies. Though malaria had still affected some villagers when I had arrived, in the eight years since, it had nearly disappeared. And just 16 years after the Atris had been defecating in the open, they now owned three toilets on the plot of their house, the third built with funds from Prime Minister Modi's *Swachh Bharat* (Clean India) initiative. 'It's not the best quality,' Akshu intimated to me about the latter.

'Maybe because they saw you already had two other bathrooms, they just couldn't put their heart into it,' I retorted.

These changes were not exclusive to the Atris. Many of their neighbors had also rebuilt their houses on concrete foundations with rooms on the ground floor, and teenagers buzzed around the village on two-wheelers. Villagers had largely switched from firewood to gas cylinders, which were cleaner burning and less labour-intensive. This accumulation of resources stood in perplexing juxtaposition with empty farm fields, now used primarily as pasture for cattle and goats.

'Why aren't you planting rice anymore?' I asked.

Akshu explained that he'd stopped a few years before. 'Someone stole our bull that year, so I decided to rent a tractor for ₹6,200 to plant the paddy. Ultimately, we got 240 kilograms of rice.'

'How much should it have been?' I asked.

'2,400 kilograms worth of grain.'

'Elephants?'

Akshu nodded. 'The food here is good. If you have the choice of *matar* paneer and plain rice, which would you choose?' Akshu showed me that elephants had figured out how to make a meal of areca trees, too. 'They have destroyed a lot this year.'

So, with agriculture now apparently unprofitable, where were people getting money for all their new stuff? Some, I learned, were drawing resources from places other than the jungle. Akshu's reputation as a stellar research assistant had spread throughout the small ecology research community in India, leading to several invitations to work around the country. While Akshu was singular in his vocation, others were also connecting to outside institutions. Government schemes were making some material advances more affordable. Thidey and others who were more educated bid for government contracts to implement local development projects. Others were finding work for businesses, NGOs, and religious organizations who wanted a presence in Buxa. Migrant labourers and educated children increasingly found jobs in nearby cities. All this helped boost a local economy including carpenters, painters, and shopkeepers.

Unfortunately, this wasn't the whole story. Buxa's jungles were still being munched up at an unsustainable rate. The Forest Department's 2015 Tiger Conservation Plan (TCP) for Buxa acknowledges the intense pressure of illicit timber felling, poaching, and the grazing of some 150,000 livestock from the villages in and around Buxa. As Akshu and I escaped the village to take walks in the jungle near his home, we saw the rampant harvesting of forest products. We ran into smugglers carrying logs to Madhubangaon; women carrying bags stuffed with *birdarrow* (a favorite fodder of elephants) from the core area; and well-dressed outsiders openly carrying bags full of aquatic snails they had pulled from the creeks outside of Malabasti. The usually upbeat Akshu grew sardonic when we spoke of his jungle. 'They've finished all but the smallest fish,' he said. 'Now maybe they will finish these snails, too.' During a visit in 2015, Akshu and I drove through Nimathi, my favorite part of the reserve outside of the core area. I wanted to cry—the thick tree cover was gone. 'It's a football field now,' Akshu remarked. When I asked if at least the core area might be faring better, Akshu retorted, 'The core area has more people than any place else.'

As identified by the TCP, population growth and consumption driven by both poverty and ambition continued to propel this loss. Between the 37 villages within Buxa and the revenue villages and tea gardens along its fringe, an estimated 255,000 people lived within 2 kilometers of the forest. The tide of non-forest development opportunities lapping at the stoop of Malabasti had not yet reached everyone there. With the tea industry still flagging, thousands of under-employed youth were constantly tempted to exploit Buxa's trees and wildlife. But to Akshu, the salient issue was that Buxa's institutions were not geared to manage these drivers in favor of sustainability or conservation. Since the government did not regulate who moved into Buxa's villages or what they did once they arrived, Akshu said there was a regular influx of migrants from all over the region that showed up, cut down some forest, and built a house. Many were friends and relatives of people already living in Buxa. He mentioned a family of recent immigrants I knew and liked, and when he saw my sympathetic reaction, he said, 'But that's another family now living off the jungle. Everything is free here! You can cut timber here, catch and sell fish for free, sell NTFP, do labour work here and there. The Panchayat provides some services, and you can even sell firewood here. And I'm seeing people who don't even have land are given compensation money for crop damage.'

I pushed Akshu a bit. 'But aren't many of the people coming here because they are poor?'

But Akshu pointed out that since there was no governance of land or forest use, there was no guarantee that only those in dire need made use of Buxa's resources. He said many people building houses in Buxa already owned three or four other homes. Retiring government officials—including Forest Department guards—would build new getaways with wood from the jungle, sometimes even within Buxa. And, he said, the burgeoning hotels, restaurants, and other large-scale development on the boundary of Buxa were built from timber and fueled by firewood from the jungle.

Akshu did concede that some who came to Buxa were poor. 'But why do they just all come live here in the forest?' he asked. 'If it were just us forest villagers, maybe we could get local jobs and work in the forest without destroying it. And we forest villagers, we would hesitate to cut trees—but the people who've come and settled here? They have no problem cutting trees. They don't know anything about the trees here. They just have come from a place where they used to cut trees, so they cut trees day in, day out. So many people shouldn't be allowed into a jungle. If they could go to another city and live there, or live in a municipal area, that would be better.'

I essentially agreed. Buxa was one of the last big patches of forest in an extraordinarily biodiverse area, and local people should get dibs on an effort at sustainable use. An open commons was a death knell for conservation—elephants, other wildlife, and trees wouldn't stand a chance in a free-for-all. But I wondered how much our desire for conservation—to escape the tragedy of the commons—sounded like xenophobia. And what alternatives were possible for poor people who came to Buxa.

Even the Forest Department's own Tiger Conservation Plan conceded that use of Buxa's resources was not properly regulated, noting several factors constraining their efforts: 'Lack of political will in shifting the human population and cattle from the core area'; 'Lack of young, energetic workforce'; 'Huge number of vacancies for all level [sic] of field staff for execution of works and monitoring.' In 2016, a senior official told The Indian Express about the situation in Buxa. 'The Forest Department is working with just 50 per cent of the sanctioned strength,' he said, adding that a quarter of the staff are nearing or past retirement age. 'Severely understaffed doesn't even begin to explain our predicament.'[3] On the one hand, perhaps hamstrung by unions, non-meritocratic systems, and funding limitations, Buxa's Forest Department leadership was under-equipped to enforce rules that prevented the overuse of resources. On the other hand, when they did try and uphold the law, they often ran afoul of the political parties: the parties protected people of various stripes that extracted resources from the forest. Parties simultaneously promised to help free smugglers from Forest Department restrictions in exchange for votes and claimed publicly to fight for human rights for forest-dwelling people. The result seems to be that there was little clarity on when political parties were promoting human rights, and when they were undermining sustainable natural resource management. According to an article published by the Press Trust of India, the West Bengal Forest Department

---

3 Ghosal, Aniruddha. 2016. 'West Bengal Polls: In Buxa Tiger Reserve, a Votebank—and No Tigers.' The Indian Express. Available at: https://indianexpress.com/article/elections-2016/india/india-news-india/in-buxa-tiger-reserve-a-votebank-and-no-tigers-2757056/ (accessed on 20 October 2021).

claimed to have killed 13 Adivasis between 2007 and 2012 while defending the forests of North Bengal, including in an instance when they were 'outnumbered and attacked by armed illegal tree fellers.' In contrast, Daanbir Baisya and other rights advocates told the press that those killed were 'innocent tribals' collecting firewood, tubers, fruits, and mushrooms.[4] Establishing what really happened in the forest was a challenge, and excessive use of force was a very valid concern. Training Forest Department operatives to protect the forest without violating human rights was clearly necessary. But if one is to believe the villagers and Forest Department officials I spoke to, the system didn't make legitimate law enforcement actions easy either. The overall trend seemed to be that Forest Department officials committed to conservation faced strong political headwinds when they tried to do their job. An open commons was tragic for wildlife, some legitimate forest users, and humanity's natural heritage at large, but it worked just fine for a variety of short-term and corrupt interests.

For a faithful democrat like myself, this all posed a striking dilemma. The same local democracy that was probably paving Buxa's roads, eradicating its malaria, and giving voice to its indigenous peoples was abetting poachers and timber mafias. Ultimately, it made sense: democracy reflects the interests of the electorate. For human beings, wildlife conservation is a long-term interest, one that feels like a luxury. And when an electorate is scrambling to escape poverty, interests are almost inevitably short-term.

---

4 Press Trust of India. 2012. 'Rights Bodies Claim Forest Guards Kill Tribals'. Zee News. Available at: https://zeenews.india.com/news/west-bengal/rights-bodies-claim-forest-guards-kill-tribals_796004.html (accessed on 4 June 2021).

I saw clearly now that the battle to save Buxa would have to engage the local people directly to be successful. Local people had to understand what was being lost. They had to *care* about what was being lost. Local people needed a way to progress socioeconomically without unsustainable extraction from the forest. And the governance regime had to be reshaped to foster sustainability, closing the open commons.

Positive coupling could provide opportunities for advancement on many of these fronts: finding ways to ensure that some local people benefitted from sustainable management not only altered the equation for people's pocketbooks, but shaped hearts and minds and influenced governance. Akshu was a rather extreme example of this—his research work obviously depended on there being wildlife in the forests, and he spent long periods with elite nature lovers, so his interest in conservation surpassed the limits that often came with poverty. But the Atris insisted that Akshu wasn't an outlier, and that it wasn't hard or unusual to get an individual to shift gears. They pointed out that the very same people that had poached and smuggled transformed completely once Arjun Oraon put them to work protecting the forest. 'Now, if you tell [one of these protectors] about a smuggling opportunity, he won't go,' Thidey claimed. 'He recognizes the jungle now. Once a person has done duty protecting the jungle, their mind will be washed. He won't ever smuggle again.'

Thidey indicated that it wasn't just a matter of economics but of self-image—like Akshu's long-time friend Moksha Chatterjee. '*Baabaabaabaa*! He took more wood than anyone else,' Thidey said. But after I left Buxa, an ecologist had hired him as a field assistant. 'She's taken him to meet the range officer and the beat officer. She's said, 'This is my assistant.' Now if the beat officer catches him pulling along some smuggled wood, it becomes a matter of prestige, doesn't it?' He was saying that Moksha would hate to be reduced from a research assistant to a criminal in the minds of the community. 'He'll never go smuggling again in his life.'

Positive coupling didn't require that everyone be hired to protect the forest. Ecotourism was another way to connect the fates of locals and of the jungle. When I left Buxa, people around Madhubangaon had started building tourist lodges. Daanbir Baisya's, with his political connections, was one of the most successful. My driver Narad Ojha had ploughed much of the money I had paid him into a lodge that had done reasonably well—that is, until it was shut down for harboring a prostitution ring. Most recently, the Atris had cobbled together funds from government schemes for widows and for aspiring homestay hosts to build a two-room guesthouse. The Atris and a couple of lucky others had also managed to secure jeeps to drive tourists into parts of the forest, and local regulations required that every jeep driver also hire a trained tour guide. These drivers and guides wanted tips, and they got tips when their tourists saw elephants. 'It's funny,' Thidey mused. 'When people have seen a muntjac, peacocks, jungle fowl, monkeys, chital deer—they come out complaining that they haven't seen anything. When they have seen a muntjac, peacocks, jungle fowl, monkeys, deer, and a leopard, they say they saw *everything*!' Tourism positively coupled a growing local elite to wildlife, often leading these local elites to actively oppose poaching. And tour guides, like researchers and locally engaged patrollers, were eyes and ears in the jungle—if bad things were happening, they could sound the alarm.

But the problem with these forms of positive coupling was one of scale. Democracy meant that policies that disserved the vast majority of legitimate stakeholders could—and should—be challenged. Simply closing an open commons by hiring some local enforcers, research assistants, and tour guides would arguably help too few people and hurt too many to survive democratic pressures. Akshu's experience as a firewatcher as well as the limited success of Daanbir's and Arjun Oraon's enforcement efforts exemplified this. But the Atri brothers and Daanbir Baisya had an answer for that, too. The best way to give more people buy-in, they said, was through the provision of local forest rights.

In 2006, under pressure from Adivasi rights' groups, the Indian Parliament passed a progressive law called The Scheduled Tribes and Other Traditional Forest Dwellers (Recognition of Forest Rights) Act—known as the Forest Rights Act or FRA—attempting to correct for colonial-era injustices by legitimizing the way in which communities had long used forests for subsistence livelihood. In addition to the recognition of individual rights to live and practice subsistence agriculture in forests, the FRA provided a set of 'community forest rights' to all adults in a village or hamlet, a hyperlocal democratic body known as the 'Gram Sabha'. If a community had traditionally gathered firewood and NTFPs, grazed livestock, or fished in certain areas of the forest surrounding their village for subsistence, the FRA required that such practices be recognized as community forest rights of the Gram Sabha, even if the area was in a national park or tiger reserve. The FRA also made efforts to regulate conservation: the right to hunt animals, even if traditional, was not recognized in the act, and the Gram Sabha was explicitly expected to 'protect the wildlife, forest and biodiversity', which in principle could mean the State could ensure that the Gram Sabha didn't overexploit such resources. But the underlying ethos of the FRA was that putting primary control of local resources in the hands of local people would lead to more social justice and conservation than leaving control in the hands of an under-resourced and often unpopular bureaucracy. If local people had the right to benefit from sustainable use of natural resources, they would sustainably use and protect the forests around them.

Highly controversial, especially among conservationists and Forest Department officials, the FRA wasn't implemented as universally as intended and, in 2018, Daanbir Baisya and other local politicians were leading the charge to make community and individual forest rights a reality in North Bengal.

'They already have community forest control like this in Nepal,' Daanbir Baisya explained. 'If you need to build a house, give an application to the Gram Sabha. The Gram Sabha will decide where there is a fallen tree. And they'll find it and give it to you—but in its place, plant 25 new trees nearby. Then you will get your wood.' As always, Daanbir's deep voice was oozing charisma. 'They totally stopped smuggling that way. We want to apply it here!'

'Right now, there's a market for *tez* leaves,' said Thidey. 'So what are people doing? They are knocking down whole trees so they can sell the leaves! So they only get profit one time. In the Gram Sabha, we can explain to people that the jungle is ours!'—that is, if they managed the trees for future years, they would be the ones to benefit. The only way to really create an ethos of local ownership would be by empowering the Gram Sabha.

Akshu believed the Forest Department was just too far removed from community realities to push for village-level sustainability. In contrast, he could literally count the number of people in his hamlet engaged in poaching and smuggling. 'There are nine.' Thidey concurred. 'A tenth is sick and might die soon.' With the knowledge of exactly who was engaged in illegal resource consumption, and the relationships they had with those people, the Gram Sabha had the potential to powerfully enforce the rules—if only they had the legitimate authority and incentive. 'You just have to invest in them,' Akshu said, speaking of the smugglers. 'Be there for them on good days and bad days—definitely, they will be converted.'

I was enthusiastically supportive of the Forest Rights Act. It didn't make sense to me that Indians had thrown out the British but then maintained that a distant government could deny the most marginalized people in the country their traditional livelihood. Besides, at least in Buxa, there seemed to be more to gain than to be lost by trying something new. But I was wary of the broad promises I heard from indigenous peoples' rights activists that the Gram Sabha Raj would automatically protect wildlife or forests. First, I wasn't sure Gram Sabhas were always truly democratic. After leaving Buxa, I had gone to see how Gram Sabhas operated in Central India. I had been surprised to find that Gram Sabhas didn't necessarily have any formal or anonymous vote. Instead, they based decisions on a perception of general consensus, and the council discussions, as villagers described them, were dominated by landed or caste elites and men. In some cases, violence or threats were used to coerce individuals—especially women—for their support. Such elite capture could jeopardize both equity and conservation.

'Establishing a Gram Sabha is easy, but using it correctly is tough,' Thidey conceded. 'In villages where there are lots of young guys and they're all involved in the illegal trade, and someone tries to say we should make a Gram Sabha to protect the jungle, well, they'll just get beaten up ... So start with all the villages that will stop smuggling—villages with fewer smugglers and more good people ... And when the other villages see the benefits of such arrangements, automatically they will switch, too.'

Akshu believed there should be checks and balances between the Gram Sabha and the Forest Department to ensure sustainability. 'Like, the old system had a *mondol*, where the village would pick a good person who would do good for everyone—for us, for the animals, for the jungle. We need to select that person. And that person, however much power the Forest Department has, should have that much power. So if the Forest Department messes something up, the *mondol* can do something. If the *mondol* messes up, the Forest Department can catch them. Like that, equal power.'

I had two other concerns about the role Gram Sabhas would play in governing the forest. Gram Sabhas could presumably promote sustainability as long as their membership was limited so that the sustainable harvest of resources—wood, NTFPs, fish—provided enough to satisfy all of them. As Akshu pointed out, when his parents immigrated in the 1960s, just 85 households occupied Madhubangaon, each responsible for contributing labour to the government's plantations. Madhubangaon's and Buxa's population had since exploded. So who exactly was going to get these forest rights? And would it be too many people to sustainably manage what was left of the jungle?

The FRA and ensuing guidelines make some clear prescriptions on this. All Adivasi families living in forests in December 2005 were entitled to the individual and community forest rights prescribed by the FRA. So even Adivasis who had moved to Buxa before 2005 from forests in, say, Jharkhand or Assam could stake a claim to their dwellings and subsistence activities. That was the easy part. Far trickier was what the FRA called 'other traditional forest dwellers', including people from so-called upper castes like the Atris. Such forest-dwellers were entitled to FRA rights if they had, since 1930, 'primarily resided in and [depended] on the forest or forest lands for *bona fide* livelihood needs.'[5] For populations that were often semi- or fully illiterate in the 1930s, demonstrating this would not be trivial. The Gram Sabha ultimately judged whose claims to rights were valid and whose weren't, so they could use discretion, giving the benefit of the doubt to people without written records or to families like the Atris that had come after the 1930s. In my mind, the Atris had a reasonable claim since they had come under the auspices of the government to work in the plantations. But I was concerned that Gram Sabhas would be cajoled, coerced, or corrupted into giving rights to families that had moved recently—basically, to too many families.

I asked Thidey, who was lobbying for forest rights in Madhubangaon, about this possibility. 'If all the people who just came from outside and settled in, say, the bazaar, without any permissions from the Forest Department—if they get forest rights too, it's just too many people, and the jungle is finished.'

'We will fight them,' Thidey said. 'We won't let them get forest rights.'

---

5 The Scheduled Tribes and Other Traditional Forest Dwellers (Recognition of Forest Rights) Act. 2006.

'Oh yeah? What if the same old people that lie about how long you've been here lie about how long they've been here? Then what will happen?'

Thidey laughed. He had grown a big belly since I'd left, and it bounced a bit. 'Then we'll all just stay very quiet.'

When I asked Daanbir about the Atris and others like them, he made clear he believed that people who had long been at home in Buxa shouldn't be thrown out. Daanbir thought for a moment, and then demonstrated his political agility with a creative suggestion for reinterpreting and implementing the FRA. 'Study the FRA closely—it doesn't require that people live in the exact same place, right? They have to have lived in the forest.' It seemed that he was saying that since Motikar's family had been jungle-dwellers in Nepal and North Bengal since before 1930, his family could qualify as forest-dwellers in Buxa.

But when I asked about the many non-tribals who had come from other jungles, Daanbir backed off. 'No, it has to be in Buxa's jungle.' Suddenly, Daanbir cracked a sly grin. 'So what are you conservationists thinking? That if villagers don't get their rights, then conservation will happen?'

'No...'

Daanbir kept going. 'My goal is that the Gram Sabha be made powerful. It's not to make me rich. The FRA says I can't rent or sell my land. It's just some security for my family. My main goal is to save the jungle, save the wildlife. Through the FRA. That's my vision.' He argued that my concerns about exactly how many people would have forest rights was missing the main point that it was effective governance that was lacking. Buxa could accommodate every family, tribal and non-tribal, that had lived in the bounds of the reserve before December 2005—farming their land, grazing their cattle, collecting firewood—but only if the Gram Sabhas were empowered to protect the forests from exploitation by outsiders, including the government and commercial interests. 'Ultimately, the villagers just need to think of the forest as theirs. Right now, they think of it as the government's.' And as long as the villagers thought that way,' he said, 'you won't be able to save the jungle.'

That brought me to my final concern. I wasn't sure I trusted anyone's assessment of what a Gram Sabha would do with its power. The Atris and Daanbir Baisya, I believed, would conserve a jungle. But unlike almost everyone else, they had also been willing to volunteer at the computer lab. It would be hard to predict the aspirations of the people of North Bengal in this age of seismic socioeconomic change. There seemed no guarantee that a traditional conservation ethic would prevent the transformation of wildlife and wood into smartphones and English-medium school fees. But perhaps a diversity of couplings might help. If some villagers were benefiting from wildlife tourism, they would cry foul if the Gram Sabha allowed hunting or unsustainable timber extraction. If conservation groups helped connect others to modern goods and services— the way Jilpa helped Akshu get medical care—perhaps the conservationists could persuade them, too, to value sustainability. And if some families were being broadly decoupled from the jungle, perhaps they would also prioritize long-term benefits attainable through sustainable realization of their forest rights.

I can't say that Daanbir persuaded me that the FRA would definitely work to restore the jungle. In 2021, Akshu called to inform me that he—and everyone else who had attained land in Malabasti, legally or otherwise, before or after 2006—had received paperwork legitimizing their land tenure under the FRA, confirming my fear that the safeguards preventing abuse of the FRA were too weak. But my concerns were always about how the FRA should be implemented, not whether it should be. Given that the FRA was a democratically established law designed to right colonial-era wrongs, and that grassroots conservationists like Daanbir supported the law, I thought it deserved a whole-hearted try. A carefully observed, well-monitored try, with scientists empowered to sound the alarm. And a place like Buxa, where the status quo had largely failed conservation, seemed like as good a place as any to give the FRA a real chance.

I found it impossible to make sense of everything going on in Buxa—to add up the development progress, the economic opportunities, the governance possibilities, the clear ecological losses, the tantalizing conservation gains. Akshu felt that the core issues plaguing Buxa had not yet been addressed, but I was humbled by how fast things changed in the region. I wouldn't hazard a guess as to whether Buxa was on its way to becoming a real tiger reserve. There was still hardly any rigorous, believable data on human and wildlife populations or interactions in Buxa and, without good numbers, effective management seemed unlikely. But with the twists and turns in the region's politics, it seemed like anything could happen.

I saw several reasons to believe that Buxa could one day be restored to some version of what it once was.

First, truth was on the march. In 2015, a report declared that no tigers had been found that year in Buxa. The news websites Scroll.in and Quartz published a post noting the irregularities in tiger DNA-testing in 2010 and 2011 and concluded that the 'most likely explanation' for what happened to the 20 tigers found in 2011 was that they 'might never have been there.'[6] The government tacitly confessed to the gravity of the problem in 2017 by launching a 'tiger augmentation program,'[7]—that is, an effort to relocate tigers to Buxa. When I stopped by the Forest Department offices in 2018 to collect the Tiger Conservation Plan, a senior official—aware that I was writing a book—told me off-handedly that there weren't any tigers in Buxa. I stared at him unbelievingly. If officials continued to be transparent about Buxa's reality, there could one day be the shared and real understanding of what needs to be done to restore the forest.

Second, I saw people of various stripes aspiring to either positively couple or decouple themselves from the jungle. Akshu, not surprisingly, was far more interested in teaching his kids English and math than about cow herding or edible forest plants. He dreamed that his children would get jobs in the city, but that then they could come back to rest and rejuvenate in his country home, away from the urban noise and pollution.

What *was* surprising was to hear similar aspirations from Bhuvan, an illiterate forest-dweller who had gathered fruits and fodder for my feeding trials from 2010–2012. When I had repeatedly tried to hire him for more regular work in the village, he had persistently turned down the lucrative offer. 'He needs to be in the jungle,' Akshu had

---

6 Chari, Mridula. 2015. 'How an Indian Wildlife Reserve Lost 20 Tigers in Three Years'. Quartz India. Available at: https://qz.com/india/424346/how-an-indian-wildlife-reserve-lost-20-tigers-in-three-years/ (accessed on 20 October 2021).

7 Roy, Esha. 2017. 'Buxa Reserve: Govt Wants to Launch Tiger Augmentation Project, Awaits Wildlife Board's Nod'. The Indian Express. Available at: https://indianexpress.com/article/india/buxa-reserve-govt-wants-to-launch-tiger-augmentation-project-awaits-wildlife-boards-nod-4675696/ (accessed on 20 October 2021).

told me. 'He is like my father. He isn't happy unless he has wandered the forests most of the day.' But, in 2018, when I asked Bhuvan whether he was teaching his young children about the jungle, he told me he was sending them to school. 'They shouldn't be like me. They should be literate, and have stable jobs.' The intergenerational loss of knowledge about nature—whether Akshu's or Bhuvan's—would be tragic. But the socioeconomic decoupling could provide some relief to the jungle. Daanbir claimed that this turn away from natural resources was an overwhelming trend. He estimated that the number of people smuggling wood from Madhubangaon had reduced by 80 per cent in five years. He said the remaining problem (at least prior to the COVID-19 pandemic) was mainly people from outside of Buxa.

I see hope, too, in nature's resilience. During my week-long visit in 2018, I saw wild pigs, sambar deer, and gaur in addition to the usual peafowl, jungle fowl, macaques, and barking deer—suggesting at least some decrease in poaching in the core area since my departure in 2012. Large numbers of chital deer had been brought to help augment the tiger's prey base, and tourists often spotted the chital alive and well in the jungle. Hari and Akshu had convinced local boys in Malabasti to put away their slingshots, telling them that tourists liked seeing birds. The cousins claimed that hornbills had returned to the fig tree near the Metal Road, and I saw some 19 great hornbills flying over the village one evening. Thanks to the connectivity of Buxa to Bhutan and Assam, it seemed that wildlife would likely come back if given the chance. And not just the small stuff. 'I think there is no need to bring tigers from outside,' Daanbir told me. 'You make an environment for the tiger, and the tiger will come itself. The type of jungle that used to be here—we need to bring that jungle back.' In December 2021, camera trap photos of a male tiger in Buxa—the first such evidence in decades—suggested that such recolonization was a possibility.

But for me, the biggest source of hope in Buxa isn't something new. It's something old. Despite all the cultural and economic changes in Buxa, many people still speak about animals as creatures that have their own life experiences, as beings with souls, as species that belong to the region. When a herd of elephants came into the village one night, there was hollering and firecracker-throwing to scare them away. But there were also smiles and excitement as villagers saw, in the beam of a high-powered flashlight, a calf scrambling up among its mother and aunts and siblings back into the forest.

'People always complain about the elephants,' Thidey said. 'But then if they don't come for a few weeks, people say, "Hey, where are the elephants? How come we haven't seen them for so long?" They miss them. That means they must like them.'

And while I know that much of what Akshu thinks and believes is a product of his unique exposure, what I think fundamentally makes him a conservationist at the core is a deep, firm—and, in my view, well-evidenced—belief that he has always had. That many animals experience their lives richly and are capable of both joy and suffering. One day, I asked him if he would think wildlife was less important if ecologists like me discovered that their functions—like seed dispersal—weren't crucial for the ecosystem, or that we humans or domestic livestock could adequately replace them.

'We do not have the right to finish them,' he responded. 'Even if we do not get that sort of benefit from them, we benefit from them a lot. Sure, sometimes they eat our crops, and if we surprise them suddenly, sometimes they will even kill a person. But, for that matter, how many people are killed by cars in the city, and sometimes planes fall from a sky. *Still* people give heaps of money to fly in a plane! They give all that money, and they just end up falling to the ground and dying.' By now I was cracking up. Akshu generally understood probability just fine. But I took his point to be that one had to accept some risks and costs to have the kind of world we want to live in. And that he wanted a world where animals' lives were respected.

Akshu isn't typical, I know. But I also know he isn't unique. Nor are Kalaivannan, Daanbir, Arjun, or Jilpa. Forest villages and cities in India and perhaps around the world must have Satyavatis and Motikars raising their children to consider the well-being of every creature with a nervous system, even if such concern doesn't always amount to full abstention from killing. It seems to me that such recognition of kindred souls in creatures with wings, tails, or trunks enables the sacrifices necessary for conservation. It is the critical mass of people championing such empathy that causes the rest of humanity to think twice, to hesitate a moment, before they strike. And, in that moment, as the world's extraordinary top primates have taken an extra breath before letting our arrows fly, just enough animals have escaped to keep the jungles of India alive—incomplete, but still alive—alongside over one billion people, deep into the 21st century.

ACKNOWLEDGMENTS

Akshu didn't see himself as a co-author of this book, but his voice and storytelling style are what make his narrative so engaging. I thank him, his family, and my neighbors and co-workers in Madhubangaon for being my teachers and allowing me the honor of chronicling their journey. Various officials of the West Bengal Forest Department stationed in Buxa also shared insights and provided support crucial for this project.

Dr Raman Sukumar, with quiet support from his administrators Nirmala S. and Palani, K., helped me get started in Indian conservation. Few academics or conservationists have thought as clearly as Dr Sukumar about the pragmatic consequences of elephant conservation in a democracy striving for justice and material progress. I hope he feels this book carries on his intellectual tradition.

I am especially grateful to Faiza Khan, my official editor and the champion for the book. I expected her to clarify and streamline my writing, but I didn't foresee that she would also bring such creativity and strategic thinking to the publication process. Prerna Vohra, my final editor, carried the baton past the finish line with clarity, patience, efficiency, professionalism. If this book is read by more than a handful of people, much of the credit goes to them. I also thank Shreya Chakraborti for her work as my managing editor, Aurodeep Mukherjee for being an incredibly attentive copyeditor, and all others at Bloomsbury India for their behind-the-scenes work on this book.

Before Faiza, I benefitted from several informal editors: Lo Kwa Mei En was my original writing mentor for this project. Tuoyang Mu, Danika Barry, and James Norton read early chapters. Ameya Nagarajan gave me the first shot at publication. The draft I sent her in 2013 was pretty bad, and she could have killed the project permanently. The combination of her (and Fazal Rashid's) unvarnished criticism and encouragement to try again were the tonic I needed to change course. Ankita Sardana and Derek Shiller provided reassuring late-stage feedback. Naman Shah offered typically unsparing, insightful revisions, and his penchant for networking made publication a reality.

Dinsha Mistree helped me find readings to better understand the relevant political science, and Nupur Kale aided with translations where I got stuck. Dr Vidya Athreya and Purnima Upadhyay fact-checked specific sections. I thank Dr Tanka Subba for pointing me towards relevant resources, and Dr Bengt Karlsson for sharing his absorbing book.

Many friends helped shape how I pitched the book: Mary Small, Phil Hannam, Vinay Sitapati, Marit Doshi, Corinne Kendall, and April Pullium among them. Mr Jonathan Cobb transformed how I approached the sales job. Dr David Wilcove and Dr Alex Dehgan helped me search for prospective publishers.

Of particular fascination to me are the people whom I have never met or even spoken with who threw their weight behind this project. I owe a special thanks to Anjan Sundaram and Dr Ramachandra Guha.

And, of course, there's my family, whom I hold responsible for all the good things I do. My parents, sister, and Kumar Mama bore the brunt of my illnesses and injuries from the field and have become heartening supporters of the book. Malathi Periamma, Rajagopalan Periappa, Anand Gopal, Bala Chitappa, Malini Chiti, Swati Balakrishnan, Kalyan Chitappa, Radha Chiti, Radhakrishnan Chitappa, and Rajasree Chiti supported me in various ways during my travels and studies.

As this project has stretched over a decade, it is inevitable that I have missed acknowledging people who helped shape this book either through encouragement or discourse. I thank my broader community for their support.

Over the last four years, my partner Laura Boffa has read and reread ... and reread drafts of the manuscript, eager to make my verbose writing more accessible. Obviously, I married Laura because of her intelligence, empathy, and obsession with fun, not because I was an aspiring writer and she was a professional editor. But I'm not going to lie—the editor thing has been a pretty great bonus.

AUTHOR BIO

 **Nitin Sekar** is a conservation scientist interested in human rights and animal welfare in wildlife conservation. His writings have been published in *Science* magazine, *Economic and Political Weekly*, *The Guardian*, and *The Indian Express*, and his research has been documented in *The New York Times*, *Washington Post* and *The Hindu*. Nitin wants you to know that, despite this incomparable record of achievement, he is a down-to-earth and fun-loving guy. For instance, he has been bowling before, and he used to have pets. Nitin currently serves as WWF India's national lead for elephant conservation.